Pascal's God-Shaped Vacuum: A Guided Tour of *The Pensées*

Peter B. Gilbert

ISBN:1461181100
ISBN-13:9781461181101

Jorge,

This is from someone that we both admire & respect. I hope you will enjoy reading it and that it will help shed light to questions we all face at some stage in our lives.

With much respect.

Joseph

For Kristi, Eleanora, Blaise, Genevieve

The photograph on the cover shows the statue *De Verwoeste Stad* ('*The Destroyed City*'), nicknamed *Stad Zonder Hart* ('*City Without a Heart*'), created by Ossip Zadkine and installed in Rotterdam in 1953

Pascal's God-Shaped Vacuum

I am grateful to my wife Kristi for her love and forbearance (much of this book was written while our kids were in diapers) and to my fellow mathematical scientist and Pascalian, Jack Snoeyink, for his generous and critical review.

-1 FORWARD

In lists of the great books of Western Civilization, one title is not a formal book at all but instead an assortment of thoughts by a 17th century French mathematician and physicist who died at the age of 39 (1623–1662). It is a record of thoughts, *Pensées*, and a collection of letters that had at first appeared anonymously. *The Provincial Letters* were a literary sensation when they broke in on the city of Paris, and though they were devoutly Christian, the wit and surprising turns of phrases would have pleased Mark Twain. Now we know who the author is and his name is Blaise Pascal; his letters and his thoughts are ours to read. He takes us on a journey into the world we think we know; but his route is by a new way that has never occurred to us.

Early on, Pascal captures our minds with his way of looking at all that is within and around us. It happens even in the way we look upward at the skies and downward at tiny specks of water. At one moment, Pascal invites us to wonder at the immensity of largeness in the universe above our heads, and in the next moment invites us to wonder at a drop of water to see the inner vastness of atomic physics with its own rotations of planets in solar systems hidden in the space of atomic and subatomic particles. Pascal anticipated both the expanding light year distances of largeness as well as the quantum mechanics of particle entanglement and information transfer both large and small. He raises the question, how do we rightly understand who we are as human beings that live in the mid place between the vastness of what appears as large and the vastness of what appears as small?

The Pensées takes us on this amazing tour with Pascal as our guide who, both as the scientist and the man, believes that the creator of everything has made himself known to us. "A king may speak rightly of power, a rich man of wealth, and God speaks rightly of God." [*Pensée* 303] Pascal believes that the one who made the eye is able to see; he who made the ear is able to hear, and that this creator cares about all that he has made. Jesus Christ is the living word of God– he is God speaking for himself. The eternal word has become flesh; Jesus is the love and truth of God, the one able to locate us and he is able to fill the God-sized space in every human life.

Pascal also takes us on a journey of discovery about ourselves, including the contradictions that collide within us. "A house in ruins is not miserable, only man is miserable. The greatness of man is great in that he knows himself to be miserable. A tree does not know itself to be miserable. It is then being miserable to know oneself to be miserable; but it is also being great to know that one is miserable... All these miseries prove man's greatness... they are the miseries of a deposed king." [*Pensées* 114, 116] *The Pensées* is totally realistic about those contradictions, but I, as a reader of his *Pensées*, am grateful to learn that Blaise Pascal himself discovered the grace and patient kindness of God. When he shares that discovery he takes me by surprise and catches my breath in a very good and healing way.

Peter Gilbert is a mathematician and scientific researcher himself and he, as much as anyone I know, understands what Blaise Pascal has written. He now invites each of us to journey along with him into the thoughts of Pascal and watch as the pieces of the puzzle of life and meaning take shape within the *Pensées*. Dr. Gilbert's book aids us in our own spiritual and intellectual quest. The title itself, *Pascal's God-Shaped Vacuum: A Guided Tour of The Pensées*, is an invitation. Peter Gilbert's own journey of discovery experienced the healing and resolving shocks of surprise and recognition when he realized that it was Christ who found him before and during what Peter thought of as his own search for truth. That discovery also happened in Pascal when he was a young adult, and his thoughts since that breakthrough have helped many men and women, young and old, realize that God's love and outstretched hands can become our own experience too.

"It is good to be weary and worn out in the vain pursuit of the true good so that we may open our arms to the Redeemer." [*Pensée* 631]

– Earl F. Palmer

December 2011

0 PROLOGUE

"What else does this craving proclaim but that there was once in man a true state of happiness, of which all that now remains is the empty print and trace? This he tries in vain to fill with everything around him though none can help, since this infinite abyss can be filled only with an infinite and immutable object, in other words by God himself."
– Blaise Pascal, *Pensée* 148

By co-founding mathematical probability, empirical science and modern journalism, and by inventing the world's first computer, public transportation system, and vacuum cleaner, Blaise Pascal had a colossal influence on shaping 21st century life. These stupefying achievements notwithstanding, Pascal himself was more devoted to other pursuits– the study of Man and God. Pascal probed the momentous questions, asking "what is a human being," this "thinking reed" with its myriad contradictory attributes; what is the meaning of our lives and our deaths? It is for these philosophical studies– not his science– for which the contemporary French principally hail their favored son (Pascal's face just completed a 40 year term on the 500 franc note), an ironic tribute coming from the proudly atheistic French. Also ironically, while Richard Dawkins among others has attacked Christianity based on Pascal's revolutionary idea to combine mathematical reasoning with probability (e.g., in *The Blind Watchmaker* and *The God Delusion*), Pascal would vehemently disagree with these atheist philosophers, and staked his life defending orthodox Christian truth.

How could one of histories' greatest scientific minds find orthodox Christianity compelling? Himself a paradox, Pascal would wield paradox as a favorite rhetorical tool in his impassioned project, now compiled in the *Pensées*, to persuade his skeptical, bored, and indifferent friends to diminish their diversionary activities and instead throw themselves into seeking God. This book takes you on a guided tour of these *Pensées*, exploring Pascal's stunningly original and incisive ideas about the human condition, and distilling practical lessons about how a person this side of the technological revolution can seriously consider Christian truth and life in the face of contemporary countervailing currents including scientism, cynicism, and entertainment culture. His thoughts have such powerful effect on modern readers that they elicited T.S. Eliot's highest recommendation, "But I can think of no Christian writer, not Newman even, more to be commended than Pascal to those who doubt, but who have the mind to conceive, and the sensibility to feel, the disorder, the futility, the meaninglessness, the mystery of life and suffering, and who can only find peace through a satisfaction of the whole being."

This book is a written form of a class on Pascal's *Pensées* that I taught at University Presbyterian Church (UPC) in Seattle. My interest in the *Pensées* began as a freshman at the University of Washington, where in a French literature class I received my first Pascal-inoculation, which led to my seeking God at UPC and coming to believe Christ a year later. This journey continued over the years with booster shots delivered as *Pensée* re-reads, discussion groups, and Pascal quotes from UPC's senior pastor, Earl Palmer. The *Pensées* tops Reverend Palmer's list of most influential books, and his regular doses of Pascal stimulated my heart and mind, along with those of thousands of others, to learn more about this 17th century genius.

What is my perspective in taking you on a guided tour? While books on Pascal's *Pensées* have been written by theologians, philosophers, historians, and French-language scholars, I have not seen tours led by scientists. Since 1994 I have worked toward the development of a preventative AIDS vaccine, spending five years on the faculty of the Harvard School of Public Health and the last ten at the Fred Hutchinson Cancer Research Center and the University of Washington. As a biostatistician and clinical trialist, I apply the theory of mathematical probability to design experimental studies to test candidate AIDS vaccines, and develop and apply novel statistical methods to analyze the data. As such, my career centers on the two intellectual areas that arguably constitute the two scientific areas on which Pascal had the greatest impact– mathematical probability and empirical science– Pascal is regarded as the father of the former field and a co-father of the latter. By living my whole professional life in the fields invented and carried forward by Pascal, I share Pascal's angle for viewing the world. As Pascal developed his mind through science, and later applied it to anthropology and theology, I come to the study of Pascal's *Pensées* via scientific training.

In addition to Earl Palmer I owe an intellectual debt to past scholars of the *Pensées*, most significantly to Peter Kreeft for his 1993 guided tour, as well as to Dick Keyes of L'Abri Fellowship for lectures and books on the interface of culture and Christianity. The "original" contribution of this book is one of arrangement, not essential material, as can be summarized by Pascal's own quip about his apologetic project (which previews Pascal's theme about the wretched hubris of Man):

> Let no one say that I have said nothing new; the arrangement of the material is new. In playing tennis both players use the same ball, but one plays it better. [*Pensée* 696]

1 PASCAL'S LIFE AND APPROACH TO WINNING SEEKERS

"All men seek happiness… This is the motive of every act of every man, including those who go and hang themselves."
– Blaise Pascal, *Pensée* 148

What are the *Pensées*? They are a collection of approximately 1000 "thoughts" that Blaise Pascal compiled on scraps of paper in preparation for a book on a comprehensive defense of the Christian religion, which was never finished. The fragments were found by family and friends after his death in 1662 and have been assembled into various orderings, the first of which appeared in 1670. I will use the Lafuma edition of 1951, as translated by Professor A.J. Krailsheimer in 1966, available as a Penguin Classic. Throughout this tour block quote *Pensées* are presented in arial font, distinguishing them from all other material given in times new roman.

Why study the *Pensées*? I believe they are helpful for people of most any religious worldview, whether atheist, Christian believer, or somewhere in between. Part of the reason for their universal appeal is they present a dazzlingly accurate portrait of the human condition that provokes fundamental questions about life that concern us all. Reading the *Pensées* is like looking into a clean mirror after previously only looking into dirty ones, and being astounded to discover that one is more frail and miserable, as well as greater and more capable of joy, than hitherto thought. Downing this strong coffee has led many to try Pascal's prescription for seeking real happiness.

I vividly recall Pascal's gripping first impression on me as an agnostic college freshman. Upon hearing Pascal's description of Man as restless, bored, apathetic, scared of death, ignorant of who made him and where he is going when he dies, a seeker of diversions in work and entertainment so as to avoid contemplating his miserable condition, I became quiet– Pascal was describing *me* and I intuited in my heart that he was on the mark. I had long felt this "infinite abyss" of unhappiness and for the first time was seeing an authentic portrait of myself.

Most apologetics are written as if we still had a predominantly Christian civilization, and use rational arguments that *pre-suppose* the listener is open to God. But many today are closed to Christianity, with no interest in seeking. For these the primary obstacle to faith is an entrenched attitude of the will, which cannot be moved by rational apologetics. Pascal is rare because he fully appreciated this reality, crafting every word in his *Pensées* to account for his interlocutor's disposition. As the first post-medieval apologist, Pascal wrote to secular society, to unbelievers rooted in entertainment culture, to ambitious pursuers of career success, to the bored and indifferent, to intellectual skeptics– in a word, to typical moderns today. Pascal was especially gifted at simultaneously employing artful prose and reasoned arguments to move both the heart and mind, with aggregate effect to set his listeners on fire to take up an interest in seeking. Pascal's approach sparks seeking by "making Christianity attractive and making good men wish it were true." [*Pensée* 12] Pascal makes his listener *hungry* before feeding him proofs of the faith (Kreeft, 1993). For Pascal, winning seekers is the essential function of modern apologetics– speaking from God's voice, he suggests that seeking is mysteriously intermingled with possessing some faith already: "You would not seek me if you did not possess me. Therefore be not troubled." [*Pensée* 929]

Outline of the Guided Tour. Following this introduction, chapters 2–4 address what Pascal called the "wretched condition" of humankind apart from God. In chapter 2 we will explore Pascal's description of the first attribute of human wretchedness without God, unhappiness. This unhappiness includes boredom, restlessness, and subjection to disease and death. Pascal observes that diversions and indifference are popular coping techniques to avoid facing these terrifying problems. Some of Pascal's most powerful prose describes humankind's insatiable appetite for diversion, as expressed, for example, through sport, entertainment, and workaholism.

In chapter 3 we will explore Pascal's thoughts on the second human attribute of wretchedness without God, being "lost in the dark." This refers to the defects in our faculties of knowing, including our limited reasoning capacity and our fanciful imagination, which thwart us from reliably grasping reality and truth. It also refers to our ignorance of ultimate questions like, "Why are we here?" and "What happens to me after I die?" Pascal leads his listener down a path to discover that "reasons of the heart," which involve faith and revelation, are needed to find a cure for his wretched condition.

In chapter 4 we will explore Pascal's description of humankind without God as empty/vain/meaningless, and as biased to love self much more than others. To Pascal this prejudice has far-reaching consequences, ranging from individual injustice to societal injustice, wherein people tend to evaluate themselves (as individuals or groups) with rose-colored glasses and judge others more pessimistically.

In chapter 5 we will probe one of Pascal's dominant themes– that human beings are paradoxically both very great and very wretched. Pascal juxtaposes descriptors of Man including thinking reed, dispossessed king, angel beast, repository of truth/sink of doubt and error, absurd god, ridiculous hero, and glorious earthworm. For Pascal, Creation, Fall, and gracious redemption/restoration are the keys to understanding this dialectical paradox:

> Man in the state of his creation, or in the state of grace, is exalted above the whole of nature, made like unto God and sharing in his divinity. But in the state of corruption and sin he has fallen from the first state and has become like the beasts. [*Pensée*131]

Indeed, Pascal's analysis of the human situation centers around Man as both great and wretched– to Pascal apart from accepting this dual condition we can understand nothing about ourselves.

In chapter 6 we will explore Pascal's *Pensées* on the question, "Why is God hidden?" God's hiddenness is often cited as a roadblock to belief in God– "If he is real why doesn't he just show himself clearly?" Pascal presents fascinating ideas about why a good God would hide himself, and, counter-intuitively, argues that the hiddenness of God makes the Christian God more believable, not less! Moreover, Pascal reasons that God's hiddenness is helpful and even necessary for Christians to grow.

In chapter 7 we will explore Pascal's most famous argument, the Wager, in which Pascal contends that it is more rational to bet on the Christian God's existence than to bet against it. Pascal addresses his Wager to open skeptics who have come to recognize their wretchedness, with objective to get them moving to vigorously seek God. While the Wager has been subjected to a barrage of criticisms, I will argue that it weathers the storm, and suggest that many of the criticisms go astray by failing to account for the Wager's context within the whole *Pensées*. I will suggest that the Wager rightfully belongs as a coherent and central component of Pascal's overall apologetic project.

In chapter 8 we will explore Pascal's description of clues and evidence supporting the rational plausibility of the Christian faith. This survey will focus on the uniqueness of Christianity compared to other religions and compared to secular scientism. As a brilliant scientist Pascal was especially well-positioned to counter secular scientism, and today's readers struggling with how a reasonable person living in our technological age can be a Christian stand to profit particularly handsomely from the *Pensées*. For these Pascal is an ultimate mentor. Compared to all other religions and philosophies, Pascal argues that only Christianity adequately explains the data about human experience; only Christianity is "worthy of reverence because it really understands human nature." [*Pensée* 12] Furthermore Pascal argues that only Christianity provides an efficacious cure for Man's wretched state. Pascal's compelling articulation of the unique relevance of Christ's gospel for our situation constitutes one of the greatest practical benefits of reading the *Pensées*– no other work better demonstrates how Jesus Christ makes the total difference in all areas of life.

In short, chapters 2 through 8 survey Pascal's demolition of the barriers holding his friends back from seeking God: (2) indifference and diversions; 3) presumptuous reason; (4) vanity and undue self-love; (5) failure to recognize Man's dual wretched-and-great condition; (6) pride; (7) fear of rolling the dice; and (8) under-investigation of the reasons to believe. Once these impediments are removed Pascal's interlocutor is in good position to seek. The last chapter synthesizes the themes in the *Pensées*, which work together to serve Pascal's singular objective to deliver his friend from his unhappy state as a "monster that passes all understanding" to a happy state of membership in Christ's body.

In this introductory chapter, Part I summarizes Pascal's life, and Part II overviews his apologetic approach in the *Pensées*. In Part III we consider *The Memorial*, Pascal's personal statement of assured faith in Christ and love for God.

Part I. Biography of Pascal

Chronology. Pascal was born in Clermont, France in 1623. Raised by his father Étienne, his mother died when he was three. Throughout his life Blaise was very close to his two sisters, Gilberte two years his elder and Jacqueline two years his younger. Gilberte's husband Florin Perier was one of Blaise's principal collaborators in conducting scientific experiments, and Blaise died in Gilberte's home under her care.

When Blaise was 23, his family encountered two pious disciples of Jansenism, a form of Catholicism. Hitherto the Pascal's were conventional churchgoers; henceforth they were enthusiastic Christians. Some have called this encounter Blaise's first conversion.

The following year, Pascal was undergoing extreme pains in sicknesses, and his physicians recommended that he cease his concentrated intellectual endeavors and seek some diversion. Pascal partook in Parisian high-society with worldly friends, who enjoyed socializing and entertainment culture, including gambling, billiards playing, dancing, and theatre going. This period of Pascal's life, a time of internal turmoil with his spiritual and worldly inclinations waging civil war, must have contributed to his acquisition of deep insight into the human condition.

When Pascal was 31, he had an intense personal encounter with God, his so-called second conversion. Thereafter he was a totally devoted Christian, and dedicated his life to loving God. This manifested itself in three ways. First, Pascal's personal life was transformed; he denounced personal pleasures and material wealth and gave generously to the poor. Second, Pascal endeavored to write a comprehensive defense of the Christian religion, to convert his worldly friends among others. And third, Pascal worked to defend the devoted spiritual community Port-Royal, an activity that is described more fully below.

Pascal died on August 19, 1662, with last words "May God never abandon me!" By seven years after his death, Gilberte and friends of Pascal had compiled hundreds of his scribbled thoughts on the Christian religion into the first edition of the *Pensées*.

Now we will survey four main attributes of Blaise Pascal.

Attribute 1: Pascal the Scientist. First, Pascal was a great scientist. As a mathematician, Pascal invented the concept of mathematical expectation and is widely regarded as the father of probability theory, a critical field in many sciences. As a physicist, Pascal conducted famous experiments supporting the existence of a vacuum. These bold experiments were revolutionary, because they directly contradicted common Aristotelian philosophical assumptions of the day. As an example of an Aristotelian assumption that Pascal would find questionable, Aristotle believed that women had fewer teeth than men. It never occurred to Aristotle to test this hypothesis by opening his wife's mouth and counting her teeth– in Aristotle's day up through Pascal's a direct empirical approach to seeking truth was not valued and was rarely used. (Kreeft, 1993) Whereas Aristotle taught that truth is found almost purely through abstract thinking, with the observation of nature contributing little, Pascal pressed the revolutionary idea that physical phenomena are correctly studied experimentally. Hence, through his vacuum experiments Pascal was a father of the empirical scientific method as a valid way to learn truth. Pascal's legacy continues today, as our society esteems empirical science (as illustrated by the fact that the licensure of medical treatments and vaccines requires a series of controlled experiments in animals and humans).

Pascal did other groundbreaking work in physics; for example he conducted experiments to determine the weight of air. As a result, today the standard international (SI) unit of pressure is named a "Pascal." Pascal is also the father of hydrostatics, inventing the hydraulic press and the syringe.

Furthermore Pascal was a father of computer science. He devised the basic binary coding system that is used in computers, and invented the world's first working computer, a mechanical adding machine. For 10 years Pascal worked diligently to design, oversee construction, and market what is now called the Pascaline. In total 50 of these adding machines were built, several of which still exist in working order. While Pascal did not realize his entrepreneurial ambition to become a 17th century Bill Gates, failing in his marketing of the Pascaline, this endeavor constitutes one example among many of how he was 350 years ahead of his time.

Also anticipating Bill Gates, Pascal was an engineer with a philanthropic bent. Pascal designed a public transport system for Paris and formed a company to build it. This horse-and-carriage system (the carrosses a cinq sols), implemented in the last year of Pascal's life, was the world's first public transportation system. Pascal developed this service out of his love for the poor, designing it such that they received all the profits. This original philanthropic achievement is particularly remarkable given that Pascal was gravely ill in the last few years of his life.

To summarize Pascal's scientific achievements, he was a father or the father of at least four fields– mathematical probability, hydrostatics, computer science, and public transportation, and accordingly numerous things have been named after him. While the descriptor genius is overused, I have never heard anyone challenge its application to Pascal– his fiercest atheist detractors invariably acknowledge his greatness in science (before lamenting his "wrong turn" to Christianity– "I will never forgive Christianity for what it did to Pascal," said Nietzsche).

Pascal's Impact on the Author. At age 18 I was confused about how a person could both be a scientist and a Christian, and confused about how an intelligent person could believe Christianity is true. The example of Pascal forever erased these doubts. Pascal convinced me that,

> It is certain that there are no grounds for laughing at those who do follow [the Christian religion]. [*Pensée* 482]

Pascal's scientific accomplishments earn him respect among today's intellectuals, giving him a platform to be heard on non-scientific topics including religion. I discovered from Pascal that my uncomfortable feeling about the incompatibility of science and faith did not have a rational basis. This feeling came from hearing people *assert* this incompatibility; for example the co-discoverer of DNA, James Watson, remarked that when he meets religious scientists, "I'm a bit embarrassed [laugh] because, you know, I can't believe anyone accepts truth by revelation." (Dawkins, 2006) Pascal helped me see that such pronouncements are more like playground sneers, aimed to embarrass people into unbelief, than like rational arguments demonstrating any real contradictions. It also struck me as obvious that my vocation as a scientist gave me no better tools for addressing my basic problems (such as my restlessness and mortality) than would other vocations.

Attribute 2: Pascal's Father Étienne. A second attribute of Blaise Pascal is that he had a wise, loving, and astute father. Blaise and his sisters were extremely close to their father. Étienne Pascal gave up his position as a lawyer and government official in Clermont to home-school his children. For the time it was a rare decision to abdicate a prestigious post in preference to educate his daughters as well as his son. Étienne was highly accomplished, fluent in Greek and Latin, and one of the leading mathematicians of the day. Étienne co-founded Marin Mersenne's Academy, the leading hub in Europe for the exchange of mathematical ideas (Mersenne was one of René Descartes' most frequent correspondents).

Étienne brought Blaise with him to regular meetings of the Academy as well as to other scientific meetings, where Blaise shined as a child prodigy. In Pascal's day leading mathematicians were celebrities. Blaise enjoyed scientific collaborations with his father, for example, he developed the adding machine to help him with his tax work. After Étienne died in 1651, Blaise's scientific activities lessened, perhaps in part because he had lost his favorite colleague.

Attribute 3: Pascal the Writer. A third attribute of Pascal is his giftedness as a writer. Following publication of *The Provincial Letters* Voltaire hailed Pascal as the greatest French prose artist, and kept the *Letters* on his bed stand. Voltaire must have *really* liked the *Letters* in light of his open disdain for Pascal's shift in intellectual work from science to religion. Today, France still hails Pascal's French as the official writing style to emulate.

Attribute 4: Pascal's Context. A fourth attribute of Pascal is that he lived during the beginning of the Enlightenment, as a contemporary of René Descartes, the father of modern philosophy. Descartes was a major player to put in motion the Enlightenment, which carried the idea that human reason alone is sufficient to solve the problems facing humanity and to achieve happiness and a just civilization– this idea is still quite influential today.

Peter Kreeft (1993) proposes that Pascal was the only major philosopher of this period who did *not* jump on Descartes' scientific method bandwagon. For Pascal, what was often passed for knowledge was more like *presumption*. Descartes claimed to know by "pure reason" that a vacuum could not exist in nature; Pascal showed this to be presumption by demonstrating experimentally the existence of a vacuum. This is akin to counting teeth to refute Aristotle's claim that women have fewer teeth than men. Pascal criticized Descartes and his admirers for their belief that pure reason could attain understanding of ultimate principles, and pointed to literature carrying this overly optimistic opinion about reason's reach. For example in *Pensée* 199 Pascal observes the ostentatious title of Pico della Mirandola's 1486 monograph, *Of All that Can be Known*.

Though Pascal sharply criticized the Enlightenment philosophers for their inflated estimation of scientific reasoning, Pascal did *not* have a low view of science. To the contrary, he thought it a potent means for obtaining knowledge, but only a certain kind of knowledge– of physical phenomena observable by the senses– which to Pascal was science's proper order of study. Pascal's criticism was not with science, but with the reductionist viewpoint that everything can be understood from a material and natural viewpoint; Pascal's beef was with *scientism*, the worldview that science is all there is. In Douglas Groothuis' (2003) words:

> Pascal thought that a materialistic and mechanistic analysis of the human person could never fully account for consciousness or for contact with a supernatural order of love or the heart.

Pascal's Impact on the Author, Continued. No wonder as an 18 year-old agnostic I found Pascal's theist approach more attractive than the cold, materialist approach of Descartes. In fact, the essay comparing Pascal and Descartes that I wrote for an in-class test in my freshman French literature class, which I still keep as a memento marking my change in life direction, reveals my awakening allure to Pascal's approach. I concluded the essay by noting that, "God was important to each of their universes, but to Pascal [God] meant everything important, and not just a cause for whatever effect Descartes wished to produce." My curiosity was piqued by Pascal's God-centered philosophy but not by Descartes', which, in Pascal's words, "would like to do without God; but [Descartes] could not help allowing him a flick of the fingers to set the world in motion; after that he had no more use for God." [Saying attributed to Pascal] Descartes' suggestion that I could find meaning and happiness through reliance on human reasoning alone resounded as over-simplified and false, whereas Pascal's comprehensive Christ-centered approach resounded as amazing, possible, and worthy of exploration. What I really wanted was happiness, wisdom, goodness; Pascal showed me that science is impotent to achieve these ends, rather the heart is required, as we will explore in chapter 3. Moreover, Descartes' suggestion to "make my chief happiness depend upon me alone" (1641 letter to Princess Elizabeth [Grayling, 2005]) resounded as futile, for it was obvious I could never bootstrap myself to real happiness. Better odds, it seemed, to take Pascal's bet to make my happiness depend on God alone.

Jesuit-Jansenist Controversy and The Provincial Letters. The event most responsible for Pascal's reputation as a hero of the Christian faith is the so-called Jesuit-Jansenist controversy. The Reformation arose in the 16th century as a protest against superstitions and abuses within the Catholic Church, and the emergent Calvinist Protestantism stressed both the corruption of humankind and salvation by grace alone. Protestantism rejected the hierarchical structure of Catholicism and swept away most of its devotional traditions. In response, the Pope approved the Society of

Jesus in 1540 (i.e., the Jesuits) as front line troops to counter the Protestant rigorism. The Jesuists reacted to Calvinism by diminishing man's corruption and emphasizing the value of works and free will for salvation, and they came under criticism for becoming worldly and morally lax. Among the critics was Catholic Bishop Cornelius Jansenius, who through his massive work *Augustinus* taught that the Catholic Church must return to grace-centered and rigorous doctrine as delineated by Saint Augustine. A convent and school at Port-Royal became the spiritual headquarters of what became known as Jansenism. In a nutshell Jansenism can be thought of as a denomination within Catholicism that sought to reform the Church to adhere to Augustine's teachings. Port-Royal was the center of this French-Augustinian movement.

Pascal's whole family had been converted to Jansenism in 1646, when Pascal was 23, and Pascal's sister Jacqueline entered Port-Royal as a nun in 1652. Blaise's total conversion in 1654 made him a devoted champion of Port-Royal for the remainder of his life, though he never officially declared himself a Jansenist, and he disagreed with some decisions of the Jansenist leader Antoine Arnauld (Connor, 2006). To Pascal the Port-Royal Society practiced Jesus' teachings with exemplary piety.

Pascal and the Port-Royal scholars criticized the Jesuits for becoming complacent, abdicating their responsibility to spiritually guide their parishioners in the ways taught in the Bible, and all too often providing chameleonic guidance that accommodated worldly desires. In response, some Jesuits attacked Port-Royal. In an effort to destroy Jansenism, the Faculty of Theology at the Sorbonne, consisting mainly of Jesuits, examined the *Augustinus*. They found it to contain heresy, and they sent seven paraphrased propositions from this work to the Pope. Pope Innocent X censured the propositions as heretical.

Beleaguered by the attacks from the Jesuits, as well as from France's king Louis XIV, the Queen mother, France's cardinal Mazarin, and many of the diocesan clergy in France (Connor, 2006), the scholars at Port-Royal pleaded with Pascal to help their cause. Pascal agreed, and set out to write a blistering satire of the Jesuits' corrupt practices and unjust persecution of Antoine Arnauld. He wrote anonymously to ordinary people, not dryly as an academic, but in a pleasant, ironic, and amusing style so that ordinary people would read the work. Most of the letters are in the form of a dialog between (the anonymous) Pascal and the "good Jesuit Father," wherein Pascal interviews the Father about the Society's methods for spiritually guiding parishioners. Pascal comes across as ethical and level-headed whereas the good Father comes across as the opposite. The longer the interview goes, Pascal becomes increasingly shocked to learn more and more rules of behavior the Society has invented to make pious living, which used to be hard, easy. With the enthusiasm of a collector of rare specimens, the Father proudly explains case after case of behaviors that used to be prohibited by the traditional Church fathers (e.g., Augustine), but, thanks to the ingenuity of the more "in tune" modern Fathers, have now been justified. For two examples, in the seventh and ninth letters the Father describes the society's imaginative rules for getting around the commandments to not kill and to not lie: "You may kill a person who has slapped you, even if he runs away, provided that you avoid doing so out of hatred or vengeance;" and, "Promises are not binding if one has no intention of being bound when making them." [Pages 109 and 142]

These examples illustrate the Society's use of hair-splitting technicalities to make easy the receipt of God's favor. In contrast to this accommodating chameleonic approach to spiritual guidance, the interviewer (Pascal) never departs from the traditional Augustinian position. Pascal's rhetoric would be winsome for readers of the letters, who, all being Catholic, would find the Society's inventions to dispense with the obligation to keep the 10 commandments– and in the end with the "irksome and tiresome" obligation to love God– as beyond the pale. Pascal's demonstration of the Society's corruption is based on meticulous reproductions of the Jesuit Father's own publications, including extensive quotations. By playing fair, which entails not spinning the Jesuits' words out of their context but instead "professing to say nothing [in the *Letters*] without certain proof," Pascal squeezes the Society into a corner with no logical course of defense. Indeed, it is difficult to conceive of a convincing reply to Pascal's devastating combination of brilliant logic and brilliant rhetoric.

The letters are extremely funny; for example in the ninth letter the good Father brags of the society's marvelous book, *Easy Piety*, and Pascal closes the letter by recommending to his friend the Society's new book, *Paradise Opened by a Hundred Easily Performed Devotions*. As Dr. Krailsheimer suggests in his introduction to *The Provincial Letters*, Pascal's critique of the Jesuits was *not* about a petty inter-denominational squabble; rather it was about fighting for the life of an authentic Christian faith; and it is certain that Pascal would not have softened his attack had he directed it against any other group of over-accommodating Christian leaders (see *Chameleon Christianity*, Keyes, 1999).

Nineteen letters appeared spanning 14 months between 1656 and 1657, which were very widely read and repeatedly condemned by the Catholic Church. These letters, now referred to as *The Provincial Letters*, were placed on the Church's Index of Forbidden Books in 1657, and Louis XIV ordered all copies of the letters collected and burned. Mazarin's secret police shut down printing companies that circulated *The Provincial Letters*, which forced their operations underground, serving only to increase their wild popularity (Connor, 2006). The vigorous efforts of Mazarin's police to determine the identity of the author were unsuccessful. Pascal's authorship did become known by 1658, but by this time the furor to chop off the author's head had died down, in part because of the Miracle of the Holy Thorn.

The famous miracle took place in March of 1656, just when the convent at Port-Royal was at its nadir of beleaguerment. Pascal's beloved 10-year old niece Marguerite (Gilberte's daughter) was suffering from a badly infected eye, with a pus- and blood-filled fistula, when nuns at Port-Royal touched the fistula with a venerated thorn that legend held was taken from the Crown that Jesus wore at the crucifixion. Later that day Marguerite showed the nuns that the fistula had disappeared. At first the nuns told no one about the miracle, and five days later they told Blaise. Blaise and Marguerite's father Florin arranged for seven doctors to examine Marguerite, who concluded unanimously it was a genuine miracle (O'Connell, 1997). The doctors spread the word throughout Paris, and such a buzz was created that even some of the powerful enemies of the Jansenists were moved and intrigued, culminating in the archbishop of Paris leading a committee of physicians and theologians to further examine the event. The committee declared Marguerite's healing an authentic miracle. The widespread fascination and acceptance of the Miracle of the Holy Thorn greatly encouraged Port-Royal and its supporters, ameliorating for the time being the ill will that had gathered against the community.

The Provincial Letters use interviewing and reporting techniques, and mark the birth of modern journalism. It was a remarkable innovation to take a political cause to the public through a gripping drama. From today's perspective this does not seem remarkable, given that society is drenched with political causes put to the public with all manner of rhetorical techniques. In Pascal's day this approach was new, however, again pointing to Pascal's originality– Pascal is a father of modern journalism.

Pascal wrote *The Provincial Letters* at great personal risk. Had his identity become known at the wrong time, he may have been put to death, and almost certainly would have been excommunicated. As a Catholic, to Pascal excommunication would have meant his spiritual death– the forfeiture of his salvation. Thus, Pascal risked his life and his salvation by defending what he saw as truth. High stakes indeed.

Pascal's approach to defending Port-Royal exemplifies a key idea expressed in the *Pensées*, Pascal's theory of orders, wherein Pascal stresses the importance of applying appropriate means for obtaining different kinds of knowledge. In particular, Pascal distinguishes between things that are appropriately known by faith and things that are appropriately known by the senses and reason. Pope Innocent X had declared the seven propositions heretical. Whether the propositions were heretical was a matter of faith, and Pascal believed in the authority of the Bible and Church fathers for judging such matters. But in matters of empirical observation, Pascal thought the senses, reason, and science are the correct means of knowing. Pascal argued that the propositions sent to the Pope were not actually contained in the *Augustinus*, and that it was outside the Pope's authority to pronounce unilaterally on matters of fact. Pascal called this misapplication of authority *tyrannical*, suggesting that an un-tyrannical process would have called upon an impartial third party of expert scholars to fact-check whether the propositions were actually in the *Augustinus*. (*Pensée* 59) Vice versa, to Pascal a scientist is qualified to judge facts and draw inferences from data, but acts tyrannically if he makes unilateral judgments on faith. Pascal saw a great danger in scientists overreaching with reason into matters of faith and ethics, and his fears came true during the next few centuries in the Age of Reason. We will further consider Pascal's theory of orders in chapter 6.

The Jesuit-Jansenist controversy ended badly for Port-Royal. In 1661 the nuns were required to sign official statements disavowing their allegiance to Jansenism. Just before the forced signing, Jacqueline died at the age of 36, of a broken heart, suggested Blaise. At the order of Louis XIV, Port-Royal was razed in 1710, its cemetery was plowed over, and the graves of its nuns were disinterred, their remains thrown into a common grave.

Jansenism survived in scattered places inside and outside France, but it would never be recognized as a legitimate element of the Catholic Church. *The Provincial Letters* live on, however, and are still widely loved. *The Provincial Letters* are a testament to a small, dissident group of faithful and truth-seeking persons who fought for reform against the dominant power by appealing to the populous, one of the earliest examples of such an activity. They also testify to Pascal's hard work, passion, and courage expended in defending truth and Christian integrity. These efforts have buttressed Pascal's reputation as a hero of the Christian faith.

Major Literary Influences. Before turning to the *Pensées* in Part II, we will consider Pascal's major literary influences. The most influential book was the Bible, which Pascal knew virtually by heart. Scripture verses written down from memory are spliced throughout the *Pensées*.

After the Bible, Augustine was Pascal's dominant influence. It is difficult to overstate the extent of Augustine's influence on Pascal, most notably on Pascal's strong sense of the necessity of revelation to understand God and ourselves, an emphasis on Original Sin and the Fall and its devastating effect to corrupt all of man's faculties, a Christ-centeredness, with Jesus Christ as the only hope for a cure from the corrupt nature that resulted from the Fall, and a view of the Christian life that is deeply devoted to God, which includes a renouncing of vain worldly pleasures and materialism, and serving the poor. During the last few years of his life, while seriously ill, Pascal gave his considerable library away, except for two books for nourishment: the Bible and Augustine's Confessions (Kreeft, 1993). As relayed by Gilberte, when Pascal was able to get out of bed, he walked the streets of Paris to talk and meet with the poor, giving them what money he had. In the last two months of his life, Pascal provided shelter to a poor family with small pox (Connor, 2006).

In a certain sense, there is nothing new in the *Pensées*– Pascal's thoughts are found in Augustine. Pascal did not intend to innovate, but rather to offer an original interpretation of Augustine's thought that would be most helpful to his secular friends, to persuade them to seek God and to provide them enough light to find God. In another sense, however, Pascal is deeply original, as he himself suggested based on his new arrangement of material [*Pensée* 696, at the end of the Prologue of this guided tour], and for the ingenious manner in which he addressed the Western mind at its transition point between medieval and modern times.

Pascal was widely read in the ancient classics and in contemporary works such as the *Essays* of the French secular skeptic Montaigne. Drawing from Montaigne's ideas and clever turns of phrase, much of the *Pensées* describe Man's unhappy condition apart from God. While Pascal and Montaigne were in accord about the restlessness, ignorance, self-love, hedonism, and vanity of the human condition, they differed totally on the matter of a cure– Montaigne explained Man's condition but did *not* offer a remedy, while Pascal explained it *and* offered a path to happiness. In fact, Pascal's two major themes of the *Pensées* are Man's unhappiness without God and Man's happiness with him. We now turn to Pascal's approach to delivering these themes.

Part II. Pascal's Apologetic Approach

Pascal outlines his two overarching theses in *Pensée* 6:

> First part: Wretchedness of man without God.
> Second part: Happiness of man with God...

Pascal uses the words "wretchedness" and "happiness" with great repetition, and to understand him it is important to consider what he meant by these terms. Peter Kreeft (1993) notes Pascal uses these words in their ancient sense. To moderns, happiness is a temporary emotional feeling. Our word "happiness" comes from the Old English "hap," which means chance, luck, or fortune; under this definition happiness is something that happens to us– it is out of our control.

In contrast, the ancients meant by happiness a state of real and permanent perfection of soul in this life and for eternity. This perfection includes an objective state of true moral goodness in which God counts a person as righteous. Such happiness is immutable– true even when sick, suffering, or asleep. It includes a peace that "rules in your heart," (Apostle Paul, Colossians 3:15) a peace impervious to circumstances, opposite to the peace the world gives that is tethered to them. Pascal proposes Christianity is attractive because it offers objective and complete happiness– Man's "true good" (Pascal borrows Socrates' term). [*Pensée* 12]

Similarly, by "wretchedness" Pascal means an objective state of the human situation that resulted from the Fall. This state of wretchedness includes 1) an ignorance about the origin and meaning of one's life, with a severely restricted capacity to apprehend truth; 2) a precarious existence– death may strike at any moment and humans are powerless to prevent it; 3) a state of restlessness and inconstancy; 4) an emptiness of being and meaning; and 5) an inclination to unduly love oneself and to fail to duly love God and neighbor.

Augustine's *City of God* shares Pascal's two theses. Augustine proposes that every person lives either in the City of Man or the City of

God, living primarily to love self or God, and life will continue on in the chosen dwelling into eternity:

> Two cities have been formed by two loves; the earthly by the love of self, even to the contempt of God; the heavenly by the love of God, even to the contempt of self. [*De civitate dei*]

Defenders of orthodox Christianity, from the Apostle Paul to C.S. Lewis and G.K. Chesterton, center their theology on the two main points of sin and salvation (Kreeft, 1993). In fact, Francis Schaefer offers the following definition of a Christian based on these two points:

> Someone who has bowed twice, once humbly in submission, because we cannot put meaning on ourselves, second in gratitude to God, for his gift of grace.

Many revisionist forms of Christianity reject one of these two truths. Modernist forms reject the "sin" point, for example scientology (developed by L. Ron Hubbard, with adherents including John Travolta and Tom Cruise) and Unitarianism, and the "de-mythologized" Christianity of Thomas Jefferson. In rejecting the sin point, most secular agnostics today have a difficult time believing the Christian tenet that every human heart is bent toward self-centeredness and is capable of wickedness–instead they suppose that bad things come from odd, exceptional criminals who are unlike the normal human being. Our generation is opposite from past ones, who readily accepted that humans are sinners, but tended to doubt salvation. Tertullian referred to the two most pervasive Christian heresies in history, licentiousness and legalism (loose-living and pharisaical self-righteousness), as the "two thieves of the gospel." These heresies can be defined by the rejection of law (licentiousness) or the rejection of grace (legalism); in contrast the orthodox Christian gospel embraces both.

To many today, the "good news" of Pascal's second part seems like "bad news;" the offer of a redeemer is irrelevant and unwelcome for people who do not think they have a sin problem and thus need cleansing. A healthy person does not feel the need for a doctor. No reasonable person would take chemotherapy if she were cancer-free, but no reasonable person would refuse it if it were the only way to become cancer-free. The first part of Pascal's apology is absolutely required to reach the second part; one must know one's wretchedness, and thus need of help, for redemption to be relevant.

Pascal outlines the method he will use to support his two central points in the second half of *Pensée* 6:

> First part: Nature is corrupt, proved by nature itself.
> Second part: There is a redeemer, proved by Scripture.

Pascal's approach to establishing the first point, the wretchedness of man without God, requires no faith or revelation from God. Man's corruption is verifiable just from watching CNN. As expressed in the book of Ecclesiastes, not faith, only experience, is needed to discover that life without God is vain. In contrast, to Pascal more than experience is needed to discover that there is a redeemer. Because of the Fall, humans are bent toward sin and only a "barely glimmering idea" of God remains; [*Pensée* 149] nature and human reason alone are not enough to discover a saving God. In order to know there is a redeemer, Pascal insists on the necessity of revelation and God's action to move the heart, and uses classical arguments to support the credibility of Christianity, including the fulfillment of prophecies, miracles, and the existence and perpetuity of the Jewish people. Pascal rejects Descartes' proposal that the things of God can be deduced from human reasoning alone. Rather, God would have to speak for himself. [*Pensée* 303]

Pascal also presents powerful arguments for the uniqueness of Christianity, with thesis that only through Christ can humanities' condition be understood and its problems solved. Henry Phillips, Professor of French at The University of Manchester, summarizes Pascal's two-part apologetic approach (Hammond, 2003):

> Pascal offers a portrait of the human condition that provokes questions whose answers will be found only in the Christian religion.

Pascal's Approach to Winning Seekers. Pascal's approach to persuading his listeners to seek God presupposes they desire happiness. The question, then, is how to find it. Pascal brings his listener to a fork in the road: Seek happiness by worldly means or by the way provided by the Church and Scripture. Two popular worldly means, which mark our time even more than Pascal's, are diversions and indifference. "Diversions" may include work, entertainment, or virtually any activity that is used to fill up life with business to avoid thinking about one's unhappy state. By "indifference" Pascal means choosing to be disinterested in the great problems (e.g., mortality) that face us. Both these strategies are evasion techniques, sticking one's head in the sand, to avoid thinking about the elephant in the room.

In chapter 2 we will tour Pascal's devastating calling out of humanity as driven to diversions and indifference. By "proving" the futility of seeking happiness through diversions and indifference, Pascal makes the other road, Christian faith, attractive. If the Christian God is real then there is a real solution– complete happiness entailing permanent joy and peace. Given the infinite value of this happiness, Pascal suggests that any reasonable person should seek after it with all their strength. Indeed, the fact/reality that every person desires happiness makes it rationally compelling to wager on seeking God (see chapter 7).

Pascal's apologetic approach aims to satisfy his friends in both their desire for happiness and their desire for intellectual rectitude. Pascal outlines his three-step strategy for winning seekers in *Pensée* 12:

> *Order.* Men despise religion. They hate it and are afraid it may be true. The cure for this is first to show that religion is not contrary to reason, but worthy of reverence and respect.
>
> Next make it attractive, make good men wish it were true, and then show that it is.
>
> Worthy of reverence because it really understands human nature.
>
> Attractive because it promises true good.

These three steps of Pascal's apology can be rephrased as follows:

Step 1. Show it is worthy of respect (not contrary to reason). The first step is to remove his listener's stumbling block– for example his mistaken belief that he cannot be both a scientist and a Christian. Earl Palmer suggests this step is effective because "respect is an inch away from faith."

Step 2. Make it attractive. Other beckoning paths to happiness, whether diversions and indifference; the theories of presumptuous philosophers; or the offerings of other religions such as deism and Islam, do not promise the "true good" promised by Christianity.

Step 3. Show that it is true. This demonstration will involve much more than the logical mind– to Pascal the heart and new habits are required.

Steps 1 and 2 preview Pascal's Wager, where the two stakes of the gamble are one's reason and one's happiness. If a person can see that Christianity is not absurd, and is attractive, then he will seek, Pascal figures. Pascal's apologetics are winsome because they appeal to his listener's human nature that deeply wants to be both happy and reasonable, as exemplified in *Pensée* 160:

> There are only three sorts of people: those who have found God and serve him; those who are busy seeking him and have not found him; those who live without either seeking or finding him. The first are reasonable and happy, the last are foolish and unhappy; those in the middle are unhappy and reasonable.

Pascal's God-Shaped Vacuum. In his "vacuum" metaphor, Pascal points to the craving we feel for happiness as a sign that humankind once experienced true happiness, when it enjoyed unbroken paradise with God in the Garden. When Adam and Eve rebelled this happiness was lost, and all that remained was an "empty print and trace," an abyss in the heart. Pascal observed people trying to fill this vacuum with anything, with wealth, power, recognition, etc., but

> ...none can help, since this infinite abyss can be filled only with an infinite and immutable object, in other words by God himself [*Pensée*148].

To Pascal, the fact that we discover an abyss in our heart is a powerful hint that our hearts were once full– for if we never had tasted glory and true happiness, how could we ache from the loss of it? The common feeling of deep restlessness and unhappiness is a clue that we once lived in a paradise with God. Man's aching heart that longs to return to Eden is Pascal's famous image of the God-shaped vacuum in every human heart. Augustine famously expresses this thought as, "...you have made us for yourself, and our heart is restless until it rests in you."

Peter Kreeft (1993) helpfully summarizes Pascal's overall approach to winning seekers in the *Pensées*. In the first part, Pascal's goal is to accurately describe the human condition, delineating its odd and enigmatic nature. In Kreeft's metaphor, Man is a "very strangely shaped lock, with weird protuberances and indentations." Man's weirdness includes his dual condition of being very great and very wretched in all areas of life, including the carnal/physical, intellectual, and spiritual arenas of reality. Pascal describes enigmatic Man as a "monster that passes all understanding." [*Pensée* 130]

In the second part of the *Pensées*, Pascal's goal is to demonstrate that Christianity is like a key, equally oddly shaped as the human lock, but which fits the lock perfectly (Chesterton also used this metaphor in *Orthodoxy*). Pascal endeavors to show that among all the philosophies and religions of the world, only the Christian religion explains the human enigma. This wins respect for Christianity, suggests Pascal, since any religion, if true, must provide a description of the human situation consistent with *all* of the observations about Man's thought life and behavior. Because the Christian model uniquely fits the human data, only Christianity can effectively transform humans from wretchedness to happiness. Pascal aims to make his friends see this grand potential of the faith, to the point that they will wager on a vigorous experiment of seeking (chapter 7).

Part III. *The Memorial*

The Memorial refers to the poem Pascal wrote during his intense personal encounter with God on an autumn evening in 1654– Pascal's "road to Damascus" experience. It was written hastily on a piece of parchment that was found sewn into Pascal's clothing by his nephew after his death.

The Memorial [*Pensée* 913]

The year of grace 1654
Monday, 23 November, feast of Saint Clement, Pope and Martyr, and of others in the Martyrology.
Eve of Saint Chrysogonus, Martyr and others.
From about half past ten in the evening until half past mid-night.

Fire

'God of Abraham, God of Isaac, God of Jacob,'[1] *not of philosophers and scholars.*
Certainty, certainty, heartfelt, joy, peace.
God of Jesus Christ.

---

[1] Exodus 3:6

God of Jesus Christ.

My God and your God.[2]

'Thy God shall be my God.'[3]

The world forgotten, and everything except God.

He can only be found in the way taught in the Gospels.

Greatness of the human soul.

'*O righteous Father, the world had not known thee*, but I have known thee.'[4]

Joy, joy, joy, tears of joy.

I have cut myself off from him.

They have forsaken me, the fountain of living waters.[5]

'My God wilt thou forsake me?'[6]

Let me not be cut off from him forever!

'And this is life eternal, that they might know thee, the only true God, and Jesus Christ whom thou hast sent.'[7]

Jesus Christ.

Jesus Christ.

I have cut myself off from him, shunned him, denied him, crucified him.

Let me never be cut off from him!

He can only be kept by the ways taught in the Gospel.

Sweet and total renunciation.

Total submission to Jesus Christ and my director.

Everlasting joy in return for one day's effort on earth.

I will not forget thy word.[8] Amen.

---

[2] John 20:17

[3] Ruth 1:16

[4] John 17:25

[5] Jeremiah 2:13

[6] Cf. Matthew 27:46

[7] John 17:3

[8] Psalm 119:16

While breaking *The Memorial* into pieces does violence to it as poetry, I will offer comments on parts of it as a way to further outline major themes in the *Pensées*.

Fire. After the preamble Pascal begins with "fire." To Pascal inspiration from God is necessary to believe; God must move the heart.

'God of Abraham, God of Isaac, God of Jacob,' not of philosophers and scholars. A theme of the *Pensées* is that intellectual effort cannot by itself lead to true knowledge of God. Faith is needed, which involves the heart as well as the mind. Pascal suggests there is profound danger in emphasizing reason as the principle faculty for knowing God, an idea championed by "philosophers and scholars" such as Descartes. Reliance on the intellect can lead to pride, inclining a person in a direction opposite to one that leads to knowledge of God. Pascal proposes that the whole person must be engaged to find God; the body, will, and heart are as important as the mind (chapter 6). One must struggle to deny the body its greedy appetites, one must habitually participate in Christian practices such as Church-going and the sacraments, and one must be teachable, including learning to accept paradoxical mysteries instead of arrogantly inventing imaginary solutions that God does not illuminate. In contrast to proud scholars who elevate the mind above the will and heart as the means to finding God, the God of Abraham, Isaac, and Jacob is a living God, who is related to primarily on the basis of submission, obedience, and faith– not reason. This fiery God cannot be fit into the mold of a philosopher's choosing. To Pascal, knowing God is not fundamentally about knowing a set of ideas, which is all that the philosophers offer; rather it is about knowing a living person.

He can only be found by the ways taught in the Gospels. This statement furthers Pascal's point about the limitations of reason for finding God; to Pascal reasoning brings little progress if not joined with listening to God's own words as taught in the Gospels. This illustrates the strong Pascalian theme of the necessity of submitting to God's revealed way to finding God.

Greatness of the human soul. This phrase captures the first piece of Pascal's theme that humans are both very great and very wretched, a "dispossessed king" in Pascal's words, or a "glorious ruin" in Francis Schaefer's.

I have cut myself off from him, shunned him, denied him, crucified him. This phrase shows Pascal's deep awareness of his own sin and culpability before God– the wretchedness half of his humanity. At times Pascal cut himself off through diversions and prideful living in Parisian society, refusing to seek God in earnest. A theme of the *Pensées* is that one must perceive and confess one's wretchedness in order to find God and walk with him. Honest self-inspection and humility are needed.

Let me not be cut off from him forever! The exclamation point underscores Pascal's terror at spending eternity without God. Pascal uses the topic of death and its permanence as a powerful smelling salt to wake his unbelieving listeners from their reality-avoidance state that is sustained by diversions and apathy– more in chapter 2.

Everlasting joy in return for one day's effort on earth. Pascal frequently draws upon the concept of infinity, and here he contrasts the infinite joy in heaven with the finite effort of obedience on earth, summed up as one day's effort. This phrase recalls Second Corinthians 4:17: "For our light affliction, which is but for a moment, is working for us a far more exceeding and eternal weight of glory." The *Pensées* make great use of the contrast between the infinite and the finite, both to set up the goal of the infinite God as supremely worth seeking after, and to humble Man's presumption. The intellectual pride of philosophers like Descartes was inflating like a balloon expanding to infinity. But to Pascal, in order to know God humans must know the limits of their knowing capacity, and acknowledge their true proportion compared to God. "What is a man in the infinite?" [*Pensée* 199] In chapter 3 we will consider *Pensées* on the topic of the disproportion of man, wherein Pascal seeks to humble his listener by portraying him as a finite creature caught between the infinitely small and the infinitely vast.

Tying together the elements of Pascal's *Memorial*, Pascal's 'joy, joy, joy, tears of joy' is, in the end, caused by God's infinite love for Pascal, as God demonstrated to Abraham personally through the symbol of fire (Genesis 15:17). To seal his special covenant with Abraham, God passed a flaming torch between two torn-apart animal halves, signifying that God himself– not Abraham– would incur the punishment if Abraham were to break the covenant. I imagine that Pascal's tears of joy flowed upon recognizing that God's supreme love was also for him.

At the end of each chapter I will commend to you a quotable *Pensée*, the "*Pensée* of the Day," selected to be practically helpful for living well. The first PoD is on the topic of Pascal's theory of orders, surveyed in chapter 6.

***Pensée* of the Day: Number 949**

It is false piety to preserve peace at the expense of truth. It is also false piety to preserve truth at the expense of charity.

Pensée 949 expresses the principle that truth is more important than physical security, which Pascal himself adhered to through his efforts in the Jesuit-Jansenist controversy. Theodore Roosevelt would agree, remarking, "If I must choose between righteousness and peace, I choose righteousness." *Pensée* 949 also expresses Pascal's view that charity (i.e., God's love, agape) is an essential component of pious truth-telling– without charity truths may be spoken for extremely selfish pursuits ignoring the interests of the hearers– in the Jesuits case, suggests Pascal, for shoring up power and self-determination.

Pensée 949 also suggests practical principles for how to respond when brethren within the church appear to be out of line with the truth of the Gospel. First, it asserts it is false piety to not address the problem; it is better to tussle over truth than to keep a false peace that allows false teaching or practice to perpetuate. Second, the parties perpetuating the false-hoods must be treated with charity. In muckraking the Jesuit Fathers, Pascal did not present a laundry list of their faults, self-righteously lording them over them. He instead crafted selected criticisms in a manner he thought helpful for opening a path to their reformation back to legitimate leaders of the church. In fact in the *Provincial Letters* Pascal expresses to the Father that, "all I want is your true good," [fourteenth *Letter*] "I simply want to make you horrified at yourselves," [sixteenth Letter] and, quoting Psalm 83:16, "Fill their faces with shame, that they may seek Your name, O Lord." [Sixteenth *Letter*] Moreover, in the eleventh *Letter* Pascal explains to the Fathers that he makes sport of them out of an obligation to love them, quoting Augustine, "For charity sometimes obliges us to laugh at men's errors so as to bring them to laugh too and avoid them." Paul's letter to the Ephesians undergirds Pascal's approach to join truth with love, wherein Paul urges speaking truth only for seeking the good of the hearer (i.e., "speak the truth in love", Ephesians 4:29).

Synthesis Points of Chapter 1

1. Pascal was a brilliant and extremely influential scientist who defended orthodox Christianity against challenges from Enlightenment scientism thinkers.
2. Pascal courageously penned *The Provincial Letters*, through which he defended Port-Royal and Christian truth at great personal risk.
3. With the *Pensées* Pascal aimed to persuade his restless, over-entertained, skeptical friends to seek God.
4. Pascal's thesis in the *Pensées* is Man's wretchedness apart from God (God-shaped vacuum in the heart) and Man's restored happiness (state of perfection/completeness) in God and the body of Christ. This restoration is accomplished by grace through faith in Jesus Christ.
5. Pascal meant by "happiness" an objective state of goodness, holiness, joy, peace– in a word the normal state for which Man was created by God. By "wretchedness" he meant the opposite objective state that resulted from the Fall. Pascal summed up Man's current state that is wretched yet still carries the trace of its original happiness as "monstrous," a composite of contradictory attributes.

2 MAN'S WRETCHED CONDTION: UNHAPPY– DEATH, DIVERSIONS, INDIFFERENCE

"Without the hope of an afterlife, this life is not even worth the effort of getting dressed in the morning."
– Prince Otto von Bismarck

"How is it that this man so distressed at the death of his wife and his only son, deeply worried by some great feud, is not gloomy at the moment and is seen to be so free from all these painful and disturbing thoughts? There is no cause for surprise: he has just had a ball served to him and he must return it to his opponent."
– Blaise Pascal, *Pensée* 522

Countless readers of the *Pensées* have been amazed at Pascal's stunning description of Man's wretched condition, which constitutes a large part of the first half of Pascal's project. In the next three chapters we will explore several great *Pensées* on Man's wretched condition. This tour will include lengthy portions of the *Pensées*, to maximize your exposure to this ingenious writer.

Upon learning that reading the following chapters will entail dwelling on one's wretched condition, you might ask: "Why would I want to do that?" Consider *Pensée* 562:

> There are only two kinds of men: the righteous who think they are sinners and sinners who think they are righteous.

According to Pascal, then, if we wish to be saints, we must know our wretched condition. This knowledge is simply required for growing in the Christian life, and Pascal is a master teacher for showing it to us. This chapter is on the first of three attributes of Man's wretched condition apart from God– his unhappiness.

Outline of Chapter 2. In this chapter we will look at some of the most powerful *Pensées*, on diversions and indifference, which Pascal saw as symptoms of Man's unhappy state without God. I have collected these particular passages because they are known for creating silence and awe in those who hear them, as with incisive clarity they demonstrate that the human condition may be less happy and less sane than we might have thought. It is important to qualify up front that these *Pensées* are addressed to unbelievers, or to those on the fence. Had Pascal finished his apology, it is likely that much of the prose would have been delivered as a dialog between the unbelieving skeptic and Pascal the Christian; such a dialog would parallel Pascal's approach in *The Provincial Letters*. Acknowledging his interlocutor's skepticism about supernatural things such as divine revelation, Pascal assumes he will process Pascal's words according to his "natural lights." This Pascalian voice that speaks to Man without God must be borne in mind to understand these *Pensées*. Although they target the unbeliever or skeptic, they are also helpful for Christians, as they expose the dangers of diversions and indifference, ubiquitous today, which wreak havoc on many a believer's integrity.

Part I. Pascal's World and His Apologetic Hook

Death as the Entry Point. To initially engage his slumbering friend, Pascal rings a deafening alarm clock in his ear:

> Imagine a number of men in chains, all under sentence of death, some of whom are each day butchered in the sight of the others; those remaining see their own condition in that of their fellows, and looking at each other with grief and despair await their turn. This is the image of the human condition. [*Pensée* 434]

Like a hook for a song, Pascal intends this graphic picture to grab attention. If our reaction is that Pascal is being pessimistic about the human situation, I think it says more about our cultural condition that we want the details of death swept away from our sight, rather than about any inaccuracy in this *Pensée*. Pascal confronts us with the plain facts that death is certain; death is often like a butchering of sorts whether by disease or accident, death can take us at any time, none of us know when;

and at unknown intervals we observe the fellow members of our species returned to the earth. Furthermore, "butchering" is not a misleading adjective describing death, considering the ravishing impact that leading causes of death have on the body, such as cancer, tuberculosis, HIV/AIDS, and auto crashes. This *Pensée* describes the condition we find ourselves in.

Why Did Pascal Start with Death? We know from Pascal's own outline of his apology that he intended to begin with this topic. Why was death at the frontline? Was Pascal merely trying his hand at scripting a horror movie? Or was this a *strategy* grounded in genuine care for his interlocutor, a strategy that Jesus himself took? To approach an understanding of Pascal's plan, let us consider the worldview of Pascal's audience, which consisted of his unbelieving, sophisticated, gambling friends that he spent much time with, especially prior to his second conversion.

Recall that Pascal's friends held the worldview of modernism, which can be defined as "that culture, brought about in the West by the Enlightenment, which replaced Christian revelation with human reason" (Jock McGregor, 2004 Portland L'Abri conference). Modernism denies the reality of the supernatural by reducing reality to the natural world; it elevates human reason to the lofty position of being the ultimate and exclusive faculty for understanding truth, for solving problems and living well; and it views the individual as autonomous and not in need of God. Modernism is also characterized by materialistic hedonism.

Modernism's Achilles Heel. The Modernist worldview provides an answer to *almost* every problem– for disease, modern medicine; for unhappiness, sport, entertainment, and antidepressants; for boredom and restlessness, work and more sport, entertainment, and strong coffee; for social problems, education. However, *modernism has no satisfying answer for death*– death remains a fact that cannot be prevented by measures devised within a materialist worldview. In the Modernist view human beings are annihilated at death, and Pascal saw this as extremely unappealing to most people. Pascal, I believe, viewed death as modernisms' weakest point. By going straightaway to his friends' Achilles heel, Pascal creates pressure to drive him to consider a different worldview that offers a more attractive answer, and in fact offers a cure. In mathematical terms, I think of death as the topic that has the greatest ratio of attractiveness in the Christian worldview compared to unattractiveness in the Modernist worldview; this, I conjecture, is why Pascal fronts his apology with death.

Whereas 19th century Western culture tended to view death as an important topic to engage, in the 20th century it evolved to increasingly displace death further away from our awareness and consciousness. As an illustration, my 18 month old daughter received a doll for Christmas 2006 that spoke an electronic prayer, with first line, "Now I lay me down to sleep, I pray Thee, Lord, my soul to keep." The traditional prayer continues with the second line, "If I should die before I wake, I pray Thee, Lord, my soul to take." However, the doll instead spoke the safe phrase, "The angels watch me through the night, And keep me in their blessed sight." While re-assuring, this revision deletes a real and momentous issue that all children face and need help with. Many children express a fear of death– is it kinder to help a child discover a potential solution to death, or to leave her alone with no guidance on this problem?

Christianity's Appeal for Addressing Death. To further explore Pascal's purpose in fronting with death, consider that in his overall apologetic strategy Pascal aims to, "First make good men wish Christianity were true," [*Pensée* 12] that is, to first wake people to *take up an interest in seeking God*. With death Pascal plays the card with the greatest odds of breaking through entrenched attitudes. For such a grim condition as being in chains awaiting execution, even an indifferent person might be moved to find the silence offered by modernism terrifying compared to the everlasting life of joy offered by Christianity. Of course, wishing something to be true does not make it so, which Pascal fully acknowledged, having devoted over half of the *Pensées* to presenting evidence supporting (but not attempting to prove) the credibility of the Christian faith. But *wishing it were true*, Pascal espouses, is a key first step in finding God.

Three hundred and fifty years later, modernism persists, primarily as a belief in science and technology and a commitment to materialist hedonism, and as such I believe death remains a pressure point for motivating contemporaries to seek God. Although I will not address it here, death may also be a pressure point for another prevalent current-day worldview, postmodernism, as this worldview purports that it is impossible to know anything about what happens after death. Death stands out as an objective reality that no purely materialistic or relativistic worldview can satisfactorily address. Peter Kreeft (1993) observes that death is unattractive for a great number of non-Christian worldviews, remarking,

> Death kills all the philosophies; only Christ kills death.

Most humans are born with an innate horrification of death, rendering many worldviews with an exposed vulnerability to this topic.

Elsewhere in the *Pensées*, where he admits God into the discussion, Pascal emphasizes the great contrast between the misery of death without God and the joy of death with God. This is evident in a letter Pascal wrote to his sisters after his father died:

> Without Jesus Christ [death] is horrible, detestable, the horror of nature. In Jesus Christ, it is altogether different, it is benignant, holy, the joy of the faithful.

This difference can be seen by comparing the writings of the famous atheist Sigmund Freud with those of the famous Christian C.S. Lewis. Freud referred to death as a "painful riddle" and said, "It is impossible not to shudder at the thought." Lewis in contrast wrote, "Can you not see death as the friend and deliverer, it means stripping off that body which is tormenting you. What are you afraid of? Has the world been so kind to you that you should leave it with regret?" Freud recoiled at death, Lewis welcomed it.

The General Horror of Death. The claim that death is quite generally horrifying to humans can be supported from a number of sources, such as the history of literature– one can find terror of death expressed by authors spanning many worldviews and faiths. Consider the haunting line from the English clergyman poet John Donne, "Ask not for whom the bell tolls; it tolls for thee." Also, let us consider the poem "Aubade," written by the venerated 20th century British atheist poet Philip Larkin at the end of his career.

> The total emptiness for ever
> The sure extinction we travel to
> And shall be lost in always. Not to be
> here
> Not to be anywhere,
> And soon; nothing more terrible, nothing more true.

In my own experience, I feel innate recoil at death. I can remember as a child lying awake, and suddenly being gripped with terror at the thought of someday being annihilated, the permanent loss of consciousness; this feeling of dread visited me as an overwhelming inevitability, and Larkin's poem captured the way I felt.

Pascal saw death as an entry point to his interlocutor's innermost being, and shot his arrow straight in. Pascal had to be dramatic and artful to penetrate through the layers of wallpaper that his friends had pasted up to insulate themselves from feelings of terror.

Part II. Diversions

I would like now to consider the first of two popular methods that Pascal observed that people use to insulate themselves from feelings of terror– diversions. To begin this discussion, consider the question that Peter Kreeft (1993) poses, "Why doesn't anybody have any time today? Where did all the time go?" Kreeft searched far and wide for an answer to this question, and discovered Pascal's answer compelling. Pascal's answer in Kreeft's words:

> We *want* to complexify our lives. We don't *have* to, we *want* to. We want to be harried and hassled and busy. Unconsciously, we want the very thing we complain about. For if we had leisure, we would look at ourselves and listen to our hearts and see the great gaping hole in our hearts and be terrified, because the hole is so big that nothing but God can fill it.

This "hole" is wretchedness and death– without the help of God, these conditions are unbearable. How does a modern unbelieving world face such terrible truth?

Pascal's answer: Multiply diversions. Our incurable unhappy condition drives us to diversions:

> Being unable to cure death, wretchedness, and ignorance, men have decided, in order to be happy, not to think about such things. [*Pensée*133]

> If our condition were truly happy, we should not need to divert ourselves from thinking about it. [*Pensée* 70]

> ...but diversion passes our time and brings us imperceptibly to our death. [*Pensée* 414]

Unhappiness Drives One to Diversions. Diversions take myriad forms, from entertainment, sports, work, even activism or religious activities; all of which, if done vigorously and continuously, can keep one's mind from thinking about death. Diversions are so omnipresent in our society it is hardly helpful to give examples; nevertheless I will provide four. First, avid sports fans illustrate the principle that diversions beget more diversions. Many fans, not satisfied merely with watching games, gamble or join fantasy sports leagues, which have become so popular that there now exist professional advisors on how to best pick fantasy players! Secondly, consider workaholism. I have struggled with this myself, and in my most honest moments I could see that it was often the aching feeling of boredom and discontentment that drove me to work harder, to erase the empty feeling. For a third example, consider TV watching. Many shows, for example crime shows, emergency room shows, or the local news, lead the viewer through a series of *exciting and agitating events*. Pascal suggests to us that we like these shows because they *sustainably prevent us from thinking about our deep problems*. Fourthly, religion can be an ultimate diversion. Many religious pursuits have been driven by motivations other than honoring God, for example by a quest for power and self-glorification. For such diversionary religious pursuits Marx's remark on religion being the opiate of the masses is apt.

On the surface it may appear that a society like America's is the happiest, because it has so many options and expressions for leisure and entertainment. But, if Pascal is right, these are *symptoms* of America's truly unhappy condition. Widespread cynicism and boredom support this. Richard Stivers suggests that boredom among young people has deepened in recent decades, from what used to be a passing mood to a sustained experience of meaninglessness, a phenomenon he calls "hyperboredom." (Stivers, 1994) To alleviate the pain of boredom many Americans feed an addiction to noise and activity. (Andrew Fellows, *Building Cathedrals within Time*, 2007 L'Abri Conference) Furthermore, relatively objective statistics support America's unhappy state– compared to other countries the U.S. has among the highest rates of depression, divorce, suicide, drug use, and violence. Nevertheless, some persons are able to avoid these problems, and may hold out that a semblance of happiness can be kept by maintaining entertainments vigorously. Pascal dashes this hope in *Pensée* 132:

> *Diversion.* If man were happy, the less he were diverted the happier he would be, like the saints and God. Yes: but is a man not happy who can find delight in diversion?
>
> No: because it comes from somewhere else, from outside; so he is dependent, and always liable to be disturbed by a thousand and one accidents, which inevitably cause distress.

I am quite sure that if we had an hour to talk together, we could generate 101 examples where our plans for enjoyment were disrupted by small accidents such as rainy weather, traffic, a flu-bug, a recipe that fell flat, etc., ranging up to more serious events such as a cancer diagnosis. Remember how some of us felt unhappy after the "accident" of the Seahawks losing the 2006 Super Bowl? The outcome of the game was something out of our control, thus fans subject their emotions to an arbitrary accident. As a sports fan many times I've found myself down after a tough loss. How fickle, what a trivial determiner of whether I am happy– yet how accurate to my strange condition. A true state of happiness, Pascal suggests, must not depend on the uncontrollable event of the wins and losses of the Mariners. Experience teaches that busily engaging in diversions does not produce lasting happiness.

Why Are Diversions So Popular? If it is clear that diversions cannot produce lasting happiness, then why are they so popular? When we learn that diversions are not the answer would we not throw them off? Well, Pascal seems to acknowledge that without the Christian God in the equation, diversions are the best we can do. We find ourselves in a state of unhappiness, ignorance, and in chains awaiting death, these are not conditions we chose, but were born into. We cannot change the facts; all we can do is decide how to respond to our situation.

> But how shall we go about it? The best thing would be to make himself immortal, but as he cannot do that, he has decided to stop himself thinking about it. [*Pensée* 134]

In an attempt at happiness some people have in fact tried to make themselves immortal, either literally through mummification or cryo-freezing, or in an imagined way through accomplishing a great deed such as conquering territories or winning a Nobel Prize. The futility of such efforts to actually prevent death is painfully obvious, which shows these activities to be merely particular diversions in the sea of diversions that we employ to stop us thinking about our afflictions. Diversions are in fact necessary for people to stave away thoughts of painful realities, because humans are not constituted to simply will themselves to stop thinking about something– in order *not* to think about one thing, it is necessary to think about *other* things (Kreeft, 1993). Hence, the multiplication of diversions. Pascal points to diversions as the deepest reason for most of the "progress" of Western civilization. Increasing complexity, technology, and busyness keep at bay thoughts of our miserable condition.

Now I will present selections from Pascal's great *Pensée* on diversions, number 136, which may be the *Pensée* most likely to take its readers breath away. Pascal opens with an abrupt assertion:

> *Diversion.* Sometimes, when I set to thinking about the various activities of men, the dangers and troubles which they face at Court, or in war, giving rise to so many quarrels and passions, daring and often wicked enterprises and so on; I have often said that the sole cause of man's unhappiness is that he does not know how to stay quietly in his room. A man wealthy enough for life's needs would never leave home to go to sea or besiege some fortress if he knew how to stay at home and enjoy it. Men would never spend so much time on a commission in the army if they could bear living in town all their lives, and they only seek after the company and diversion of gambling because they do not enjoy staying at home...
>
> Imagine any situation you like, add up all the blessings with which you could be endowed, to be king is still the finest thing in the world; yet if you imagine one with all the advantages of his rank, but no means of diversion, left to ponder and reflect on what he is, this limp felicity will not keep him going; he is bound to start thinking of all the threats facing him, of possible revolts, finally of inescapable death and disease, with the result that if he is deprived of so-called diversion he is unhappy, indeed more unhappy than the humblest of his subjects who can enjoy sport and diversion.
>
> The only good thing for men therefore is to be diverted from thinking of what they are, either by some occupation which takes their minds off it, or by some novel and agreeable passion which

> keeps them busy, like gambling, hunting, some absorbing show, in short by what is called diversion.
>
> That is why gaming and feminine society, war and high office are so popular. It is not that they really bring happiness, nor that anyone imagines that true bliss comes from possessing the money to be won at gaming or the hare that is hunted: no one would take it as a gift. What people want is not the easy peaceful life that allows us to think of our unhappy condition, nor the dangers of war, nor the burdens of office, but the agitation that takes our mind off it and diverts us. That is why we prefer the hunt to the capture.

Here Pascal provides insight into why unemployment is so painful– it is sitting on the sidelines of the hunt.

> That is why men are so fond of hustle and bustle; that is why prison is such a frightful punishment; that is why the pleasures of solitude are so incomprehensible. That, in fact, is the joy of being a king, because people are continually trying to divert him and procure him every kind of pleasure. A king is surrounded by people whose only thought is to divert him and stop him thinking about himself, because, king though he is, he becomes unhappy as soon as he thinks about himself.

Pascal observes that because the royal and the rich do not have to work to survive, they have more time to think about themselves. This might be part of the explanation why suicide rates are much higher among the rich than the poor– the poor must stay busily working to survive, but a king "becomes unhappy as soon as he thinks about himself."

> That is all that men have been able to devise for attaining happiness; those who philosophize about it, holding that people are quite unreasonable to spend all day chasing a hare that they would not have wanted to buy, have little knowledge of our nature. The hare itself would not save us from thinking about death and the miseries distracting us, but hunting it does so...
>
> It is wrong then to blame them; they are not wrong to want excitement– if they only wanted it for the sake of diversion. The trouble is that they want it as though, once they had the things

> they seek, they could not fail to be truly happy. That is what justifies calling their search a vain one...
>
> When men are reproached for pursuing so eagerly something that could never satisfy them, their proper answer, if they really thought about it, ought to be that they simply want a violent and vigorous occupation to take their minds off themselves, and that is why they choose some attractive object to entice them in ardent pursuit. Their opponents could find no answer to that,
> (Vanity, pleasure of showing off. Dancing, you must think where to put your feet.)
> but they do not answer like that because they do not know themselves. They do not know that all they want is the hunt and not the capture. The nobleman sincerely believes that hunting is a great sport, the sport of kings, but his huntsman does not feel like that. They imagine that if they secured a certain appointment they would enjoy resting afterwards, and they do not realize the *insatiable nature of cupidity*. They think they genuinely want rest when all they really want is activity...

Pascal points out that cupidity, that is, greed, is insatiable by nature. On his deathbed, John D. Rockefeller was asked if there was anything he would change about his life. He replied: "To have made more money." Despite greed's infinite desire, people commonly believe that if only they obtain more money, power or prestige, then they will be happy. The prophet Isaiah laments this vain pursuit of happiness: "Why do you spend money for what is not bread, and your wages on what does not satisfy?" [Isaiah 55:2]

Pascal continues *Pensée* 136:

> They have a secret instinct driving them to seek external diversion and occupation, and this is the result of their constant sense of wretchedness. They have another secret instinct, left over from the greatness of our original nature, telling them that the only true happiness lies in rest and not in excitement. These two contrary instincts give rise to a confused plan buried out of sight in the depth of their soul, which leads them to seek rest by way of activity and always to imagine that the satisfaction they miss will come to them once they overcome certain obvious difficulties and can open the door to welcome rest.

> All our life passes in this way: we seek rest by struggling against certain obstacles, and once they are overcome, rest proves intolerable because of the boredom it produces. We must get away from it and crave excitement...
>
> Man is so unhappy that he would be bored even if he had no cause for boredom, by the very nature of his temperament, and he is so vain that, though he has a thousand and one basic reasons for being bored, the slightest thing, like pushing a ball with a billiard cue, will be enough to divert him.
>
> 'But,' you will say, 'what is his object in all this?' Just so that he can boast tomorrow to his friends that he played better than someone else. Likewise others sweat away in their studies to prove to scholars that they have solved some hitherto insoluble problem in algebra. Many others again, just as foolishly in my view, risk the greatest dangers so that they can boast afterwards of having captured some stronghold. Then there are others who exhaust themselves observing all these things, not in order to become wiser, but just to show they know them, and these are the biggest fools of the lot, because they know what they are doing, while it is conceivable that the rest would stop being foolish if they knew too.
>
> A given man lives a life free from boredom by gambling a small sum every day. Give him every morning the money he might win that day, but on the condition that he does not gamble, and you will make him unhappy. It might be argued that what he wants is the entertainment of gaming and not the winnings. Make him play then for nothing; his interest will not be fired and he will become bored, so it is not just entertainment he wants. A half-hearted entertainment without excitement will bore him. He must have excitement, he must delude himself into imagining that he would be happy to win what we would not want as a gift if it meant giving up gambling...

Pascal observes that the gambler does not play for the winnings, nor just for the fun of playing. Rather, he plays for the *self-delusion* that winning money will make him happy. If he actually wins he is not happy for long, but if he plays with the hope of winning, then he can be happy for a long time, both through the diversion of playing and through the delusion that true happiness will come if he wins. This rushing to diversions to delude himself about a road to happiness reveals an emptiness of the human heart without God, the vacuum theme we will explore further in chapter 4. The self-deluded gambler illustrates a principle that Peter Kreeft (1993) expresses as,

We are happy only climbing the mountain, not staying peacefully on the summit; only chasing the fox, not catching it; only courting, not marrying; only traveling, not arriving; only fighting wars, not keeping a boring peace.

After winning three Super Bowls, the decorated New England Patriots quarterback Tom Brady may have reflected this reality with his remark, "You know what my favorite ring is– the next one– that's my favorite."

Pascal concludes *Pensée* 136:

> He must create some target for his passion and then arouse his desire, anger, fear, for this object he has created, just like children taking fright at a face they have daubed themselves.
>
> That is why this man, who lost his only son a few months ago and was so troubled and oppressed this morning by lawsuits and quarrels, is not thinking about it anymore. Do not be surprised; he is concentrating all his attention on which way the boar will go that his dogs have been so hotly pursuing for the past six hours. That is all he needs. However sad a man may be, if you can persuade him to take up some diversion he will be happy while it lasts, and however happy a man may be, if he lacks diversion and has no absorbing passion or entertainment to keep boredom away, he will soon be depressed and unhappy. Without diversion there is no joy; with diversion there is no sadness. That is what constitutes the happiness of persons of rank, for they have a number of people to divert them and the ability to keep themselves in this state.
>
> Make no mistake about it. What else does it mean to be Superintendent, Chancellor, Chief Justice, but to enjoy a position in which a great number of people come every morning from all parts and do not leave them a single hour of the day to think about themselves? When they are in disgrace and sent off to their country houses, where they lack neither wealth nor servants to meet their needs, they infallibly become miserable and dejected because no one stops them thinking about themselves.

Let us consider further Pascal's suggestion that a king will be unhappy if he is "not surrounded by people who are incredibly careful to see that the king should never be alone and able to think about himself." [*Pensée* 137] A king's ignorance about how to be happy when left quietly in his room suggests that riches, power, and glory do not bring happiness. Pascal may have had King Solomon in mind, the probable author of Ecclesiastes:

> Ecclesiastes shows that man without God is totally ignorant and inescapably unhappy, for anyone is unhappy who wills but cannot do. [*Pensée* 75]

The Bible describes Solomon as the wealthiest, most powerful, and wisest king in Israel, yet in Ecclesiastes he proclaims the emptiness and unhappiness of life without God.

King Cole Porter. As a modern example of a "king," consider the life of Cole Porter (1891–1964), the great American Broadway songwriter who composed musical gems including, "What is this thing called love?" and "Night and Day." Porter's songs are often associated with happiness; his melodies and lyrics have been making Americans smile, whistle, and hum for three generations. On the surface, Cole Porter seemed happy himself; after all, for most of his life he was rich, famous, and influential.

Porter was known for his luxurious elegance. In John Lahr's words in a 2004 New Yorker article [July 12&19]:

> ...with his valets, his 16 dressing gowns, his Art Deco Paris house, with zebra rugs on marble floors, his Venetian palace, where he composed in a ballroom hung with Teopolos– personified the myth of American abundance... Porter's songs evoked an adult existence– a world of pleasure, travel, wealth, and promiscuity.

As pointed out by Southborough L'Abri director Dick Keyes, secular American ambition has typically focused on three pursuits: money, recognition, and power. Cole Porter was at the top in all three for much of his life. According to the worldview of the American dream, Porter should have been the happiest man in America. How, then, can the following Porter lyrics and excerpts from the New Yorker article be explained? In "Poor Young Millionaire," Porter wrote: "I'm tired of being, /Tired of sporting, /Tired of flirting, /Tired of courting,.../Tired of being/ Tired, tired, tired." In Lahr's words:

Songwriting was Porter's antidote to the entropy of self-indulgence. 'He worked around the clock,' Moss Hart, who collaborated with Porter on 'Jubilee' (1935) said. 'He used work as a weapon to shield himself from a boredom whose threshold was extremely low. He could withdraw and disappear before one's eyes with an almost sinister facility.'

Lahr goes on to observe:

> Many of his melodies, written in haunting minor keys, express a palpable sadness that his public persona kept hidden. 'The thrill when we meet / Is so bittersweet / That, darling, it's getting me down,' he wrote in 'Get Out of Town.' In 'Down in the Depths,' he noted, 'Why, even the janitor's wife / Has a perfectly good love life / And here am I / Facing tomorrow / Alone with my sorrow.' Promiscuity and songwriting were Porter's antidepressants, at once an expression of and relief from his neediness– the 'oh, such a hungry, yearning burning inside of me' that he wrote in 'Night and Day.'... 'Wouldn't It Be Fun,' written for a 1958 TV production of 'Aladdin,' was Porter's last song, and it carries a bitter autobiographical aftertaste: 'Wouldn't it be fun not to be famous, /Wouldn't it be fun not to be rich! / ... Wouldn't it be fun to be nearly anyone / Except me, mighty me!'

What do we conclude about the happiness of kings? Is this elite life of Cole Porter, marked with restless activity to stave away boredom and misery exceptional? Or is it emblematic of the general human condition that is unhappy without God?

Boredom. To Pascal, Porter's boredom is the normative condition of modern man without God, which explains why many do not know how to stay quietly in their room.

> *Boredom.* Man finds nothing so intolerable as to be in a state of complete rest, without the passions, without occupation, without diversion, without effort.
>
> Then he faces his nullity, loneliness, inadequacy, dependence, helplessness, emptiness.
>
> And at once there wells up from the depths of his soul boredom, gloom, depression, chagrin, resentment, despair. [*Pensée* 622]

There is a danger here to mistake Pascal as being pessimistic or cynical. To the contrary, by jarringly awakening us to perceive our unhappiness without God, Pascal gives us what we need most. Pascal explicitly calls this medicine "good" in *Pensée* 631:

> It is good to be tired and weary from fruitlessly seeking the true good, so that one can stretch out one's arms to the Redeemer.

Qualifying Pascal's Point About Diversions. Let me offer a further qualifier about Pascal's study of diversions. We are *not* to infer that activities such as sports, entertainment, work, art, etc. are intrinsically bad and should be avoided by Christians. To the contrary Pascal's own life shows he valued the pursuit of excellence in many areas, and the Bible proclaims that all areas of life are important, all are made by God who called them all good, and activities within each area are valuable and worthwhile the extent to which they honor God. Rather, Pascal's point is that *diversions are a false solution to our fundamental problem of unhappiness*, and they are dangerous because they are seductive and deceptive. Diversions are anesthesia against painful truth and reality; they keep us busy to stop us from turning to God to address our ailments. Pascal states this perfectly in *Pensée* 166:

> We run heedlessly into the abyss after putting something in front of us to stop us seeing it.

Pascal's approach to shock his listener to go beyond diversions reminds me of my love-hate relationship with flying on airplanes. I used to only hate it– my base fear of crashing, agitation from being jostled about in turbulence, the helpless condition of being caught in the sky with only one way to make it through. However, Pascal taught me the value of these flights. Like Pascal's shocking portraits, the plane-rides drive me to think of life and death, and I sometimes find myself grasping for the Psalms, running to God faster than when I am securely bolted (seemingly) to the ground. In a word, in the air I feel my need for God more plainly; the discomfort induces me to seek God. This benefit may be similar to the benefit Pascal received from his perpetual illness, which he wrote about in his prayer asking to make appropriate use of his sickness (available in Houston, 1997).

If I am running heedlessly into the abyss, I will thank Pascal for kindly pointing it out, for this awareness dissolves the delusionary power of diversions, freeing me to seek real happiness.

Part III: Indifference

I would like now to consider the second of two popular strategies that Pascal observed people use to stave away thoughts of grim realities of the human condition– indifference.

Peter Kreeft (1993) suggests that indifference, not hate, is the opposite of love. A person who passionately hates God is closer to coming to relationship with him than a person who does not care, for it is easier to re-direct a flame than to create it. The life of the Apostle Paul illustrates this point: as a "perfect" Pharisee Paul persecuted the Christians with zeal, and after conversion, he preached the Gospel with equal zeal. Paul cared deeply about his religious work as a Christ-hater and then as a Christ-lover. Had Paul been disinterested in religion, a "double conversion" would have been necessary– not only would Paul need to become convinced that Christ is the Lord, he would also need a change in disposition.

By describing passionate truth seeking as necessary for finding God, the Bible acknowledges the impossibility of accessing God from a stance of indifference. In a letter to the Israelites captive in Babylon, Jeremiah reports the Lord declaring, "...you will find Me when you seek Me with all your heart." [Jeremiah 29:13] A person who does not care to seek is not even on the playing field to find God, and it is the apologist's task to spark a desire for truth seeking.

Many in the West today are in need of a Pascalian spark. Until recently apathy has been considered a character flaw, but today many accept it as normal and some have even proposed it as a virtue. In 2003 journalist Jonathan Rauch introduced the term "apatheism," describing it as a "disinclination to care all that much about one's own religion, and an even stronger disinclination to care about other people's." Rauch called apatheism "a major civilizational advance," useful for its potential to restrain destructive behaviors of religious zealots. This notion that apathy holds more promise than seeking religious truth illustrates the depths to which a large segment of our culture is steeped and stained in indifference.

Pascal set out to awaken his apathetic friends to seek in his major *Pensée* on indifference, number 427. We will consider this essay in the remainder of Part III. Before engaging it, let us consider the meaning of a phrase Pascal uses, "immortality of the soul." Pascal likely accepted a Cartesian dualism in which the immortal soul is supposed nonmaterial and distinct from the material body. Modern neuroscience challenges this dualism, however, supporting a unified body-soul monism, one version of which has been coined "non-reductive physicalism." (Brown, Murphy, and Malony, 1998) Christians holding the non-reductive physicalist position believe in the resurrection of the body-soul unity and its everlasting life. Pascal's chief concern in *Pensée* 427 is for everlasting life, irrespective of a dualist or monist position, so that readers holding either position (or a third one) need not be diverted from the point of Pascal's argument.

In *Pensée* 427 Pascal addresses whether there is life after death:

> ...The immortality of the soul [whether there is life after death] is something of such vital importance to us, affecting us so deeply, that one must have lost all feeling not to care about knowing the facts of the matter. All our actions and thoughts must follow different paths, according to whether there is hope of eternal blessings or not, that the only possible way of acting with sense and judgment is to decide our course in the light of this point, which ought to be our ultimate objective.
>
> Thus our chief interest and chief duty is to seek enlightenment on this subject, on which all our conduct depends. And that is why, amongst those who are not convinced, I make an absolute distinction between those who strive with all their might to learn and those who live without troubling themselves or thinking about it.
>
> I can feel nothing but compassion for those who sincerely lament their doubt, who regard it as their ultimate misfortune, and who, sparing no effort to escape from it, make their search their principal and most serious business.
>
> But as for those who spend their lives without a thought for this final end of life and who, solely because they do not find within themselves the light of conviction, neglect to look elsewhere, and to examine thoroughly whether this opinion is one of those which people accept out of credulous simplicity or one of those which, though obscure in themselves, none the less have a most solid and unshakable foundation: as for them, I view them very differently.

This negligence in a matter where they themselves, their eternity, their all are at stake, fills me more with irritation than pity; it astounds and appalls me; it seems quite monstrous to me.

In this fragment Pascal was specifically appalled at Montaigne's expression of open indifference to the question of whether there is an afterlife. [*Pensée* 680] Not caring about whether one will go to bliss, eternal torment, annihilation, or some other unknown state, is psychologically insane, Pascal suggests; given the infinite difference one's post-death state makes to one's happiness, it is literally insane to not care. It is like receiving a cancer diagnosis and not even asking the doctor if it is treatable! Such behavior is so odd that Pascal does not hesitate to call it monstrous.

Importance of the Question Is there Life After Death? But why should the question of immortality totally alter "all our actions and thoughts?" Even if there is no afterlife, one might argue, it is still meaningful to "enjoy life" and to "live a good and moral life" in the time that we have.

The reflections of the philosopher Thomas Morris (1992) help clarify Pascal's assertion. First, the existence of an afterlife is a motivation for living morally. Descartes acknowledges this in his *Meditations*, "Few would prefer what is right to what is useful, if they never feared God nor hoped for an after-life." This is a start toward understanding the question.

Second, Morris considers diverse persons in history who shared Pascal's view that whether there is an everlasting afterlife is of ultimate importance. These include Alfred Lord Tennyson, who wrote,

If there is no immortality, I shall throw myself into the sea.

At first read, this sentiment did not make sense to me; if this life is all there is, then I might care even more to savor life while it lasts! Later I comprehended it when I read the following from the Marxist writer Leszek Kolakowski:

If personal life is doomed to irreversible destruction, so are all the fruits of human creativity, whether material or spiritual, and it does not matter how long we, or our own performances, might last. There is little difference between the work of Giovanni Papini's imaginary sculptor carving his statues in smoke for a few seconds' duration, and Michelangelo's 'immortal' marbles.

In other words, all that does not last has infinitely diminished meaning, like an artist completing a painting on the deck of the Titanic, or like Solomon calling life meaningless because it is here today and gone tomorrow. Kolakowski points to immortality as an essential conveyor of meaning and true happiness. Woody Allen agrees, as recorded by Frank Rich in a 1977 *Esquire* interview:

> I always see death's head lurking. I might be sitting at Madison Square Garden, at the most exciting basketball game and they're cheering and everything is thrilling, and one of the players is doing something very beautiful, and suddenly I think, 'he's only 28 years old and this is as good as it's ever going to be for him.' The fundamental thing behind all motivation and all activity is the constant struggle against annihilation and against death. It's absolutely stupefying to realize you're going to die and it renders everyone's accomplishments meaningless, for, as Camus wrote, It's not only that he dies, or that man dies, but you struggle to do a work of art that will last and then you realize that the universe itself is going to die, and that destroys all meaning.

The Apostle Paul also seems to agree, "If in this life only we have hope in Christ, we are of all men most miserable." [I Corinthians 15:19] If there is immortality, then anything good, true, or beautiful in this life has permanent significance. As Earl Palmer has quipped, if you are 80 years old, it's not too late to take up the saxophone, because there will be eternity to continue playing.

Continuing *Pensée* 427, Pascal ratchets up the importance of caring about everlasting life:

> This negligence in a matter where they themselves, their eternity, their all are at stake, fills me more with irritation than pity; it astounds and appalls me; it seems quite monstrous to me. I do not say this prompted by the pious zeal of spiritual devotion. I mean on the contrary that we ought to have this feeling from principles of human interest and self-esteem. For that we need only see what the least enlightened see.

> One needs no great sublimity of soul to realize that in this life there is no true and solid satisfaction, that all our pleasures are mere vanity, that our afflictions are infinite, and finally that death which threatens us at every moment must in a few years infallibly face us with the inescapable and appalling alternative of being annihilated or wretched throughout eternity.
>
> Nothing could be more real, or more dreadful than that. Let us put on as bold a face as we like: that is the end awaiting the world's most illustrious life. Let us ponder these things, and then say whether it is not beyond doubt that the only good thing in this life is the hope of another life, that we become happy only as we come nearer to it, and that, just as no more unhappiness awaits those who have been quite certain of eternity, so there is no happiness for those who have no inkling of it.

Pascal's phrase "nothing could be more real, or more dreadful than that" echoes Philip Larkin's line "nothing more terrible, nothing more true." These essentially identical sentiments expressed three centuries apart from opposite worldviews testify to a sort of universal and timeless importance to the question of what happens after death.

Pascal next expresses astonishment at the ability of his friends to sustain indifference about the matter:

> It is therefore quite certainly a great evil to have such doubts, but it is at least an indispensable obligation to seek when one does thus doubt; so the doubter who does not seek is at the same time very unhappy and very wrong. If in addition he feels a calm satisfaction, which he openly professes, and even regards as a reason for joy and vanity, I can find no terms to describe so extravagant a creature.
>
> What can give rise to such feelings? What reason for joy can be found in the expectation of nothing but helpless wretchedness? What reason for vanity in being plunged into impenetrable darkness? And how can such an argument as this occur to a reasonable man?
>
> 'I do not know who put me into the world, nor what the world is, nor what I am myself. I am terribly ignorant about everything. I do not know what my body is, or my senses, or my soul, or even that part of me which thinks what I am saying, which reflects about everything and about itself, and does not know itself any better than it knows anything else.

> 'I see the terrifying spaces of the universe hemming me in, and I find myself attached to one corner of this vast expanse without knowing why I have been put in this place rather than that, or why the brief span of life allotted to me should be assigned to one moment rather than another of all the eternity which went before me and all that which will come after me. I see only infinity on every side, hemming me in like an atom or like the shadow of a fleeting instant. All I know is that I must soon die, but what I know least about is this very death which I cannot evade.
>
> 'Just as I do not know whence I come, so I do not know whither I am going. All I know is that when I leave this world I shall fall for ever into nothingness or into the hands of a wrathful God, but I do not know which of these two states is to be my eternal lot. Such is my state, full of weakness and uncertainty. And my conclusion from all this is that I must pass my days without a thought of seeking what is to happen to me. Perhaps I might find some enlightenment in my doubts, but I do not want to take the trouble, nor take a step to look for it: and afterwards, as I sneer at those who are striving to this end– (whatever certainty they have should arouse despair rather than vanity) I will go without fear or foresight to face so momentous an event, and allow myself to be carried off limply to my death, uncertain, uncertain of my future state for all eternity.'

Many today share the proud indifference of Pascal's friends; as one example a character in the TV show *Lost* exclaimed, "I looked death in the face and said 'whatever man'." Pascal observes that the indifferent person's method of handling death is "limp" and inconsistent with reason– any reasonable person should take an interest in whether there is a real solution to overcome death. All the modernists can offer is the consolation prize that "your accomplishments will live on in the memories of others." I have always found this answer limp, because if the soul dies permanently, then after death the person is no different from dust; he never again can think, feel, relate, reflect. This conclusion is in fact held by the Nihilist worldview, which accepts the meaningless of life and death; and within this worldview indifference is a reasonable and coherent position. But what a difficult and unattractive worldview to actually hold! Pascal knew that most human hearts are unsatisfied with purposelessness, and presses this point as he continues:

> Who would wish to have as his friend a man who argued like this? Who would choose him from among others as a confidant in his affairs? Who would resort to him in adversity? To what use in life could he possibly be turned?
>
> It is truly glorious for religion to have such unreasonable men as enemies: their opposition represents so small a danger that it serves on the contrary to establish the truths of the religion. For the Christian faith consists almost wholly in establishing these two things: The corruption of nature and the redemption of Christ. Now, I maintain that, if they do not serve to prove the truth of the redemption by the sanctity of their conduct, they do at least admirably serve to prove the corruption of nature by such unnatural sentiments.
>
> Nothing is so important to man as his state: nothing more fearful than eternity. Thus the fact that there exist men who are indifferent to the loss of their being and the peril of an eternity of wretchedness is against nature. With everything else they are quite different; they fear the most trifling things, foresee and feel them; and the same man who spends so many days and nights in fury and despair at losing some office or at some imaginary affront to his honour is the very one who knows that he is going to lose everything through death but feels neither anxiety or emotion. It is a monstrous thing to see one and the same heart at once so sensitive to minor things and so strangely insensitive to the greatest. It is an incomprehensible spell, a supernatural torpor that points to an omnipotent power as its cause.

With "supernatural torpor" and "divine cause" Pascal refers to the Garden of Eden and the consequence of Original Sin, God's curse on humanity, which led to Man's backwards priorities. Hence humankind's great sensitivity to trivial things like hitting a billiard ball with just the right massé, and insensitivity to great things like the immortality of the soul. Pascal calls Man's reversed priorities a "strange disorder," [*Pensée* 632] and took it as empirical evidence for the biblical account of the Fall and Original Sin (addressed in chapter 4).

After expressing more astonishment at the strange indifference of his friends, Pascal moves to his concluding take-home point for them– that all reasonable people will seek God:

> Do they think that they have given us great pleasure by telling us that they hold our soul to be no more than wind or smoke, and

> saying it moreover in tones of pride and satisfaction? Is this then something to be said gaily? Is it not on the contrary something to be said sadly, as being the saddest thing in the world?...
>
> There is no surer sign of extreme weakness of mind than the failure to recognize the unhappy state of a man without God; there is no surer sign of an evil heart than failure to desire that the eternal promises be true; nothing is more cowardly than to brazen it out with God. Let them then leave such impiety to those ill-bred enough to be really capable of it; let them at least be decent people if they cannot be Christians; let them, in short, acknowledge that there are only two classes of persons who can be called reasonable: those who serve God with all their heart because they know him and those who seek him with all their heart because they do not know him...

Pascal ends *Pensée* 427 by observing that all people are susceptible to being strangely indifferent– all may fall into this pit, with God's gift of grace providing the only way out. Consequently, Christians are obliged to graciously help their friends escape their complete indifference and become seekers.

> But as this religion obliges us always to regard them, as long as they live, as being capable of receiving grace which may enlighten them, and to believe that in a short time they may be filled with more faith than we are, while we on the contrary may be stricken by the same blindness which is theirs now, we must do for them what we would wish to be done for us in their place, and appeal to them to have pity on themselves, and to take at least a few steps in an attempt to find some light...

I love the manner in which Pascal delivers his case for seeking– not with force, threats, or self-righteousness– but with gentleness.

Part IV. Dangers of Diversions for Believers

I would like to conclude this chapter by offering three reflections on dangers of diversions for believers.

For background on this topic, I will expand on the point that most activities that qualify as diversions are not bad in themselves. Rather, each activity can be done as a diversion, or as a good activity that honors God. For one example, consider regular weekend recreational getaways in the Pacific Northwest. Such activities may be honoring to God, for example they may be helpful for worship, prayer, reflection, building up relationships and health. Eighteenth-century New England pastor Jonathan Edwards found his daily nature walks in New England immensely helpful for communing with God and comprehending God's love for his creatures (Marsden, 2003). On the other hand, nature excursions may be a diversion from facing one's problems or responsibilities. Habitual hikes could dishonor God for a variety of reasons; for example they might prevent one from fulfilling responsibilities to family, work, or neighbor; or one could worship nature itself rather than God. An activity is diversionary, and leading away from God, *if it is done trusting in the activity itself as a remedy for unhappiness.* This leads to the first and most fundamental danger of diversions.

Danger of Diversions 1: Rooting One's Happiness in Diversions, Not God. By definition diversions are ultimately unsatisfying, because they are distractions, escapes from facing grim realities. Diversions do not fill the hollow core within. Finding happiness in diversions instead of in God constitutes a basic malfunction of a healthy relationship with God, which is meant to be an abiding in and enjoyment of him.

In his confession to God, Saint Augustine describes all diversionary activities as sorrows:

> For whatever way the soul of man turns, it is fixed upon sorrows any place except in you, even though it is fixed upon beautiful things that are outside of you and outside of itself... For the soul... loves to rest in things it loves. But in such things there is no place where it may find rest, for they do not endure. They flee away... (*The Confessions*, Book 4, Chapter 10)

Therefore, the pleasures found in diversions are restless and fleeting. Pascal gives a reason why seeking happiness outside of God is restless:

> What causes inconstancy is the realization that present pleasures are false, together with the failure to realize that absent pleasures are vain. [*Pensée* 73]

That is, we are aware of our unhappiness in the present moment, yet hold the false belief that if we can just tweak it in the right way, then real happiness will ensue (examples: I'm tired of my shoes, new ones will make me happy; My job or boyfriend is tedious, a new one will make me happy). Yet when the change is made we soon again feel our unhappiness. Psychology research supports Pascal's explanation for our restlessness. For example, Professor David Myers (2000) surveyed research on the happiness of Americans suggesting that extremely positive events do not typically lead to greater happiness. In particular, lottery winners are no happier than the average American. More generally, Dr. Myers reports research supporting that money is only weakly connected to happiness, suggesting that chasing after wealth cannot bring happiness. Real income of the average American doubled during the time-period of study, 1970 to 1993, but it was accompanied by "less happiness, more depression, more fragile relationships, less communal commitment, less vocational security, more crime, and more demoralized children." Some economics studies also conclude that money does not bring happiness, for example as argued by Sagoff (1990).

To Pascal, the grass-is-greener or escalating-wealth syndrome is vain, and recognizing one's restless pursuits can be a helpful diagnosis to spark a return to the only source of true rest. I find it helpful to cultivate an awareness of when I am engaging in diversions in a vain attempt at happiness, which functions like a high temperature on a spiritual thermometer, alerting me to seek rest in Christ. Biblical authors concur with Pascal about the only source of true happiness, for example as expressed in Psalm 119:2, "Happy are those who keep his decrees, who seek him with their whole heart."

Danger of Diversions 2: Crowd Out Time for the Means of Grace. A second danger of diversions is that they may crowd out time for the means of grace. By means of grace I mean activities that God provides for us to receive his grace and to sanctify us, ranging from prayer, Bible study, fellowship, singing hymns and spiritual songs; as well as play, work or artistic endeavors that are done in a way honoring to God. Contrary to being means of grace, diversions often operate as counter-influences that harm one's will to listen to God and honor him.

No one articulated this more profoundly than Jonathan Edwards in his great philosophical work *Freedom of the Will*. Edwards argues that at every moment of a person's life, he or she must do (is compelled to do) whatever is their strongest desire at that moment (Pascal concurs, writing in the eighteenth *Provincial Letter*, "the will invariably inclines towards what gives it greatest pleasure.") Add to this the Apostle Paul's suggestion that believers possess two natures that war against one another, the Old Man that desires sinful gratifications and the New Man in Christ that desires loving God. Because the will is determined by one's strongest desire, it follows that feeding the New Man (i.e., filling life with activities that promote love of God) is necessary for achieving godly living. The more the New Man is fed and the Old Man is starved, the more likely it is that the desires will be inclined to love God and neighbor. But if the Old Man is fattened up with vastly more food than the New Man, then in Edward's view it is *inevitable* that the person will follow after sin. Hence a danger in diversions. If Edwards is right about the will, then we have deduced a spiritual law: multiplying diversions that feed the Old Man will lead to compromise in the living of life under the Lordship of Christ. Pascal expresses it this way: "if we do not hunger for spiritual things we find them boring." [*Pensée* 941] Therefore, if we are preoccupied with hungering after diversionary earthly things, we risk cultivating a lack of hunger for spiritual things, and thus become bored with the means of grace. And this boredom is deadly dangerous, as the constant feeding of the New Man is the only way to grow in grace.

The Psalmist put it this way:

> Blessed is the man who walks not in the counsel of the ungodly...but his delight is in the law of the Lord, and in His law he meditates day and night. [Psalm 1:1–2]

These verses suggest that investing in means of grace leads one toward blessedness, whereas the alternative investment in diversions leads one away from blessedness.

Danger of Diversions 3: Expend One's Compassion on the Unreal. A third danger of entertainment-type diversions like TV and theatre-going is that one can expend one's compassion and emotional currency on the unreal. Going regularly to the Opera, the Seattle Repertory Theater, and to movies may regularly wrench one's heart at witnessing tragedies, heroism, etc., and tears of compassion may be shed at the theatre. However, Pascal concurs with Augustine, who points to a danger of theatre-going– a person can feel that they have discharged their duty of compassion to the poor simply by feeling compassion at the theatre, even though they may never actually feed, cloth, or befriend a poor person! (*The Confessions*, Book 3, chapter 2) Life can pass with all one's compassion expended on actors and images on a screen.

C.S. Lewis also warns Christians about the danger in feeling compassion but not translating the feeling into compassionate action. In *The Screwtape Letters*, the mentor-devil Screwtape writes letters to his apprentice under-devil, Wormwood, instructing him on how to ensure that his human patient ends up in Hell. In Chapter 13, Screwtape is furious at Wormwood, because Wormwood's patient has just re-converted to Christ. Screwtape writes:

> Let him do anything but act. No amount of piety in his imagination and affections will harm us if we can keep it out of his will... The more often he feels without acting, the less he will be able ever to act, and, in the long run, the less he will be able to feel.

Pervasive entertainment can operate invisibly as a dulling mechanism that prevents believers from exercising real duties to love God and neighbor.

Pensée of the Day: Number 136

With the PoD, Pascal succinctly expresses his answer to the question of why Man is unhappy apart from God:

> I have often said that the sole cause of Man's unhappiness is that he does not know how to stay quietly in his room.

Pascal observed that many of his fellow Frenchmen did not know how to enjoy living quietly. When they rested they would almost immediately become bored, and to relieve the boredom they would throw themselves into agitated activity. If a man were truly happy he would know how to stay contentedly at home without diversions. The experience that he does not "proves" that happiness eludes him.

Synthesis Points of Chapter 2

1. Pascal begins the *Pensées* with the fact of death to grab his listeners' attention. Death is a pressure point for most non-Christian worldviews (particularly modernism), because they do not offer satisfying solutions to the problem of death.

2. Like Solomon in Ecclesiastes, Pascal shows that an examination of human experience demonstrates that humankind is unhappy (including restlessness and boredom) without God.
3. Diversions and indifference are popular strategies for trying to achieve happiness without God. Pascal observes that these pursuits are symptoms of underlying unhappiness– they "prove" our unhappiness.
4. Pascal urges that once we recognize diversions and indifference as false solutions to our unhappiness, if we are reasonable we will seek with great effort a true solution in God. Pascal contrasts the "empty good" offered by presumption, diversions, and indifference with the "true good" offered by Christianity. This is the second point of Pascal's apologetic approach– to make Christianity attractive because it promises true good, the objective state of happiness.

3 MAN'S WRETCHED CONDITION: LOST IN THE DARK– CANNOT FIND THE TRUTH

"There is a plague on Man, the opinion that he knows something."
– Michel de Montaigne (1580, *Essays*)

"What we know is always vanishingly small."
– Bertrand Russell

"Imagination magnifies small objects with fantastic exaggeration until they fill our soul, and with bold insolence cuts down great things to its own size, as when speaking of God."
– Blaise Pascal, *Pensée* 551

In chapter 2 we looked at Man's wretched condition of being unhappy. In this chapter we consider Man's wretchedness in terms of his severely limited capacity to find truth.

Outline of Chapter 3. In Part I, we will look at the entertaining *Pensée* 44, famous for demonstrating the power of the mental conception Pascal calls imagination, and that imagination frequently leads to error. This *Pensée* describes several features of Man that severely handicap his capacity to find truth. In Part II, we will explore *Pensée* 199, which Pascal titled the *Disproportion of man*. In this *Pensée* Pascal takes his listener through a roller coaster tour of the extremely intricate physical universe, with aim to place Man's capacity to comprehend reality into perspective. In so doing Pascal seeks to deflate Man's presumption, and make possible the growth of humility that is necessary for receptiveness to God. In this essay Pascal emphasizes the limitations of reason, and we will examine other *Pensées* on this topic.

In Part III we will look at Pascal's statements on the importance of faith for knowing God. Moreover, we will explore Pascal's thoughts on the relationship between faith and reason, and how they both play an important role in knowing God. But they must be wielded in the appropriate way– too much emphasis on faith at the expense of reason, or too much emphasis on reason at the expense of faith, leads to disorder, Pascal posits, and thus may distort the Christian religion and lead one away from knowing God.

These *Pensées* will lead to Part IV, on Pascal's discussion of knowing God with our hearts– to Pascal the principle way of knowing God. The chapter will end at the place where Pascal hoped for his reader to arrive– at a place of humility, of recognition that human-generated reasoning alone is feeble for finding God. Rather, a teachable, open heart that carefully listens to God's revelation is the essential ingredient. Pascal was convinced that apart from receiving revelation about Christ, it is impossible to know God or even ourselves.

Part I. Imagination: Prince of Error

Essay on the Imagination: Pensée 44. *Pensée* 44 is an apparently completed essay on the imagination, and more generally on sources of human error. The human condition is not well suited to reliably finding truth, Pascal suggests. In this grand *Pensée*, Pascal seeks to demonstrate this with vivid imagery, fitting to his subject. By the word "imagination" Pascal does not mean creative or compassionate mental imagery, which may be appropriate and helpful for art, generosity, and other good endeavors; rather he means something like fancy– a mental conception of something that is believed real but is often illusory.

> *Imagination.* It is the dominant faculty in man, master of error and falsehood, all the more deceptive for not being invariably so; for it would be an infallible criterion of truth if it were infallibly that of lies. Since, however, it is usually false, it gives no indication of its quality, setting the same mark on true and false alike...

Old wives tales illustrate the inclination of imagination to concoct supposed truths. "If an expecting mother likes salty foods while pregnant, then it's a boy, if sugary, then a girl," true or false? False. "Chicken noodle soup helps the sick get well," true or false? True. The first wives tale is false, the second is true, and the imagination is quite willing to believe in both of them. The imagination is deceptive because it is quick to accept something, yet is a poor judge of whether it is really true.

> Who dispenses reputation? Who makes us respect and revere persons, works, laws, the great? Who but this faculty of imagination? All the riches of the earth are inadequate without its

> approval. Would you not say that this magistrate, whose venerable age commands universal respect, is ruled by pure, sublime reason, and judges things as they really are, without paying heed to the trivial circumstances which offend only the imagination of weaker men?
>
> See him go hear a sermon in a spirit of pious zeal, the soundness of his judgment strengthened by the ardour of his charity, ready to listen with exemplary respect. If, when the preacher appears, it turns out that nature has given him a hoarse voice and an odd sort of face, that his barber has shaved him badly and he happens not to be too clean either, then, whatever great truths he may announce, I wager that our senator will not be able to keep a straight face...

This passage is similar to C.S. Lewis' description in *The Screwtape Letters* of the Christian whose faith is challenged by the double chin of the fellow worshipper in the next pew. Based on no rational evidence, the imagination boldly draws a connection between possessing too many chins and the health of one's soul. Another example comes from the famous televised 1960 presidential debate between Richard Nixon and John Kennedy. Nixon's haggard appearance with a 5-o'clock shadow was said to cost him a great many votes. Is fast-growing beard-hair predictive of poor presidential skills? The imagination of some believed this to be true– for these it was not reason, but vain imagination, which cast their vote.

> Reason never wholly overcomes imagination, while the contrary is quite common. Our magistrates have shown themselves well aware of this mystery. Their red robes, the ermine in which they swaddle themselves like furry cats, the law-courts where they sit in judgment, the fleurs de lys, all this august panoply was very necessary. If physicians did not have long gowns and mules, if learned doctors did not wear square caps and robes four times too large, they would never have deceived the world, which finds such an authentic display irresistible. If they possessed the true justice, and if physicians possessed the true art of healing, they would not need square caps; the majesty of such sciences would command respect in itself. But, as they only possess imaginary science, they have to resort to these vain devices in order to strike the imagination, which is their real concern, and this, in fact, is how they win respect...

A case can be made that it was not until the mid 1800s, when Pascal's fellow Frenchman and devoted Catholic Louis Pasteur developed the germ theory of disease, that the science of medicine had advanced to the point where doctors' practices were usually more beneficial than harmful. For one historical example of a prestigious physician who applied the craft of medicine based on imaginary science with tragic consequences, consider the death of George Washington.

In December 1799, Washington developed a sore throat while on his daily horse ride. Several physicians were called to Washington's side, including the prominent Dr. James Craik. Dr. Craik and his colleagues diagnosed fever, swelling, and painful swallowing, and prescribed bleeding as a remedy. When the patient did not improve after the first pint of blood was removed, another pint was prescribed. As the condition worsened more and more bleeding was prescribed. In all Washington was bled about five pints of blood. Current-day doctors believe that these bleedings were either the cause of Washington's death, or, at a minimum, aggravated the disease and hastened his demise. Custis George Washington Parke (1860) recalls the affair:

The manly sufferer uttered no complaint, would permit no one to be disturbed in their rest on his account, and it was only at daybreak he would consent that the overseer might be called in, and bleeding resorted to. A vein was opened, but no relief afforded. Couriers were dispatched to Dr. Craik, the family, and Drs. Dick and Brown, the consulting physicians, all of whom came with speed. The proper remedies were administered, but without producing their healing effects; while the patient, yielding to the anxious looks of all around him, waived his usual objections to medicines, and took those which were prescribed without hesitation or remark. The medical gentlemen spared not their skill, and all the resources of their art were exhausted in unwearied endeavors to preserve this noblest work of nature.

Pascal also suffered from his doctors; during the last few years of his life, as he was laid up in bed with severe toothaches, migraines, and digestive problems, physicians hovered around him prescribing medications that inflicted nearly as much pain as his natural ailments. René Descartes was bled on his death bed, and while Descartes' medical science was advanced enough to lead him to resist this treatment until he was too weak to protest, Descartes' own prescription for his pneumonia was liquid tobacco mixed with warm wine. (Grayling, 2005) Molière, Pascal's contemporary, satirized the impotence of the medical profession in his comedy about a hypochondriac (*The Imaginary Invalid*, 1673), and in the next century Voltaire remarked,

> Medicine is something a doctor prescribes a patient while waiting for nature to cure the disease.

Interestingly, even though the science of medicine has now advanced to the point of producing truly effective remedies, doctors still wear white coats. Patients imagine that a doctor in a white costume has greater skill than one without one. The imagination still plays an important role in the patient-physician relationship.

Pascal concludes *Pensée* 44 with these words on the imagination:

> Such, more or less, are the effects of this deceptive faculty, apparently given to us for the specific purpose of leading us inevitably into error. We have plenty of other principles of error...

Other Principles of Error. The thesis of *Pensée* 44 seems to be that "Man has no exact principle of truth, and several excellent ones of falsehood." A list of these principles can be derived from this *Pensée*: (1) imagination; (2) longstanding impressions; (3) charms of novelty; (4) the war between senses and reason; (5) illness, and (6) self-interest.

After imagination, consider the capacity for longstanding impressions to mislead. Once something false is believed, it can become lodged in the brain and resist removal. Third, charms of novelty have the same power to deceive– think of the human tendency to be fascinated with the new and bored with the old. This inclination creates a bias for new things– if a novel medicine is presented to us we are tempted to presume it better than the standard medicine. Our wishful hopes cause a prejudiced judgment.

Fourth, truth is sought with both the senses and reason, and these faculties compete to create confusion.

> The two principles of truth, reason and the senses, are not only both not genuine, but are engaged in mutual deception. The senses deceive reason through false appearances, just as they trick the soul, they are tricked by it in their turn: it takes its revenge. The senses are disturbed by passions, which produce

false impressions. They both compete in lies and deception... [*Pensée* 44]

To illustrate the senses' deception of reason, consider the laboratory sciences, wherein most instruments used for identifying biological entities are subject to measurement error. Scientific inferences rely on the accuracy of the measurements, and the extent to which errors exist and are not detected or are not properly accounted for destabilizes the reasoning process. Many a dissertation topic has been switched after the student discovers that the exciting observation that stimulated it turned out to be a mistake! More generally, information gathered by the senses can always turn out to be an illusion.

The passions' disturbance of the senses is evident when peoples' self-interests color their interpretation of data. A businessman's greed inclines him to overlook certain figures in his accounting books. A hypochondriac's fear of death (such as the imaginary invalid's fear) prevents him from noticing that he has no symptoms of illness. John Medina (University of Washington bioengineering professor, founding director of the Talaris Research Institute and of the Brain Center for Applied Learning Research at Seattle Pacific University, and popular author of *Brain Rules* and other scientific books) observes that an attribute of a lousy scientist is 'caring' about what the data show– by *wanting* to find a certain result, an investigator's senses are subjugated to his passions. In *Pensée* 44 Pascal suggests there are no perfect scientists– none of us can extricate our passions entirely from our pursuit of truth.

I will further illustrate this mutual deception with Pascal's example. Based on her senses, a child, upon seeing that a box is empty, may come to believe that a vacuum exists. However, her senses may mislead her– there could be air in the box but the child does not know this. On the other hand, at school her Cartesian teacher tells her that a vacuum does not exist, that the senses were wrong, and this false impression must be corrected. Thus, the child is taught that it is reasonable for her to conclude that a vacuum does not exist. What then shall the child believe? The child is stuck, with her senses telling her one thing and reason telling her another, and she has no way to discern the correct answer. Pascal enquires, "Who then is the deceiver, the senses or education?" Pascal provides other examples, and suggests that errors commonly arise from confusion created by different signals coming from the senses and from reason.

The fifth principle of error is illness.

> We have another principle of error in illnesses, which impair our judgment and sense. If serious illnesses do considerable harm, I have no doubt that the less serious ones have a proportionate effect... [*Pensée* 44]

Alzheimer's disease is a serious illness that obviously impairs judgment, but lesser ailments, even garden-variety colds, take smaller but real tolls on judgment [e.g., Smith (1989) reviews effects of colds and the flu on various human performances].

Pascal continues with a sixth source of error, self-interest:

> Our own interest is another wonderful instrument for blinding us agreeably. The fairest man in the world is not allowed to be judge in his own cause. I know of men who, to avoid the danger of partiality in their own favor, have leaned over to the opposite extreme of injustice. The surest way to lose a perfectly just case was to get close relatives to commend it to them. Justice and truths are two points so fine that our instruments are too blunt to touch them exactly. If they do make contact, they blunt the point and press all round on the false rather than the true... [*Pensée* 44]

Why does Pascal belabor the point that human beings are riddled with principles of error, and are not constituted to reliably find the truth? Why harp on the ignorance of Man? *Pensée* 45 summarizes where he is heading:

> Man is nothing but a subject full of natural error that cannot be eradicated except through grace.

By demonstrating that leaning on one's own faculties and understanding is unreliable for finding truth, Pascal hopes to persuade his friend to seek truth elsewhere, outside of himself. Pascal is heading toward the necessity of God's breaking into the human life to give it some knowledge of truth, toward the necessity of gracious revelation. More later on this major theme of the *Pensées*.

Part II. Limitations of Reason

In *Pensée* 199, Pascal marvels at the physical universe, contrasting Man's minuteness compared to the "infinitely large" world of galaxies, and Man's hugeness compared to the "infinitely small" world of sub-atomic matter. In this essay Pascal seeks to baffle his listener with impenetrable mysteries of nature, to show him the limits of what human reasoning by itself can understand. Most scientists of Pascal's day had a very optimistic view about the scope of what science and reason could grasp, and Pascal sought to humble their presumption. They overreached in myriads of areas including religion– for example Descartes wrote to the Faculty of Theology in Paris proposing that all that can be known of God can be shown by reasons drawn from nowhere but ourselves. Furthermore, in a letter to Marin Mersenne, the director of the Mathematics Academy co-founded by Étienne Pascal, Descartes wrote,

> I dare to boast that I have found a proof of the existence of God which I find fully satisfactory and by which I know that God exists more certainly than I know the truth of any geometrical proposition. (*Meditations*)

Departing radically from previous apologetic approaches, Descartes asserted that human reason alone, apart from revelation, could prove grand matters such as God's existence and the immortality of the soul.

Let us listen to Pascal's answer to this kind of boldness in *Pensée* 199:

> *Disproportion of man...* Before going on to a wider inquiry concerning nature, I want him to consider nature just once, seriously and at leisure, and to look at himself as well, and judge whether there is any proportion between himself and nature by comparing the two.
>
> Let man then contemplate the whole of nature in her full and lofty majesty, let him turn his gaze away from the lowly objects around him; let him behold the dazzling light set like an eternal lamp to light up the universe, let him see the earth as a mere speck compared to the vast orbit itself to be no more than the tiniest point compared to that described by the stars revolving in the firmament. But if our eyes stop there, let our imagination proceed further; it will grow weary of conceiving things before nature tires of producing them...
>
> The whole visible world is only an imperceptible dot in nature's ample bosom.

Current data on the immense size of the universe validate Pascal's point– the farthest galaxies we see are 12 to the ninth power light-years away, and a light-year is 5.88 times 10 to the twelfth miles. Moreover, in describing the whole visible world as an "imperceptible dot," Pascal anticipated what science would later show, that by any conceivable metric the universe is almost totally empty (e.g., if the sun were the size of the period at the end of this sentence, then the nearest star to it would be about ten miles away, with other stars hundreds and thousands of miles away).

> No idea comes near it; it is no good inflating our conceptions beyond imaginable space, we only bring forth atoms compared to the reality of things. Nature is an infinite sphere whose centre is everywhere and circumference nowhere...

The original form of Pascal's "infinite sphere" quotation, well known in Pascal's day, read that "God is an infinite sphere...," not nature (Kreeft, 1993). Why did Pascal modify the famous quote by swapping God for nature? Kreeft suggests that Pascal made this switch in order to characterize modern Man in the Enlightenment as divinizing nature and naturalizing God. That is, replacing "in God we trust" with "in science we trust," staking its hope for security and prosperity not on the trustworthiness of God's promises, but on the promise of science.

Enlightenment thinkers proposed that humans would be able to understand and conquer nature, to the point that nature could be utilized to bring about a delivery of humankind from suffering. Pascal aims to show that they were being wildly optimistic, first of all because their instruments (their minds and their scientific techniques) for apprehending nature are much blunter than they think. Secondly, even if reasoning could achieve a firm grasp of the natural world, these thinkers were yet more wildly unrealistic to imagine that reasoning could adequately address matters impervious to evaluation as phenomena in the physical world, including questions of meaning, wisdom, and goodness:

> If natural things are beyond [reason], then what are we to say about supernatural things? [*Pensée* 188]

We will return to this thought in Part III.

Pascal goes on in *Pensée* 199 to describe the infinitely small, proposing that the microscopic is equally incomprehensible to Man as the astronomic. Pascal describes "man in nature" as

> a nothing compared with the infinite, a whole compared to the nothing, a middle point between all and nothing, infinitely remote from an understanding of the extremes; the end of things and their principles are unattainably hidden from him in impenetrable secrecy.

Here we can begin to see Pascal's purpose in *Pensée* 199, to show his friends that they know less than they think they do. This objective becomes clearer as the *Pensée* continues.

> For who will not marvel that our body, a moment ago imperceptible in a universe, itself imperceptible in the bosom of the whole, should now be a colossus, a world, or rather a whole, compared to the nothingness beyond our reach? Anyone who considers himself in this way will be terrified at himself, and seeing his mass, as given him by nature, supporting him between these two abysses of infinity and nothingness, will tremble at these marvels. I believe that with his curiosity changing into wonder he will be more disposed to contemplate them in silence than investigate them with presumption...

Be humble, limited reason! Pascal exclaims. Pascal was writing to Francis Bacon, Thomas Jefferson's hero and the Father of modern science who lived just prior to Pascal, as well as to nearly all other 17th century scientists that followed Bacon, who also were over-confident. I imagine Pascal saying, "Apart from grace, the only thing infinite about Man is his presumption."

In our day, I imagine that scientists are on average less arrogant than they were 350 years ago, partly because many important scientific problems have resisted solution. In my own work in trying to develop an AIDS vaccine, how little basis I have for arrogance when the march of the HIV/AIDS pandemic continues largely unabated to the clip of 17,000 new HIV infections globally each day! The title of a 2003 book by Jon Cohen succinctly expresses the inability of science to yet deliver a vaccine: *The Wayward Search for an HIV Vaccine*.

Despite myriad scientific failures, arrogance and presumption surely remain as ugly attributes of some scientists today. A few decades ago

Stephen Hawking was pursuing The Theory of Everything, a unifying theory that could explain everything. On the face of it this statement is stunningly bold, and in Hawking's later years, he abandoned this search (impacted by Kurt Gödel's famous Incompleteness Theorem), apparently accepting the overreaching ambition of his quest.

Unlike his contemporaries, Pascal saw clearly that science is deeply limited by Man's finite mind and his disproportion compared to the practically infinite universe:

> ...our intelligence occupies the same rank in the order of intellect as our body in the whole range of nature. [*Pensée* 199]

That is, just as our bodies are imperceptible dots in the physical universe, so our minds are imperceptible dots in the intellectual universe, comprised of the mind of God and possibly the minds of other created beings. Pascal sought to correct the unrealistic optimism of modern science, and thereby motivate his friends to seek answers from God. Pascal knew it was the arrogance of his friends that kept them from seeking, and out of love for them he sought to bring them low. Only then would they have ears to hear from God. In Peter Kreeft's (1993) words, the purpose of this spectacular *Pensée* is to give us a "slap in the face, to teach us the wisdom of wonder, silence and humility. [This *Pensée*] is not designed to fill our heads, but to bow them."

Pascal believed that the mysteries of the infinite God and his creation are beyond us, and while it is worthwhile to pursue what knowledge can be obtained through science, we must accept that many mysteries lie beyond our grasp in an unattainable quarry. "The author understands– no one else can... Let us then realize our limitation." [*Pensée* 199] To imagine that all mysteries can be known invites error, since it leads to over-simplified solutions to complex realities. Gross over-simplifications beget grossly false solutions. Given the immense complexity of physical reality it seems only possible to perceive narrow low-dimensional slices of the whole. Nobel-prize winners may correctly explain small parts of an organism or physical system examined in isolation, but the whole entity, of a higher order of complexity, remains unknown.

Pascal's technique, to humble his friends and move them to seek, resembles God's response to Job's litany of questions. In paraphrase, God told Job: "Consider your proportion relative to me, Job, my ways are higher than your ways, and my thoughts higher than your thoughts... as a finite creature of mine, how can you expect to fully understand my ways?

Be humble and listen to me...otherwise you will not be able to learn from me." Pascal recognized that in order for his interlocutor to listen to God, he must first stop his arrogant presumption. Only then will his ears be open to the opportunity to know God and himself. The Psalmist expresses this reality as, "The fear of the Lord is the beginning of wisdom." [Psalm 111:10] Without stopping to listen openly, there is little hope to grow in wisdom.

I find it intriguing that one of the greatest scientists in history was acutely aware of the limitations of his craft– lesser scientists do not recognize these limits. There is a principle here: the wise recognize their own ignorance, and acknowledge the limits of their capacity for knowing.

Danger of Scientism. By calling out the limits of science, Pascal by no means bashed science, rather, he bashed *scientism*, the worldview that elevates reason as the primary or sole faculty of knowing to the exclusion of the heart. Pascal saw this worldview as profoundly dangerous for society and for a person's spiritual condition. The danger for society can be seen in the dark-side of technology. In the 20th and 21st centuries there are painfully many examples of technology being used as a means for perpetrating violence and destruction. Robert Oppenheimer, the father of the atomic bomb, deeply regretted helping build the bomb, and spent much of his post world war II life in a sort of repentance, working for the elimination of nuclear weapons. As technological capacity has expanded, so has the scale on which violence can, and has, been wielded. Although Descartes believed that technology, if developed using his mathematical method, would lead to the elimination of human suffering, Pascal saw through Descartes' naïve Utopianism, perceiving it as terribly dangerous. In *Pensées* 16 and 427 Pascal observes that the failure to recognize the wretchedness of Man is the surest sign of a weak mind and Man's greatest weakness, and in *Pensée* 97 he calls the refusal to acknowledge one's faults an evil, because it involves deliberate self-delusion. As such, Pascal must have viewed Descartes as a foolish, proud, and self-deceived man who dangerously played with fire. Intellectual pride was Descartes' blind spot.

Next, Pascal suggests that the scientism worldview is dangerous for a person's spiritual health, because reason in isolation is impotent to arrive at knowledge about morality. Pascal foresaw that replacing God with science would open the door to dehumanizing ideologies such as Nazism, which have been justified by appealing to scientism. Writing 350 years after Pascal, Marilynne Robinson laments the sour fruits of scientism,

> The modern fable is that science exposed religion as a delusion and more or less supplanted it. But science cannot serve in the place of religion because it cannot generate an ethics or a morality. It can give us no reason to prefer a child to a dog, or to choose honorable poverty over fraudulent wealth. It can give us no grounds for preferring what is excellent to what is sensationalistic. And this is more or less where we are now. [*The Death of Adam*, essay *Darwinism*]

Pascal matched his belief that excluding faith is perilous with action. To illustrate this, consider an incident in 1647, when Pascal was 24. A priest near Pascal's home, Saint-Ange at Crosville-sur-Cie, was preaching that God could be found and related to purely by reasoning, without the requirement of faith. Finding this teaching heretical, Pascal and two fellow young admirers of the Jansenist leaders Saint-Cyran and Antoine Arnauld followed Jesus' three-tiered recipe (Matthew 18:15–17) for admonishing Saint-Ange. When the cleric would not repent, they took the case to the archbishop, who in response removed Saint-Agne as priest but stopped short of declaring him a heretic (Connor, 2006, page 96). Pascal's congruent coupling of beliefs with actions is also demonstrated by his deep involvement in the Jesuit-Jansenist controversy.

A sub-fragment within *Pensée* 199, which has been called *vanity of science*, further reveals Pascal's belief that scientific knowledge is less important than other kinds of knowledge:

> Knowledge of physical science will not console me for ignorance of morality in time of affliction, but knowledge of morality will always console me for ignorance of physical science.

Someday when I learn I am afflicted with an incurable disease, my ability to write scientific papers will not console me. But my knowledge that God loves me, and the revealed hope for a new and perfect body someday, will. What I need is the revealed knowledge that God will restore me and the world to a paradise, a different order of knowledge than what is obtained through reasoning. In *Pensée* 919 titled *the mystery of Christ*, Pascal expresses this thought as,

> Physicians will not heal you, for you will die in the end, but it is I who will heal you and make your body immortal.

In Pascal's theory of orders (addressed more fully in chapter 6), Pascal describes three realms of reality, those of the body, mind, and heart. Pascal observes that scientific knowledge is derived through means proper to the first two orders, through the collection of data by the senses, and through reasoning to derive inferences based on the data. He then proposes that faculties different from these are needed to acquire knowledge in the order of the heart– in particular the heart itself is the essential faculty for knowing God. In Part IV we will look at Pascal's famous *Pensées* on the heart.

Pascal's Purpose in Pensée 199: Make the Listener Feel He is Lost in the Cosmos. With *Pensée* 199 Pascal aims to make his listener feel like an alien lost in an unfeeling, cold, dying universe. As an Enlightenment thinker Pascal's listener believes the natural world is all there is, and Pascal wishes for him to feel deeply dissatisfied with this inhospitable home. In the *City of God*, Augustine also shows people that they feel like aliens and wanderers, restless sojourners, and their deepest desire is to find a warm and lasting home. The only truly satisfying and forever home is in God, and by jolting our awareness of this reality, Augustine and Pascal seek to rekindle our desire to look for it.

Part III. Faith and Reason

We will now look at the *Pensées* in which Pascal discusses faith and reason, and proposes they must both be used, in an appropriate way, to know God. We begin with *Pensée* 183:

> Two excesses: to exclude reason, to admit nothing but reason.

To this point we have considered the second excess listed here, the Cartesian exclusive reliance on reason as the sole method of knowing, which I have called scientism. In *Pensée* 183 Pascal suggests that the opposite excess, to exclude reason altogether (which may be called fideism), is equally dangerous. By discarding reasoning as a means to knowledge, fideism cripples both science and religion. In fact a strict fideism undercuts the possibility of science, for example by pre-assuming that it is not a valid or worthwhile enterprise to conduct medical research in the pursuit of cures. It also cripples Christianity because the truths of the faith are made real to its followers partly through reasoned arguments instilled into the mind, involving history and logic. Therefore reason must not be neglected, but used in the right way.

By instigating the now-prevalent idea that all reality is unknowable and that reason is divorced from reality, Emmanuel Kant was an important carrier of the idea "to exclude reason." In Peter Kreeft's (1993) words,

> In this post-Kantian climate, reason, no longer anchored in reality, floats on a subjective sea, blown by every wind: sociological, psychological, 'politically correct', or even hormonal.

Christian Faith Does Not Contradict Reason. *Pensée* 173 expands Pascal's recommendation to embrace both faith and reason:

> If we submit everything to reason our religion will be left with nothing mysterious or supernatural. If we offend the principles of reason our religion will be absurd and ridiculous.

Here we see that Pascal believed that for a religion to be credible, it must never flatly contradict reason, all of its doctrines and truths must not be disproved by reason. For a hypothetical example, if the historical resurrection of Jesus Christ's body was definitely disproved, then Christianity would be discredited, and Pascal could not believe it.

Young Earth Creationists illustrate a group of Christians that may "offend the principles of reason," thereby impeding the scientifically-minded from belief. By teaching that the earth is only thousands of years old, this perspective neglects a major body of geological and other physical evidence supporting a vastly older earth. Ignoring these data can make Christians look anachronistic and ridiculous, building for Christianity a reputation that it can only be believed by the simple-minded who suspend their reason. In the eighteenth *Provincial Letter* Pascal quotes Saint Augustine's admonishment of the Christians of his day who taught doctrines that contradicted scientific information:

> It is disgraceful and dangerous for an infidel to hear a Christian, while presumably giving the meaning of Holy Scripture, talking nonsense. We should take all means to prevent such an embarrassing situation, in which people show up vast ignorance in a Christian and laugh it to scorn... If they find a Christian mistaken in a field which they themselves know well, and hear him maintaining his foolish opinions about the Scriptures, how then are they going to believe those

Scriptures in matters concerning the resurrection of the dead, the hope of eternal life, and the kingdom of heaven? (*The Literal Meaning of Genesis*, Book 1, Chapter 19)

Pascal adds a similar quote from Saint Thomas, "Thus, we should be making our religion an object for their scorn, and indeed closing the door on their conversion." Applying this to my work, if I talk like a fool about natural things like vaccines, then how will you believe me when I talk about my friendship with God? Being foolish in the first arena ruins my credibility for the second.

Pascal thought that tenets of the Christian faith never contradict data–no one has yet observed phenomena, nor devised an experiment, which falsify them. While *The God Delusion* (2006) may seem to falsify Christian claims, a closer look suggests its line of attack has less to do with reasoning than with laughing the faith to scorn. The nature of Christian faith is such that the senses and reason are unable to contradict it:

> Faith certainly tells us what the senses do not, but not the contrary of what they see; it is above, not against them. [*Pensée* 185]

The Outer Limits of Reason. Pascal goes on to observe that a vast portion of reality is impenetrable by reason.

> Reason's last step is the recognition that there are an infinite number of things which are beyond it. It is merely feeble if it does not recognize that. If natural things are beyond it, what are we to say about supernatural things? [*Pensée* 188]

Examples abound of things beyond reason. Two grand-daddy problems that have always stumped philosophers and scholars are an explanation for consciousness, and an explanation for the relationship between mind and body. Pascal marvels at the second of these puzzles in *Pensée* 199, quoting Augustine:

> The way in which minds are attached to bodies is beyond man's understanding, and yet this is what man is. (Saint Augustine, *City of God*)

For a third example of matters beyond reason, I will come back to my own work as a vaccine research scientist. There are approximately 35 licensed vaccines for infectious diseases, such as polio, measles, and flu, but for most of these vaccines, scientists do not understand how they work. In addition, after 30 years of research on HIV/AIDS, we still do not know how HIV infection, which usually replicates in a person without causing symptoms for several years, eventually breaks out and causes AIDS and death. We do not understand these mechanisms because the immune system is deeply complex, with hundreds of cell types communicating through a multi-factorial chemical signaling system. The more we study the immune system the more we discover of its intricate complexities. It is likely that some key immune players have not even been discovered yet, let alone have their function within the multi-factorial immune system explained. The more I study infectious diseases, the more I appreciate that my understanding is an imperceptible dot in the space of knowledge. My reason would have to be feeble if it did not recognize that.

As difficult as it is for reason to apprehend natural things, Pascal suggests it is even more difficult for it to grasp supernatural things. At least nature can be studied with the senses. Augustine considers God's incomprehensibility to be inherent to who God is, remarking, "If you understand him, he is not God." (Sermo 52) Montaigne put it this way: "Human reason goes astray... especially when she concerns herself with matters divine."

How can reason comprehend the soul? Or explain the meaning of life? These questions are beyond reason's reach. Pascal's statement that supernatural things are farther beyond reason than natural things mirrors a question that Jesus posed to Nicodemus: "If I have told you earthly things and you do not believe, how will you believe if I tell you heavenly things?" [John 3:12]

In summary, given the finitude of Man's reasoning capacity, the essentially infinite complexity of the natural world, and the incapacity for reasoning to evaluate the supernatural world, on what grounds can the human animal imagine that he can possess complete understanding?

Part IV. Knowing Through the Heart

A thesis of the *Pensées* is the central role of the heart for knowing truth, especially truth about God. A prominent geneticist, National Institutes of Health director, and Christian, Francis Collins, previews this Pascalian theme in *The Language of God* (2006):

> It also became clear to me that science, despite its unquestioned powers in unraveling the mysteries of the natural world, would get me no further in resolving the question of God. If God exists, then He must be outside the natural world, and therefore the tools of science are not the right ones to learn about Him. Instead, as I was beginning to understand from looking into my own heart, the evidence of God's existence would have to come from other directions, and the ultimate decision would be based on faith, not proof.

Pascal's Meaning of the Word Heart. What did Pascal mean by the heart? Peter Kreeft (1993) summarizes Pascal's meaning of heart in four points. First, the heart is the intuitive mind, which knows self-evident first principles. The intuitive mind "just knows" something is true. For example, the fact we exist– we know this intuitively. Or, the law of non-contradiction in logic, which states that A and not A cannot both be true at the same time. We intuit immediately that this law is true, but cannot prove it: it can only be accepted as an axiom. Reasoning is unable to prove or disprove first principles; they can only be believed by intuition.

Second, the heart is what perceives God by faith. As in *Pensée* 424:

> It is the heart which perceives God and not the reason. That is what faith is: God perceived by the heart, not by the reason.

I think of point 2 as a subcategory of point 1, because through faith the heart intuits that God is near. This kind of knowledge is not acquired through deductive logic; it is more like a sensation or feeling, something different from reason.

Third, the heart is what hopes– the heart hopes for love from a parent, for redemption from God, for a friend to never abandon us. Hope is beyond reason because it is not possible for reasoning to assure the hoped-for event, simply because the event has not yet happened; things hoped for cannot be seen.

Fourth, the heart is the will, which chooses to love and honor God, or to disobey and dishonor God. The heart is the seat of the will. Kreeft (1993) notes that the Apostle Paul's list in I Corinthians 13:13 of the three greatest things, faith, hope, and love, are all found in the heart. Therefore the heart is the greatest faculty, our most important part.

Knowing Through the Heart. With those definitions of the heart, let us turn to *Pensée* 110.

> We know the truth not only through reason but also through our heart. It is through the latter that we know first principles, and reason, which has nothing to do with it, tries in vain to refute them... We know that we are not dreaming, but, however unable we may be to prove it rationally, our inability proves nothing but the weakness of our reason, and not the uncertainty of our knowledge, as they maintain...

At this moment, I feel certain I am not dreaming. But if you ask me to prove it, you will only get back a blank stare. I have no argument for it; "I just know" is the best I can do. The dominant philosophers of Pascal's day were skeptics, who would conclude that we do not know whether we are awake or dreaming, and we cannot know. "Because our reasoning ability cannot prove it, therefore it cannot be known," goes their argument. Pascal called to the carpet this fallacious deduction, pointing out that it is not an argument at all, but rather the *assumption* that reason is the only way to obtain knowledge. The fact that our reason is too weak to prove whether we are awake says nothing about the reliability of the heart for knowing this. Our heart may very well know we are awake, despite its inability to prove it logically. Pascal accepts that the heart's knowledge of first principles is sure, remarking, "I pause at the dogmatists' only strong point, which is that we cannot doubt natural principles if we speak sincerely and in all good faith" [*Pensée* 131]

Pascal elaborates as *Pensée* 110 continues:

> For knowledge of first principles, like space, time, motion, number, is as solid as any derived through reason, and it is on such knowledge, coming from the heart and instinct, that reason has to depend and base all its argument. The heart feels [intuits] that there are three spatial dimensions and that there is an infinite series of numbers, and reason goes on to demonstrate that there are no two square numbers of which one is double the other. Principles are felt [intuited], propositions proved, and both with certainty though by different means. It is just as pointless and absurd for reason to demand proof of first principles from the heart before agreeing to accept them as it would be absurd for the heart to demand an intuition of all the propositions demonstrated by reason before agreeing to accept them...

The Hungarian physical-chemist turned philosopher-of-science Michael Polanyi wrote about "tacit knowledge," a term he coined for the pre-logical phase of learning, which consists of a range of conceptual and sensory information and images that can be brought to bear in an attempt to make sense of something. Polanyi proposes that tacit knowledge, different from rational knowledge, is of central importance in human discovery and creativity. This conjecture is consistent with Pascal's view about the central important of intuition/the heart for knowing. As an illustration, Mozart "discovered" beautiful melodies in his mind, and then applied his training to write the notes down. Similarly, many great mathematicians describe their breakthrough results as suddenly appearing, being "apprehended in an instant." After the heart apprehends the result, reason steps in to supply a proof. To Polanyi and Pascal, all of reason's work stands on the shoulders of intuition/the heart, and commonly the essential insight is achieved by the heart.

In *The Abolition of Man* (1943), C.S. Lewis expresses alarm about a philosophical perspective, gaining popularity in his day, which debunks all philosophies that assert the existence of objective values. This relativistic/subjectivist point of view commits the "absurd" error of "demanding proof of first principles from the heart." Aligned with Pascal, Lewis insists that any non-absurd worldview must at bottom depend on a dogmatic belief in un-analyzable first principles. For example, science is only rational under the un-provable first principle that laws of nature are constant (*Miracles*, chapter 13). Lewis believed the subjectivist error so dangerous that his book's thesis warns that this error, carried to its logical conclusion, will abolish Man as Man: all that makes him human– such as his capacity to love goodness and truth– will be lost. "It is no use trying to see through first principles," Lewis concludes.

Fallibility of the Heart's Knowing. While Pascal believed the heart to be a powerful means for obtaining knowledge, he also recognized its fallibility– like the other faculties many snares interfere with its truth-finding capacity. In *Pensée* 975 Pascal compares the imagination with the heart:

> Men often take their imagination for their heart, and often believe they are converted as soon as they start thinking of becoming converted.

For example, consider a person who is petrified of death and learns that Christianity promises everlasting life. He could believe he is converted purely out of fear, imagining he has faith in an attempt to alleviate his fear of death. Such imaginings may indeed be a first step to seeking and eventually finding authentic faith, but here Pascal notes that this is not an automatic process that can be invoked by pressing a button. Pascal suggests it is easy to mistake one's imagination for one's heart; consequently, reliably discerning truth through the heart requires an openness to learn from God and the habitual practice of means of grace. Humility, which involves shedding presumption, is needed to find truth through the heart.

Supremacy of the Heart for Knowing God. Pascal's grand *Pensée* 110 on the heart concludes as follows:

> Those to whom God has given religious faith by moving their hearts are very fortunate, and feel quite legitimately convinced, but to those who do not have it we can only give such faith through reasoning, until God gives it by moving the heart, without which faith is only human and useless for salvation.

While recognizing that reason is a vitally important tool for helping people come to faith, Pascal stresses that reason can never substitute for saving faith, which is a gift from God. The author of Hebrews put it this way, "Jesus is the author and finisher of our faith." [Hebrews 12:2] God's movement is required to produce faith, which cannot be drummed up by the effort of human reason alone. Pascal was deeply concerned that philosophers and religious leaders of his day were teaching that God could be found through reasoning alone. This is dangerous, Pascal warns, because it neglects the fact that faith is the essential ingredient for a Christian, and faith is a "gift of God and not of reason." (Henry Phillips)

Let us now turn to what may be the most famous *Pensée*:

> The heart has its reasons of which reason knows nothing: we know this in countless ways. [*Pensée* 423]

To understand *Pensée* 423, first note that, as considered in Part III, Pascal is not putting down reason– he is not a fideist. Pascal's passionate scientific work late into his life supports this. To the contrary of denigrating reason, in this *Pensée* Pascal elevates the heart as having its own stalwart reasons. How do we know a Mozart sonata is sublime? How do we recognize a great story? How do we know our mother loves us? In each case the senses and reason are certainly involved, for example we can observe our mother's cooking for us, tending to us when we are sick, paying for our college tuition, etc. But this kind of evidence is inconclusive, for in principle a robot could be programmed to do these tasks. This evidence cannot be neatly written down as a set of statistics and a sequence of logical steps for testing a hypothesis in a scientific experiment. Rather, to Pascal the primary means of knowing my mother's love is through the heart, it is intuited with faculties including emotion, feeling, and wonder; not proved by solving a mathematical equation. John Medina proposes there are two ways of knowing– through observation/reasoning, and through relationships. Knowing through the heart almost always involves relationships, and Dr. Medina suggests this knowledge is real.

And for the grandest question of how we know God loves us, again the senses and reason play an important role, by observing that we have been provided food, shelter, recovery from the flu, some loving friends, some opportunities, etc. But this kind of evidence is infinitely distant from a full proof that we are beloved. For this we must have supernatural grace and faith, operating directly on our heart. [*Pensée* 424]

Pascal goes on in *Pensée* 423 to observe that it is the heart's decision to love God or to refuse to love God:

> ...I say that it is natural for the heart to love the universal being or itself, according to its allegiance, and it hardens itself against either as it chooses. You have rejected one and kept the other. Is it reason that makes you love yourself?

There is a sort of justice in the heart, not reason, deciding allegiance to God or self. Consider that our reasoning ability is something largely out of our control– genetics partly determine our intelligence, and the family and socioeconomic condition we are born into affects the opportunities we have for educational development. Therefore some people inherit superior reasoning powers to others. Would it be fair for those born brilliant and placed into the best schools to be favored for entering God's kingdom? Peter Kreeft (1993) suggests that since reason is a largely inherited trait, it would be unfair for it to decide heaven or hell.

On the other hand, the heart may be less influenced by genetics and the environment– anecdotes abound of people born into depraved families who chose a radiant path of service, and vice versa of people born into advantaged Christian families who chose idleness or a life lived for self-indulgence. The worldwide Christian church over the course of history includes the entire spectrum of intelligences and environmental situations, ranging from the brilliant born with educational opportunity, such as Pascal, Chesterton, Isaac Newton, etc.; to the majority of the world's Christians today who live in developing countries, many of whom have not had the opportunity to learn to read. Each person, no matter what genes or circumstances they are born into, has a heart that may will to love God or not, and those with disadvantaged inheritance are not disadvantaged at the level of the heart. In fact, Jesus observed that the well-born have no advantage for entering the kingdom of God, and that it is particularly difficult for the rich to enter. Pascal suggests that irrespective of being advantaged or disadvantaged intellectually, it is the heart that decides and not the reason. [*Pensée* 424]

Pensée of the Day: Number 172

> The way of God, who disposes all things with gentleness, is to instill religion into our minds with reasoned arguments and into our hearts with grace, but attempting to instill it into hearts and minds with force and threats is to instill not religion but terror.

How clear an expression of true religion! *Pensée* 172 reminds me of the grace I received in 1992 when, as a 22 year old, I was mugged at knife-point on the day I arrived in Amsterdam to begin volunteer work at the Christian youth hostel Ebenhaezer. I was shaken, especially as I did not know a soul in the city. But my co-volunteers whom I met later that day consoled me with a hand crafted card that paraphrased *Pensée* 172, "God's love is as fresh as flowers, and comes to us as gently as a dove."

This PoD links with Chapter 1's PoD, which concludes, "...it is also false zeal to preserve truth at the expense of charity..." [*Pensée* 949] God's truth must be delivered with gentleness and charity; to deliver it with force destroys its legitimacy. *Pensée* 172 serves as a self-diagnostic tool for how well we carry the truths of the gospel.

Synthesis Points of Chapter 3

1. Humans have a severely limited capacity to apprehend truth, and because of the Fall, are inclined toward fanciful imagination and

presumption. Therefore, left to themselves, humans are prone to making errors, both about natural things and supernatural things, yet they under-recognize their fallibility.

2. In particular, Pascal perceived that Enlightenment thinkers greatly erred in imagining that science could solve our deepest problems including unhappiness (i.e., our "nullity, loneliness, inadequacy, dependence, helplessness, emptiness" [*Pensée* 622]).
3. Because of 1. and 2., it behooves humans to look for help by listening to God. Do not rely on ourselves; cultivate silence and spend time listening to God.
4. In Man's origin the mind (reason) and the heart were perfect and harmonious faculties for obtaining knowledge, but after the Fall they both became error prone and competitors. While modern skepticism sides with reason and denigrates the heart as impotent for obtaining knowledge, Pascal venerates it as our principal faculty for obtaining knowledge in the most important realms of reality including for grasping first principles, beauty, goodness, ourselves, and God.

4 MAN'S WRETCHED CONDITION: EMPTY AND INCLINED TO LOVE ONLY SELF

"I have seen all the works that are done under the sun, and indeed, all is vanity and grasping for the wind."
– King Solomon, Ecclesiastes 1:14

"The better one is, the worse one becomes, if one ascribes this excellence to oneself."
– Saint Bernard, *Sermons on the Canticle*, 84.

"An inch or two of cowl can put 25,000 monks up in arms."
– Blaise Pascal, *Pensée* 18

In the past two chapters we considered Man's wretchedness in his being unhappy and lost in the dark. We now survey Man's wretchedness in his vanity and undue self-love.

Outline of Chapter 4. By vanity, Pascal meant the same thing Solomon meant in Ecclesiastes– a vapor, vacuous-ness, emptiness, meaninglessness, nullity. In this chapter, in turn we will look at three vain attributes considered by Pascal: human justice, human reason, and a self-centered self-love. Pascal believed there are such things as true justice, true reasoning, and an appropriate way to love oneself. But like Augustine he emphasizes the sweeping impact of the Fall– after being expelled from God's fellowship, Man, left to himself, had a severely weakened ability to practice true justice, to reason accurately, and to love others as much as himself.

This chapter probes the nadir of the human plight, the depths of the hollowness and foulness of the heart of man. As such it completes the three-chapter description of the bad news of Man's wretchedness apart from God. Take heart, though– at the end of this chapter we will begin to explore Pascal's *Pensées* proclaiming the good news– that through Jesus Christ humankind can be restored from vanity to fullness, from a lover of self alone to a lover of God and neighbor.

Part I. Vanity of Human Justice

We begin with Pascal's *Pensées* on the vanity of human justice.

> I spent much of my life believing that there was such a thing as justice, and in this I was not mistaken, for in so far as God has chosen to reveal it to us there is such a thing. But I did not take it in this way, and that is where I was wrong, for I thought that our justice was essentially just, and that I had the means to understand and judge it, but I found myself so often making unsound judgments that I began to distrust myself and then others. I saw that all countries and all men change. Thus, after many changes of mind concerning true justice I realized that our nature is nothing but continual change and I have never changed since. And if I were to change I should be confirming my opinion. [*Pensée* 520]

Pascal observes that he, his friends, and societies repeatedly change their minds about what is just. The data also suggest that figuring out what is truly just is a daunting task for human beings. For one example, consider the controversial Iraq war II. I suspect the readership holds a wide range of perspectives about whether launching the American operation in Iraq was just. Some, I expect, would passionately seek to justify one position, others the opposite position. Moreover, many have changed their minds about the justice of the war. Perhaps the only point of consensus we could reach is that there is a wide scope of opinions on what is right. The continual change of what people consider just constitutes Pascal's first proof of the vanity of human justice.

Justice Depends on a River. Pascal's second proof of the vanity of human justice observes that what people consider just depends arbitrarily on geography. *Pensée* 51 describes a dialog between two opposing soldiers:

> 'Why are you killing me for your own benefit? I am unarmed.' 'Why, do you not live on the other side of the water? My friend, if you lived on this side, I should be a murderer, but since you live on the other side, I am a brave man and it is right.'

Princes and rulers wage war, often for their own reasons that have little to do with the welfare of their subjects, and each expects their subjects to kill those of the other. Within each country it is considered noble to kill a man from the other country, and cowardly not to. At the same time it is considered murder to kill a man from the same country. Therefore it is a river, the border between nations, which determines whether killing is just or unjust. Pascal elaborates this observation:

> Could there be anything more absurd than that a man has the right to kill me because he lives on the other side of the water, and his prince has picked a quarrel with mine, though I have none with him? [*Pensée* 60]
>
> On injustice: The absurdity of the eldest son having everything. 'My friend, you were born on this side of the mountain, so it is right that your elder brother should have everything.' [*Pensée* 9]

Essay on the Vanity of Human Justice: Pensée 60. Now let us turn to Pascal's most complete *Pensée* on the vanity of human justice, which carries both the idea that what is considered just changes, and what is considered just is determined arbitrarily by custom.

> What basis will he take for the economy of the world he wants to rule? Will it be the whim of each individual? What confusion! Will it be justice? He does not know what it is. If he did know he would certainly never have laid down this most commonly received of all human maxims: that each man should follow the custom of his own country. True equity would have enthralled all the peoples of the world with its splendour, and lawgivers would not have taken as their model the whims and fancies of Persians and Germans in place of this consistent justice. We should see it planted in every country of the world, in every age, whereas what we do see is that there is nothing just or unjust but changes colour as it changes climate. Three degrees of latitude upset the whole of jurisprudence and one meridian determines what is true... It is a funny sort of justice whose limits are marked by a river; true on this side of the Pyrenees, false on the other. [*Pensée* 60]

Pascal observes that countries define rules of justice based on accepted customs, which are often derived from whim and fancy. Since customs differ among countries, a river or mountain range determines what is considered just.

There are No Universally Accepted Rules of Justice. Continuing *Pensée* 60:

> They confess that justice does not lie in these customs, but resides in natural laws common to every country. They would certainly maintain this obstinately if the reckless chance which distributed human laws had struck on just one which was universal, but the joke is that man's whims have shown such great variety that there is not one.
>
> Larceny, incest, infanticide, parricide, everything has at some time been accounted a virtuous action...

Here Pascal addresses the topic of whether there are universal ethical principles ("natural laws"). The finding that some actions have been considered unjust by all cultures and all times would support their existence. However, to Pascal the data do not indicate this. Although researchers have identified moral codes that have been believed by most nations at most times, Pascal suggests there is not a single truly universal and unchanging moral code– exceptions can always be found. Child sacrifice was considered right by many civilizations for thousands of years. Many today consider it right to kill selected ethnic groups, and to enslave women and to kill them for upholding honor. (Kristoff and WuDunn, 2009) For much of U.S. history many citizens felt it right to enslave people based on race, and to allocate voting rights by race and gender. Many Americans consider it right for an individual to accumulate and autonomously control massive wealth. The data do not support the existence of universally accepted rules of justice.

True Justice Exists. Later in *Pensée* 60 Pascal broaches the topic of true justice:

> ...There no doubt exist natural laws, but once this fine reason of ours was corrupted, it corrupted everything...

This assertion confirms that Pascal believed there is such a thing as true justice, that is, absolute universal justice (what C.S. Lewis calls Moral Law in *Mere Christianity*). As an orthodox Christian Pascal believed the creator God defines what is absolutely just, and these rules are true everywhere and for all time. Similarly, in *Pensée* 520 Pascal asserts that true justice exists, and that we can understand it "so far as God has chosen to reveal it to us," through Moses and the prophets, conscience, reason, and other sources.

Corruption of Reason Perpetuates Injustice. However, in his statement in *Pensée* 60, Pascal points to the corruption of human reason as a cause of why humans, left to themselves without God's help, have only a weak ability to apprehend what is true justice, let alone practice it. Pascal believed that consequent to the Fall, Man's reasoning capacity became corrupted to the point that he was no longer able to understand God's justice on his own– only through God's revelation, through the ten commandments and the like, could understanding be acquired. As a result, attempts to create justice through purely human reasoning/philosophizing invariably fail, a conjecture supported by the history of political movements that sought justice through the autonomous power of individuals or societies, but in practice backfired. For examples, Rousseau's philosophy, which purported the power of the individual for creating justice, is now credited with facilitating the European bloodshed of the twentieth century, whereas Marxist-Lenin communism, which purported the power of society for creating justice, led to millions dead and oppressed.

Power Determines Rules of Justice. Pascal suggests that, alongside Man's corrupt faculty of reasoning, Man's desire for power is a cause of why humans have not practiced any universal rules of justice:

> The only universal rules are the law of the land in everyday matters and the will of the majority in others. How is that? Because of the power implied... [*Pensée* 81]

Therefore what really determines rules of justice is power– whoever has authority makes the rules. Power-seekers tend to seize upon any available pretext to achieve their objectives. Robinson (2005) suggests that Stalin and Hitler appropriated the prestige of science to help their cause to purge society of undesirable folk, "Their scale and relentlessness have been owed to the disarming of moral response by theories authorized by the word 'science,' which, quite inappropriately, has been used as if it meant 'truth'." Similarly, Robinson suggests that lords in the

Middle Ages leveraged the prestigious institution of their day, the church, to justify the Crusades. "We never do evil so fully and cheerfully as when we do it out of [religious] conscience," suggests Pascal. [*Pensée* 813]

Pascal observes that power determines justice not only for totalitarian states, but also for democratic states where power rests with "the will of the majority." In a democracy or republic, if the majority believes something is right, then representatives will be elected that hold their views, and in time the laws of the land will reflect their beliefs. The legality of abortion in the United States provides one example– no ethical principles were invoked in the Roe versus Wade decision, rather the will of a large segment of Americans led to the result. And why are speed limits 70 miles per hour? Is it because objective statistical analysis of safety and fuel economy data demonstrated the optimality of this limit in some sense? Similarly, given the results of studies supporting the danger of cell-phone driving [e.g., Strayer et al.'s (2006) comparison of the cell-phone driver to the drunken driver], why is it still legal in many states? Hard statistics on elevated accident, injury and death rates do not necessarily persuade the will of the majority, who may prefer convenience and an imagined safety to reasoned conclusions from the data.

Difficulty in Making Might Obey Right. Later in *Pensée* 81 Pascal writes,

> …As men could not make might obey right, they have made right obey might. As they could not fortify justice they have justified force.

The thesis of Plato's Republic is that for republics to be run well, wisdom and power must join. (Kreeft, 1993) Unfortunately, as Pascal observes, this cannot be sustained in practice, except for a short while under a rare wise leader and circumstance like Winston Churchill and World War II. In general, humankind has been unable to make might obey right. Pascal begins to address why in *Pensée* 103, which opens with the words:

> Right without might is helpless, might without right is tyrannical.

To interpret this, consider Pascal's definition of "tyranny" as

> ...the desire to dominate everything regardless of order... Tyranny is wanting to have by one means what can only be had by another. We pay different dues to different kinds of merit; we must love charm, fear strength, believe in knowledge.
>
> These dues must be paid. It is wrong to refuse them and wrong to demand them of others. So these arguments are false and tyrannical: 'I am handsome, so you must fear me. I am strong, so you must love me'... [*Pensée* 58]

Pascal suggests that the right and appropriate reason to love someone is that they are lovely and lovable, and a wrong and inappropriate reason to love someone is that they are strong. If a brutal man commands his wife to love him because otherwise he will hurt her, he behaves tyrannically.

I will now apply this discussion to Pascal's phrase in *Pensée* 103, "might without right is tyrannical." Might is based on strength and should be feared, whereas right is based on qualities that are acknowledged even in the absence of strength; right is believed because it is aligned with a value or a criterion that is believed for some reason. Right governance should be based on wisdom. But might without right is based on strength, and is upheld by keeping people afraid. This is tyrannical because right governance should be based on belief in the wisdom of the governors, not on fear of the governors. Fear is a far easier basis for ruling to sustain than belief; *The Grand Inquisitor* scene in Dostoyevsky's *The Brothers Karamazov* expresses this theme.

The remainder of *Pensée* 103 further addresses the difficulty in making right rule:

> Right without might is challenged, because there are always evil men about. Might without right is denounced. We must therefore combine right and might, and to that end make right into might or might into right.
>
> Right is open to dispute, might is easily recognized and beyond dispute. Therefore right could not be made mighty because might challenged right, calling it unjust and itself claiming to be just. Being thus unable to make right into might, we have made might into right.

The central phrase here is, "Right is open to dispute, might is easily recognized and beyond dispute." This is might's advantage. It is straightforward to instill fear by shows of power, for example by public executions. But it is hard work to persuade the majority to believe wisdom; this requires a willingness to put self-interest behind the public good, and the hard work of educating the majority, made especially hard by the frailty of reasoning as noted above. For only if the majority is persuaded to follow wisdom can wisdom's rule be sustained. But "there are always evil men about," so right without might will always be challenged in short order. Therefore for the majority of nations and eras might without right has ruled, as the path of least resistance, the flow of water downstream.

Problem of Relativity in Ethics. Pascal points to another challenge to identifying true justice: there is no agreed upon standard:

> When everything is moving at once, nothing appears to be moving, as on board ship. When everyone is moving towards depravity, no one seems to be moving, but if someone stops he shows up the others who are rushing on, by acting as a fixed point. [*Pensée* 699]

Pascal raises a serious problem in ethics, the relativity of standards. If "everyone is moving towards depravity," and we use our fellow passengers aboard ship as guides for ethics, then we will end up staying on the course to depravity. Some fixed point, a constant standard not aboard ship, is needed to hope to find true justice. But based on human beings alone, how can this fixed point be found? Pascal begs the answer that without God, it is impossible. This *Pensée* hints at a fallen world that has lost its guide.

My senior pastor in the late 1990's at Park Street Church in Boston, Dr. Gordon Hugenberger, observes that sin makes true righteousness– that is a fixed point– seem odd. He offers a definition of sin as, "that which makes wickedness seem normal, and righteousness seem odd." If everyone is moving towards depravity, it follows that doing the right thing will sometimes stand out as abnormal. This serves as a practical warning to me: if I never feel like I am stopping in a rushing stream, going against the current, I may be complacently floating down the river with others in the wrong direction.

Pascal reinforces his point about the relativity of ethics apart from God's revelation:

> Those who lead disorderly lives tell those who are normal that it is they who deviate from nature, and think they are following nature themselves; just as those who are on board ship think that people on shore are moving away. Language is the same everywhere; we need a fixed point to judge it. The harbour is the judge of those aboard ship, but where are we going to find a harbour in morals? [*Pensée* 697]

Pascal poses the question of how can we find true, absolute ethics? Pascal's modern interlocutor will likely answer, "Nowhere, ethics are relative." Pascal may have wished for him to live with this answer for a while, to become dissatisfied with it, to the point that he will seek a true harbor. To Pascal God and the Scriptures alone constitute this fixed point. We must know this harbor in order to find true ethics, as illustrated by a quote from Seneca, "You must know for which harbor you are sailing in order to catch the right wind to get you there."

Peter Kreeft (1993) contributes the following commentary on *Pensée* 697:

> The whole question is: What is the true standard of naturalness and normalcy in morality? What is the absolute to which everything is relative?... The very things that lead many *away* from God– the problem of evil, injustice, ignorance, and relativity– are what Pascal uses to drive us in desperation to his arms. The atheist argues: 'If there were a God, how could there be injustice?' To which Pascal replies: 'If there is injustice, there must be true justice for it to be relative to and a defect of; and this true justice is not found on Earth or in man, therefore it must exist in Heaven and God.'

Kreeft then observes that Pascal offers this argument not as a proof, but as a prod to encourage seeking. With this prod, Pascal does what he does best, raising a paradoxical question, "How could a good God allow injustice?" He then reveals how this paradox is a clue for the truth of Christianity. He turns a piece of evidence seemingly against Christianity into a piece of evidence supporting it.

Summary of the Vanity of Human Justice. To conclude Part I, the following summarizes Pascal's reasons for why human justice is vain: (1) rules for justice change over time; (2) there are no universal rules of justice; (3) human reasoning, which is charged with identifying justice, is impaired; (4) power and might greatly influence what is considered just; and (5) there is no agreed upon standard for defining what is just.

Part II. Vanity of Human Reason

As in Part I it was important to distinguish between justice in essence versus justice in practice; so to in Part II it is important to distinguish between reason in essence versus reason in practice. Just as true justice exists and is great, Man's reasoning capacity exists and is great– indeed Pascal wrote copiously about reason's prestigious role in making Man infinitely greater than all else in the known universe (e.g., Man as "thinking reed," elaborated in chapter 5). But, just as Man's ability to practice true justice is very weak, so also is his ability to practice reason. Reason is weak in practice because other attributes of human nature tend to overpower its influence.

Pascal knew that reason alone would not persuade most of his Modernist listeners to seek and believe Christ. From the materialist viewpoint of the Modernist it is folly to think that an invisible God made us and has spoken into human history in miraculous and mysterious ways. Thus reason– or, more precisely, pretentious reason– was more of a barrier to faith than an aid for most of Pascal's listeners, as is the case for many today. By providing a realistic account of reason's capacities, Pascal aimed to deflate his interlocutors' pretensions about it, and hence to acknowledge its frailty. In so doing Pascal hoped to open them up to go beyond reason and consider what God has to say. Pascal sought to break through the Enlightenment assumption that only an unreasonable person can be open to revelation.

We will now look at *Pensées* in which Pascal describes why reason in practice is weak: Reason is pushed around by passions such as fear and greed (aided and abetted by fanciful imagination); it only works if conditions are just right; it is not fully in our control; and it wields less influence on behavior than ingrained habits.

Reason Pushed Around by Passions. Pascal's first point on the vanity of human reason is that passions challenge the ability of reason to operate reliably, and vice versa.

> This internal war of reason against the passions has made those who wanted peace split into two sects. Some wanted to

> renounce passions and become gods, others wanted to renounce reason and become brute beasts...[*Pensée* 410]

The first group, for reason, is idealistic, with father Plato. This philosophy suggests looking at the soul and disciplining it in ways that acknowledge the input from reason as more appropriate than from passions. This discipline involves exercising self-control over sex, lust, pride, greed, etc. While Plato recognized that achieving this self-control was difficult, Pascal went much farther by declaring it impossible apart from grace. The second group, for the passions, is animalistic, with major representative Freud. Freud and others saw that Plato and the idealists were naïve to think that reason was strong enough to prevail over the passions. Their solution is to throw away reason altogether, and to follow one's passions. This approach is de-humanizing, because it denies Man's dignity in thought, and proposes that people become just like animals, like the beasts of the field.

Pascal concludes *Pensée* 410 by commenting on the war between these two groups:

> But neither side has succeeded, and reason always remains to denounce the baseness and injustice of the passions and to disturb the peace of those who surrender to them. And the passions are always alive in those who want to renounce them.

I will derive two points from this. First, reason essential is great, because when the Freudian advice to act like a beast is put into practice, the reason in Man's nature objects, creating a sense of guilt that cannot be eradicated. Second, reason in practice is weak, because the passions that vie to dominate reason cannot be extinguished by sheer will power. The Apostle Paul expresses this reality in his letter to the Romans, writing of his wrestling against his passions, even as a faithful disciple of Christ [Romans 7:14–25]. Pascal suggests that a person who relies on reason as his or her sole guide will continually face an internal civil war against the passions.

Illustrations of Passions Dominating Reason. Our first illustration of passions dominating reason is the struggle of those who wish to lose weight. I leave it to the reader to reflect on the myriad passions/appetites that out-compete the voice of reason that tells us to eat less and move more. Our second illustration is long-term retirement investments. Reason would suggest that 40-year olds should not pull their retirement investments out of the market due to a short-lived bear market, yet the sky-is-falling fear has gripped many to do just this.

Our third illustration is in the area of child safety. Based on auto safety data, economist Steven Levitt presented evidence that, compared to buckling up in the back seat, car seats for older babies are only slightly helpful, if at all, for lowering the risk of child death (Levitt and Dubner, 2005). Yet most states require car seats for the first several years of life, and it is conventional wisdom that any good parent must take their appropriate use with the utmost gravity, and many parents take their cars to the fire or police department to make sure the car seats are correctly installed. Fear, in the hands of marketers and lobbyists of car seats, is one of the passions that influences parents and lawmakers to elevate car seats to their current lofty status. But with hundreds of millions of dollars spent on car seats each year and marginal returns in increased safety for older babies, reason did not play the lead role in creating this situation. Reason would suggest requiring car seats only for the ages for which their benefit is supported by the data, and allocating the saved money in myriad other ways that save more children's lives.

For a less subtle example, in the mid-1990's legislation was proposed to require every dentist in the U.S. to buy special equipment to lower the risk of transmitting HIV to dentists or their patients. The proposal sprung from a firestorm created by a single case of HIV transmission from a dentist to a patient in Florida, even though the transmission event was never causally linked to unclean dental equipment. The new equipment would cost a dentist upwards of $10,000, for preventing a hypothetical risk that is less probable than the life-time risk of being struck by lightning. With the simplest cost-benefit analysis any economist would find it grossly unreasonable to require the equipment.

For a final illustration, which personally alarms me given my profession, is the fact that in 2008 the National Institutes of Health spent only several-fold more on HIV vaccine development than on anthrax vaccine development. The one bioterrorist attack with anthrax in U.S. history led to five suspected deaths among U.S. postal workers in 2001. In contrast, millions have died of HIV infection and over 40 million are currently infected. (www.unaids.org) The HIV pandemic is probably the worst plague in human history and is still expanding. Then how come a great deal more money is not injected into HIV compared to anthrax vaccine development? I submit it is more because of irrational fear than reason– following the scare of the suspected anthrax deaths the attending media coverage struck a chord with the imagination and fears of Americans, leading to the asymmetrical funding for anthrax vaccines. More broadly, a large portion of the National Institute of Allergy and Infectious Diseases' budget is mandated for bio-terrorism prevention, despite the fact that beyond the anthrax episode no other American lives have been lost through this means (the two other known bio-warfare attacks are General Cornwallis' foiled attempt to infect George Washington's troops with smallpox in the battle of Yorktown; and the German's thwarted attempt to infect American horses with glanders during World War I).

If reason decided how money is allocated to health sciences, then money would be spent proportionally to the risks and consequences of different diseases, to minimize the total amount of morbidity and mortality. But money is allocated quite differently. Fear and other passions play a key role, supporting Pascal's point that reason is relatively weak and is easily pushed around by the passions.

Reason Only Works Under a Narrow Set of Conditions. Pascal's second point on the vanity of human reason is that the mind can reason well only under a restrictive set of conditions.

> If we are too young our judgment is impaired, just as it is if we are too old.
>
> Thinking too little about things or thinking too much both make us obstinate and fanatical.
>
> If we look at our work immediately after completing it, we are still too involved; if too long afterwards, we cannot pick up the thread again.
>
> It is like looking at pictures which are too near or too far away. There is just one indivisible point which is the right place.
>
> Others are too near, too far, too high, or too low. In painting the rules of perspective decide it, but how will it be decided when it comes to truth and morality? [*Pensée* 21]

Pascal expresses similar thoughts in *Pensée* 199 on the disproportion of man:

> Our sense can perceive nothing extreme; too much noise deafens us, too much light dazzles; when we are too far or too close we cannot see properly; an argument is obscured by being too long or too short; too much truth bewilders us...

And in *Pensée* 48, Pascal tells us,

> ...Do not be surprised if his reasoning is not too sound at the moment, there is a fly buzzing round his ears; that is enough to render him incapable of giving good advice.

In these *Pensées* Pascal observes that conditions must be just right in order to think well. Reasoning only works if a person is physically and mentally healthy and in a certain age range, if done in the right timing, without distractions; if the amount of light and sound is in a certain range; and if the facts are put before the mind in the right proportion. Reason is not a robust faculty, it depends sensitively on outer conditions, and it can only comprehend a narrow range of reality. Most of reality is missed by our minds.

Reason is Largely Out of Our Control. A third point Pascal makes on reason's weakness is that we only have limited control over it.

> Thoughts come at random, and go at random. No device for holding on to them and not having them.
>
> A thought has escaped: I was trying to write it down: instead I write that it has escaped me. [*Pensée* 542]

Commenting on this *Pensée*, Peter Kreeft (1993) considers Plato's comparison of the mind to an aviary and thoughts to birds. When we reach in the aviary to grab a bird, it might fly away, and we grab another bird instead. The observation that our thinking depends on the firing of synapses that we only partially control shows an inherent instability of reason. Kreeft writes:

> The highest and most God-like thing in us– that which understands eternal Truth– is subjected to the lowest thing in us, random chance, which neither understands nor is understood. This is more evidence for the Fall, another example of our looking suspiciously like disinherited princes.

Pascal suggests that the greatest of human institutions are also subject to random chance. He makes this point by observing that the demise of the Roman Republic, governed by the august body of reasoning senators including Marc Antony, was hastened by a random genetic event that caused Antony to fall in love with the foreign queen Cleopatra, giving Octavian the advantage he needed to defeat Antony and usher in the new era of Imperial rule:

> Cleopatra's nose: if it had been shorter the whole face of the earth would have been different. [*Pensée* 413]

Reason is Weaker Than Habit. The last point of human nature that tends to overpower reason that we will consider is habit.

> For we must make no mistake about ourselves: we are as much automaton as mind. As a result, demonstration is not the only instrument for convincing us. How few things can be demonstrated! Proofs only convince the mind; habit provides the strongest proofs and those that are most believed. It inclines the automaton, which leads the mind unconsciously along with it... [*Pensée* 821]

Pascal proposes we are both mind and machine, and both are important for acquiring knowledge and for acting on it. Furthermore, habit has a stronger influence on behavior than reason, because the automaton or machine nature of Man is easily habituated, and once the machine is convinced by habit, often the mind will follow its lead. Pascal goes on in this *Pensée* with an example of a habituated belief.

> Who ever proved that it will dawn tomorrow, and that we shall die? And what is more widely believed? It is, then, habit that convinces us and makes so many Christians...

Reason is unable to prove that the sun will rise tomorrow– it would not be contrary to reason if the sun did not rise. Rather, the fact that we experienced the sun rise in all our days past makes us *assume* it will also rise tomorrow; this assumption is based on habit, not reason. C.S. Lewis called this un-provable assumption the "principle of the Uniformity of Nature," and demonstrated that only by accepting it can we infer that the sun will dawn. (*Miracles*, chapter 13) The great German physicist Max Planck also expressed this fact, remarking, "We have no right to assume any physical laws exist, or if they have existed up to now, that they will continue to exist in a similar manner in the future."

Continuing *Pensée* 821:

> In short, we must resort to habit once the mind has seen where the truth lies, in order to steep and stain ourselves in that belief which constantly eludes us, for it is too much trouble to have the proofs always present before us. We must acquire an easier belief, which is that of habit. With no evidence, art or argument it makes us believe things, and so inclines all our faculties to this belief that our soul falls naturally into it. When we believe only by the strength of our conviction and the automaton is inclined to believe the opposite, that is not enough. We must therefore make both parts of us believe: the mind by reasons, which need to be seen only once in a lifetime, and the automaton by habit...

Here Pascal extends his point that both reason and habit are essential for cultivating and sustaining faith in God and relationship with him. It is naïve to think that reason by itself can sustain faith, suggests Pascal– a contrary inclination of our machine nature tends to overrule our mind's conviction. If a person believes in her head that she should do something, but not in her gut and heart, then she likely will not do it– the habituated body must be ready to act. This has far reaching applications, encouraging us to foster automatic habits of engagement with the means of grace.

Illustrations of Beneficent Habits. For an example, consider two college students who are exploring Christianity at the Inn (University Presbyterian Church's college ministry), each whose minds have been convinced of the importance of going to church on Sundays. One of these students has been attending the 10 o'clock service every Sunday, with a group of other Inn-goers, who attend church together. The other student has no ingrained habit of church going, and relies on his conviction when he awakes on Sunday morning. Some Sundays he wakes up feeling like jumping out of bed and going to church, other Sundays he wakes up feeling tired or concerned about his homework or more interested in watching a football game. Even though in his mind he understands equally well as the other student the importance of going to church, because he is not also habituated to attend, his attendance is sporadic.

For another example, consider tithing. Suppose a woman studies the reasons to tithe given by the Old and New Testaments, and becomes convinced that she should tithe at least 10%. She writes a check to UPC the first Sunday after she completes her Bible study on tithing. Six months later, she forgets the details of the arguments given by Moses, Paul, and others about why she should tithe. She hears a friend suggest that tithing does not really matter. She leads a very busy life, and does not find herself searching the Scriptures again to re-discover the arguments of why to tithe. This is Pascal's point that it is "too much trouble to have the proofs always present before us." If she relies only on her reason, her tithing may become sporadic or cease. On the other hand, if she allows tithing to become automatic, tithing will happen with regularity. It is not necessary for her to recall Moses' commands each month, all that is needed is to set up direct-deposit! Twenty years later she may have never revisited the biblical proofs, but like a machine has consistently tithed. The reasons do not need to stay in view, only the habitual inclination to tithe. More generally, I expect Pascal would urge believers to embrace all disciplines that cultivate spiritual growth. Pascal would commend tutorials such as Richard Foster's (1998) that aim to help us develop habits of meditation, prayer, fasting, study, service, confession, worship, and other means of grace.

Pascal concludes *Pensée* 821 with the observation that,

> Reason works slowly, looking so often at so many principles, which must always be present, that it is constantly nodding or straying because all its principles are not present. Feeling does not work like that, but works instantly, and is always ready. We must then put our faith in feeling, or it will always be vacillating.

Vanity of Human Reason and Pascal's Wager. Pascal's thoughts on the importance of habit and the machine play an important role in his Wager– his argument that the expected payoff of believing in Christ is infinitely greater than the expected payoff for not believing (elaborated in chapter 7). Here I will preview the central position of habit in the Wager's conclusion.

If you are a little familiar with Pascal's Wager, then you might think that its conclusion is that a person should bet on the Christian God; that he or she should place his faith in Jesus Christ and become a Christian. This is a common misconception, however, as the Wager's actual conclusion is quite different. Indeed, Pascal's conclusion is that a person, even though he does not believe, should *act as if he believes*– to engage in the habits of a true believer, which will involve curtailing his greedy appetites, attending Church, praying, serving neighbors and the poor, etc.

Pascal recognized that it is not possible for a person to make herself believe, but she can act is if she believes. *Pensée* 821 therefore echoes the conclusion of Pascal's Wager, in proposing that cultivating the habits of true believers can lead to the sprouting and growing of real faith.

Conclusion from Parts I and II: Nullity (Vacuum) of the Human Condition. We conclude Pascal's characterization of the vanity of the human condition with *Pensée* 806, wherein Pascal calls out Man apart from God as a null set, possessing no real substance– nobody is home. Pascal points to the horrifying attribute of the human being that he prefers manufacturing an imaginary existence to facing the real one; he creates and sustains an illusion of being perfect rather than facing the painful reality of being full of faults.

> We are not satisfied with the life we have in ourselves and our own being. We want to lead an imaginary life in the eyes of others, and so we try to make an impression. We strive constantly to embellish and preserve our imaginary being, and neglect the real one. And if we are calm, or generous, or loyal, we are anxious to have it known so that we can attach these virtues to our other existence; we prefer to detach them from our real self so as to unite them with the other. We would cheerfully be cowards if that would acquire for us a reputation for bravery. How clear a sign of the nullity of our own being!

Pascal suggests that, in response to his dissatisfaction with his real being, Man makes up an imaginary being, and constructs a meaning for it. If one strives constantly to do this, the logical conclusion is that the real person himself has no being. Here again Pascal diagnoses Man's wretched condition in strong terms– apart from God Man is a vacuum. Moreover, in *Pensée* 806 Pascal observes that no one accepts being a nothing, and therefore it is normative human behavior to embellish an imaginary self.

Man's strivings to fill his emptiness through the manufacturing of meaning helps explain many areas of human sociology. Some athletes take steroids to build meaning from success and fame; some executives cheat and steal to build the same meaning; some people volunteer to fight in wars to attain purposeful work without doing the requisite homework to evaluate whether the war is just; some terrorists plan mass murder to make themselves count for something; some people engage in reckless sex and violence to build a feeling of tangible-ness, etc. On this thought line Peter Kreeft (1993) proposes that trying to escape the "nullity of our own being" is the deepest explanation for why people use violence.

Part III. Self-love

What did Pascal Mean by "Self-love?" To begin on self-love, I will address what Pascal meant by the term. Here Dr. Kreeft makes the important point that this self-love is very different from self-respect. Pascal believed people should respect themselves, regarding themselves as possessing intrinsic value and dignity (as we will see Pascal express in the next chapter). This dignity derives from being made in God's image.

Distinguished from self-respect, self-love is sin, self-centeredness, Man's belief in himself as being his own God, his own good and goal. Man's original sin in the garden entailed proudly turning inward toward himself, rebelling against the central place God meant to hold in his life. This self-centered self-love Pascal decries ignores God and neighbor and is concerned only with self.

Original Sin. Pascal's adherence to the orthodox Christian doctrine of original sin is key for understanding Pascal's thoughts on self-love. This doctrine states that the first sin of Adam and Eve led to the universal infection of the human race with the disease of being inclined to unjustly exalt themselves– hence being "born unfair:"

> It is untrue that we are worthy to be loved [preferentially] by others. It is unfair that we should want such a thing. If we were born reasonable and impartial, with a knowledge of ourselves and others, we should not give our will this bias. However, we are born with it, and so we are born unfair...
>
> This bias towards self is the beginning of all disorder, in war, politics, economics...
>
> The will is therefore depraved. We are born unfair...
>
> [*Pensée* 421]

The devastating consequence of original sin is that all people are partial judges for themselves. This bias toward self is the beginning of all disorder, Pascal purports, affecting all spheres of life.

The doctrine of original sin is anachronistic to most Westerners today. Many still hold the Enlightenment worldview that hails the doctrine of Progress, to which the notion of original sin is inadmissible. To this rebuff Pascal might reply: "look at the data." Look at human history and all the evil that men do. More specifically, we consider two clues from Pascal's *Pensées* for the rational plausibility of Original Sin.

Mark of Original Sin: Man's Concupiscence. Pascal frequently uses the word concupiscence, which can be defined as the habit of selfishly demanding to gratify all one's desires; it is the habitual inclination to pursue self-gratification above other pursuits. More specifically, concupiscence is often rendered in English translations of the New Testament as "evil desire," which is a translation of the Greek word *epithumiai*. Tim Keller reminds us that this evil desire does *not* mean a desire for something evil, but rather a desire for something good that is made into something evil. Therefore concupiscence/evil desire is an idolatrous *over-desire* (or lust), and this is always the meaning of the term used by New Testament authors (e.g., Galatians 5:16, Ephesians 2:3, 4:22; Colossians 3:5; James 1:14; 1 Peter 2:11, 4:2; I John 2:16). [Tim Keller, February 3, 2002 sermon *Resting Grace* in the sermon series *Practical Grace; How the Gospel Transforms Character*] Elsewhere Pascal observes that concupiscence has three forms, in the areas of sensual pleasure, pride, and intellectual curiosity. [*Pensée* 145] Examples of over-desire include lust for sex, power, money, fame, and reputation. When his brother-in-law Florin Perier prepared to build a very large house, Pascal and his sister Jacqueline warned him of over-desire, advising him "to build much less than he intended, and only what is actually necessary... lest it may happen that he may be far more prudent and bestow much more care and pains in the building of an earthly house than he is obliged to bestow on that mystic tower..." [Letter to Pascal's sister Gilberte] The opposite of concupiscence/over-desire is the old-fashioned virtue of temperance– the satisfaction of a desire to just the right point, but not beyond it (when is the last time you heard the word temperance? The loss of such valuable words is in itself a mark of our concupiscence. [McEntyre, 2009].

In *Pensée* 616 Pascal suggests the all-pervasive influence of concupiscence:

> Concupiscence has become natural for us and has become second nature. [*Pensée* 616]

We observe this reality about our second nature, Pascal suggests, which begs the question as to what is its cause? To Pascal no theory is more consistent with the data than the event of Original Sin; Adam and Eve's original over-desire for more autonomy than what God deemed appropriate initiated their race's habit of pursuing over-desires. To sustain this habit, Man had to convince himself that the heedless pursuit of over-desires is right and normal– perceiving nothing wrong with it– and to do so he developed a superlative ability to self-deceive. This inclination to self-deceive then provides a further clue for the rational plausibility of Original Sin. For if this doctrine is correct, then we would expect Man to be blind to his own sinful inclinations, perceiving himself as wise and in the right, and will find ridiculous the notion that he himself is born unfair. And this is just the effect we observe. Therefore the fact that we naturally find Original Sin ridiculous is expected if this doctrine is true, constituting a clue for its rational plausibility.

Mark of Original Sin: Postmodernism. Some of Postmodernisms' major conclusions about the reality of the human condition are well-explained by the doctrine of Original Sin, constituting another clue for its rational plausibility. Postmodernism levied a strong critique of modernism, including in the areas of knowledge and truth, the self, and meta-narratives (Wright, 1999). Modernists believe that humans can know things objectively about the world, and that people have a strong identity derived from themselves, as expressed by Descartes' famous assertion "I think, therefore I am." Furthermore, modernism tells the meta-narrative that the use of human reason will bring about a new era of prosperity and happiness for the world. Postmodernism challenged these positions, pointing out that when Modernists speak of objective knowledge they are really expressing their subjective perceptions about reality, that Modernists have no grounds for proposing that meaningful identity can derive from self-assertion, and that modernism's promise to usher in a new era of blessing has proven totally false. N.T. Wright summarizes this critique:

> This huge overarching story [of modernism] ... has now been conclusively shown to be an oppressive, imperialist and self-serving story; it has brought untold misery to millions in the industrialized West and to billions in the rest of the world, where cheap labor and raw materials have been ruthlessly exploited.

Most postmodern positions do not accept Pascal's second point that "there is a redeemer, proved by Scripture," because they think humans are incapable of attaining such knowledge. However, many postmodern critiques concur with Pascal's first point that Man is wretched without God; hence they arrive at a conclusion about the human condition that is predicted by the doctrine of Original Sin. For example, in the story of the Fall, Genesis describes Adam and Eve's expulsion from the garden as radically cutting off their ability to know truth, separating them from their source of true identity, and expelling them from the only meta-narrative that can suit them. These are perhaps the three central conclusions drawn by postmodernism about the human condition. By affirming Pascal's first point, postmodernism usefully corrects arrogant modernisms' failure to recognize Man's wretchedness without God. The fact that theists like Pascal and contemporary postmodern philosophers both observe the same wretched attributes of the human condition constitutes another clue for the rational plausibility of Original Sin. Similar to scientific knowledge, which builds through independent replicate experiments, discovery of the same facts based on different techniques, contexts, and perspectives supports the veracity of those facts.

While the doctrine/theory of Original Sin can never be proved, this theory makes predictions about human behavior, and the ample data over the centuries consistent with the theory corroborate it [this framework for corroborating theories follows the work of Sir Karl Popper (1959)].

Essay on Self-love: Pensée 978. We turn to Pascal's grand complete essay on the nature of self-love. In it Pascal addresses the question of why is it that most people get defensive when their faults are pointed out? Why is correction such a bitter pill to swallow? I will present parts of *Pensée* 978 and pause for comment as we make our way through it.

> The nature of self-love and of this human self is to love only self and consider only self...
>
> But what is it to do? It cannot prevent the object of its love from being full of faults and wretchedness: it wants to be great and sees that it is small; it wants to be happy and sees that it is wretched; it wants to be perfect and sees that it is full of imperfections; it wants to be the object of men's love and esteem and sees that its faults deserve only their dislike and contempt.

> The predicament in which it thus finds itself arouses in it the most unjust and criminal passion that could possibly be imagined, for it conceives a deadly hatred for the truth which rebukes it and convinces it of its faults. It would like to do away with this truth, and not being able to destroy it as such, it destroys it, as best it can, in the consciousness of itself and others; that is, it takes every care to hide its faults both from itself and others, and cannot bear to have them pointed out or noticed...

If a person fairly assesses himself, then he will discover faults, and acknowledge that criticisms of these faults are accurate and appropriate. However, Pascal observes that a human self is so averse to acknowledging its faults that it "conceives a deadly hatred for the truth which rebukes it and convinces it of its faults." That is, a person erects facades and masks to hide his faults from others and from himself. As such, Pascal proposes that Man would rather live in the illusion of being "great, happy, perfect, loved, and esteemed" than to face his real miserable situation. In chapter 2 we explored two particular strategies for sustaining an illusion and avoiding looking at the truth: diversions and indifference. Pascal calls the hatred for the truth "deadly," because only by facing the truth, and recognizing one's wretchedness, will a person recognize he is sick and needs a doctor.

Continuing *Pensée* 978:

> It is no doubt an evil to be full of faults, but it is a still greater evil to be full of them and unwilling to recognize them, since this entails the further evil of deliberate self-delusion. We do not want others to deceive us; we do not think it right for them to want us to esteem them more than they deserve; it is therefore not right either that we should deceive them and want them to esteem us more than we deserve...

Pascal observes an asymmetry about how people feel about the truth. To illustrate, suppose I am running for a political office. If a piece of truth makes my opponent look bad, I love the truth, and I wish to shout it from the roof tops. But if a piece of truth makes me look bad, I hate the truth; I suppress it and hide it from others. This example translates to countless other settings. My asymmetrical feelings about the truth, loving or hating it depending on whether it helps me or somebody else, proves that I am biased toward self.

This *Pensée* suggests to me an exercise for self-examination. Think of someone you spend much time with, say, a colleague at work. If he insists that he is a better worker than you plainly know him to be, how do you feel? I would feel annoyed and embarrassed for him for his inflated view of himself. I want him to receive a judgment no better than he deserves. But what about the judgment of myself? Suppose my boss tells me I am near the bottom of merit among my colleagues. My first thought will be, "There must be something wrong with his judgment; he is missing some of my good qualities." Thus when I honestly evaluate my feelings, I discover that I want (at best) a fair judgment for others and a lenient one for me. This constitutes empirical psychological evidence that my nature is unjust in its evaluation of myself compared to others. Or, if you have multiple children, consider whether they tend to judge themselves more favorably than their siblings. Do you find them to be unprejudiced judges?

Continuing, Pascal describes the feelings we would have if we were truly just judges:

> Thus, when they merely reveal vices and imperfections which we actually possess, it is obvious that they do us no wrong, since they are not responsible for them, but are really doing us good, by helping us to escape from an evil, namely our ignorance of these imperfections. We ought not to be annoyed that they know them and despise us, because it is right that they should know us for what we are and despise us if we are despicable.
>
> These are the feelings which would spring from a heart full of equity and justice. What then should we say of ours, seeing it quite differently disposed? For is it not true that we hate the truth and those who tell it to us, and we like them to be deceived to our advantage, and want to be esteemed by them as other than we actually are?
>
> Here is a proof of it which appalls me. The Catholic religion does not oblige us to reveal our sins indiscriminately to everyone; it allows us to remain hidden from all other men, with one single exception, to whom it bids us reveal our innermost heart and show ourselves for what we are. There is only this one man in the world whom it orders us to disillusion, and it lays on him the obligation of inviolable secrecy, which means that he might as well not possess the knowledge of us that he has. Can anything milder and more charitable be imagined? And yet, such is man's corruption that he finds even this law harsh, and this is one of the

> main reasons why a large part of Europe has revolted against the Church.
>
> How unjust and unreasonable the heart of man is, that he should resent the obligation to behave towards one man as it would be right, in some ways, to behave towards all! For is it right that we should deceive them?

Here Pascal observes Man's resistance to openly confess sins. If the human heart embraced truth, then it would be commonplace for people to speak openly about their faults. But what we find in society is very different. The Catholic Church, an institution more intentional than most at trying to cultivate honest confession, was only able to create a system that extracts the mildest kind of confession. In other contexts, how often do you hear people fully offering a disillusioned picture of their innermost hearts? Short of a transformation by God, Pascal suggests, a person's natural hatred of the truth renders him unwilling, and even unable, to engage in honest confession.

Pensée 978 continues:

> This aversion for the truth exists in differing degrees, but it may be said that it exists in everyone to some degree, because it is inseparable from self-love...

Here Pascal draws a connection between self-love and the hatred of truth. A self-centered man hates the truth when it points out his faults. Thus the greatest problems plaguing humankind, hating the truth instead of loving it, and unduly loving self instead of God and neighbor, are inextricably intertwined. In the second part of the *Pensées* Pascal points to a simultaneous cure for both diseases; this cure is like a potent drug regimen, which though challenging to take, is fully efficacious to cure both HIV and cancer.

Consequence of Self-love/Aversion for the Truth: Can Make One Unwilling and Unable to Provide Honest Critiques. Pascal goes on to observe that self-love makes it hard to deliver criticism:

> It is this false delicacy which makes those who have to correct others choose so many devious ways and qualifications to avoid giving offence. They must minimize our faults, pretend to excuse them, and combine this with praise and marks of affection and esteem. Even then such medicine still tastes bitter to self-love,

> which takes as little of it as possible, always with disgust and often even with secret resentment against those administering it.
>
> The result is that anyone who has an interest in winning our affection avoids rendering us a service which he knows to be unwelcome; we are treated as we want to be treated; we hate the truth and it is kept from us; we desire to be flattered and we are flattered; we like being deceived and we are deceived.
>
> This is why each rung of fortune's ladder which brings us up in this world takes us further from the truth, because people are more wary of offending those whose friendship is most useful and enmity most dangerous.

Pascal suggests that a real friend, who tells us the truth about ourselves, is the most valuable thing in the world. Yet undue self-love causes one to avoid real friendships, preferring to remain deluded about one's right condition. In America, the infection of undue self-love has led to a pandemic of lonely isolation, which has accelerated over the past 50 years, with sharp drops in social connections, membership in groups, and in time spent with friends and family [e.g., see Putnam's (2000) aptly named book, "Bowling Alone"]. Research suggests this isolation-pandemic has exacted heavy tolls in health. Pascal's *Pensée* helps reveal the cause, diagnosing our intrinsic condition acquired at the Fall that has led to so many distressing symptoms. Pascal continues:

> A prince can be the laughing-stock of Europe and the only one to know nothing about it. This does not surprise me: telling the truth is useful to the hearer but harmful to those who tell it, because they incur such odium. Now those who live with princes prefer their own interests to that of the prince they serve, and so they have no wish to benefit him by harming themselves...

Here Pascal directly answers the question I opened with: "Why are we defensive at criticism?" To Pascal it is because of our unfair self-love, which finds criticism a bitter and unwelcome medicine. A particular consequence is that it is very hard for an inferior to provide honest criticism of a superior. The story of the Emperor with no clothes illustrates Pascal's principle– no subject in the Emperor's kingdom would dare to tell him that he was a laughingstock for parading about in the buff– they would not dare for fear of retribution. It took a small child, who had not yet comprehended the human heart's aversion to honest critique, to tell the Emperor he was naked. Pascal's principle is also illustrated by King Saul's expression of exasperation when he discovered that all of his servants concealed from him Jonathan's betraying pact with Saul's enemy David: "All of you have conspired against me, and there is no one who reveals to me that my son has made a covenant with the son of Jesse; and there is not one of you who is sorry for me or reveals to me that my son has stirred up my servant against me, to lie in wait, as it is this day." [I Samuel 22:8]

It can be instructive to look at our own lives to see if Pascal's principle applies. Do you find it easy to critique your boss or spouse openly and honestly? Or do you find yourself restricting feedback to affirmative comments and perhaps flattery? The more difficult it is to wield an honest critique, the more on target Pascal's analysis may be.

Pascal concludes his essay on self-love by summarizing the hollowness and foulness of Man's heart (apart from transformation by God):

> This misfortune is no doubt greater and more common among those most favoured by fortune, but more modest people are not exempt, because we always have some interest in being popular. This human life is nothing but perpetual illusion; there is nothing but mutual deception and flattery. No one talks about us in our presence as he would in our absence. Human relations are only based on this mutual deception; and few friendships would survive if everyone knew what his friend said about him behind his back, even though he spoke sincerely and dispassionately.
>
> Man is therefore nothing but disguise, falsehood and hypocrisy, both in himself and with regard to others. He does not want to be told the truth. He avoids telling it to others, and all these tendencies, so remote from human justice and reason, are naturally rooted in his heart.

In Contrast to Society, the Bible is Replete with Frank Truth Telling. Despite humankind's great sensitivity to being criticized or corrected, the Bible is replete with statements from God and others frankly pointing out faults. Moses regularly harangued the stiff-necked Israelites, and Jeremiah and the other prophets constantly pointed out their wayward ways. They used direct language (often in poems) with no minimization or flattering praise, for example the prophets called the people prostitutes with other Gods. John the Baptist called the religious leaders broods of vipers, and Jesus called them vipers and whitewashed tombs. Such stark truth telling must have startled the onlookers, given that these leaders had reputations as the most righteous ones. Jesus also frequently delivered frank words of correction to his disciples, and Paul filled his letters with admonitions for the churches to repent in myriad specific ways. The Bible's routine use of frank truth telling about faults is extraordinarily odd compared to what goes on in society. This juxtaposition makes Pascal's point– that apart from God, truth telling is odd, because Man reviles it; but in God's kingdom, truth is normative and loved. Without God there is only deception and falsehood and with God there is only truth. By showing his interlocutor what he is really like without God, Pascal aims to persuade him to seek.

Summary of Humankind's Vanity and Self-Love, and Onward to Its Redeemability. To summarize, Pascal observes that Man's notion of justice has greatly varied over time, within geography, and within a person. *Pensée* 61 summarizes the shifting sands of Man's idea of justice, "Justice is as much a matter of fashion as charm is." The fact that might has trumped right in the governments of most nations for most of human history reflects the absence of a true and consistently practiced justice. Pascal's objectives in surveying Man's ubiquitous practice of injustice are to stimulate searching for true justice in God and to provide paradoxical evidence that true justice indeed exists in God. Pascal employs similar logic in *Pensée* 734, considered further in chapter 8, where he suggests that the large number of false miracles "proves" the existence of true ones, and likewise the large number of false religions proves the existence of a true one.

Pascal's thoughts on the vanity of human reason are closely connected to those on the vanity of human justice, because a main factor thwarting Man's practice of justice is the weakness of his reasoning faculty for discerning what constitutes true justice. Passions like fear, pride, and greed, or non-rational elements like the imagination and habit, tend to wield greater influence on a person's beliefs and actions than reason, Pascal suggests.

Furthermore, Pascal puts forward that Man's undue self-love, that is his exclusive love of self, is the root cause of both the vanity of human justice and the vanity of human reason. By definition, loving self exclusively means being unfair to others and therefore being unjust (*Pensée* 617). And, if a person loves only himself, then he cannot be fully influenced by reason, because reason is supposed to be unbiased. Rather, a lover of self alone will tend to use reason only as it serves his interests, and abandon it otherwise.

Why did Pascal paint a withering portrait of the vanity of human justice, reason, and self-love? The reasons seem to be his views (1) that our awareness of these wretched characteristics, together with our idea of perfection, constitutes a powerful clue for our creation by God and subsequent fall; and (2) that our greatest weakness is the lack of awareness of our vanity and wretchedness. To Pascal, a person's empty and wretched state is the one thing he absolutely must know in order to become a seeker of God's help. Therefore, like the biblical authors who frankly point out faults and needs, Pascal's motivation is concern for his friends– he knew the kindest thing he could do for them was to show them clearly their true condition. Pascal is like a crewman on a sinking ship who, out of concern for his passengers, shouts the message that the ship is going down and all aboard must immediately get aboard the lifeboats. Pascal's task may be even more important than saving a person from death to life– by sounding a clarion call to seek Jesus Christ Pascal hopes to turn empty lives into full lives, vain lives into meaningful lives.

What is more, if we keep the second half of the *Pensées* in view, with its theme that there is a redeemer, it becomes clear that Pascal believed that justice, reason, and love are redeemable. They are not doomed to permanent vanity. Rather, Pascal believed that with God's help, human efforts in justice, reason, and love are worthwhile endeavors, imbued with meaning and virtue. Pascal's life itself supports these points. His courageous writing of *The Provincial Letters* to try to reform the Jesuits' corrupt practices shows he believed true justice exists and is worth struggling for. His work in science and literature demonstrates his belief in the value of reasoning with excellence; in particular his ambitious project represented in the *Pensées* shows he believed reason has an important role to play in winning seekers. Lastly, Pascal believed that once one's heart is changed by God, then one can be freed from the shackles of exclusive self-love– once given faith a person can actually love God, neighbor, and even enemy. Pascal himself showed this in countless ways including by avoiding pursuits of personal prestige, co-developing a public transport system to benefit the poor, and by living modestly and giving almost all his belongings to the poor. Moreover, in his *Pensées* on the body of Christ, Pascal suggests the path forward for achieving appropriate self-love; for example in *Pensées* 368 and 374:

> *Members. Begin there.* In order to control the love we owe ourselves, we must imagine a body full of thinking members (for

> we are members of the whole), and see how each member ought to love itself, etc. [*Pensée* 368]

> If the feet and hands had their own wills, they would never be properly in order except when submitting the individual will to the primal will governing the whole body. Otherwise they would be disorganized and unhappy, but in desiring only the good of the body they achieve their own good. [*Pensée* 374]

I believe Pascal is most accurately seen as a realist– he was realistic about how corrupt Man is without God, and how angelic Man can be through the redeeming and sanctifying work of Christ. In a word, consider the prayer of Catholic Bishop Lesslie Newbigin,

> Lord Jesus, I admit that I am weaker and more sinful than I ever believed, but through you I am more loved and accepted than I ever dared hope. [*The Gospel in a Pluralist Society*, 1989]

Pascal had such clear sight that he grasped better than most just how bad the bad news is, and how good the good news is.

***Pensée* of the Day: Number 148**

The PoD famously observes the vanity of Man's heart without God, an infinite vacuum that Man craves to fill (where "craving" may be rendered as "epithumiai"/over-desires) , yet only God, not vain diversions, can fill it:

> What else does this craving proclaim but that there was once in man a true state of happiness, of which all that now remains is the empty print and trace? This he tries in vain to fill with everything around him though none can help, since this infinite abyss can be filled only with an infinite and immutable object, in other words by God himself.

This *Pensée* sums up the place to which Pascal wishes to take his listener in the first part of the *Pensées*, a place where he *feels* his emptiness apart from God. Pascal hopes for his friend to discover within himself the gaping hole in his heart, and to recognize that his attempts to fill it with presumption, diversions, and embellishing an imaginary being fail, because these things are not his "true good." Only his true good, his unchanging Creator, can possibly fill the infinite abyss in his heart.

Recognizing that only God may be able to fill this abyss will open his listener to the Wager's challenge to give the Christian faith a try.

Synthesis Points of Chapter 4

1. Pascal believed that apart from God, humankind is vain/empty, with no source of meaning or identity.
2. Pascal observed that consistent rules of justice are not practiced. Apart from God humankind does not know what true justice is; therefore custom, power, a river, fancy, fashion determine what is considered just.
3. Pascal believed that the Fall severely impaired humankind's reasoning capacity. Reason is pushed around by passions, imagination, circumstances, random events, habit, undue self-love.
4. Pascal held the orthodox doctrine of original sin, that humans have an innate self-centeredness, they are born unfair. This undue self-love causes an aversion to the truth about themselves. To Pascal Original Sin is the key to explain human history.
5. Pascal dwelt on the wretchedness of Man because he knew his listeners must know their malady in order to be open to seeking a remedy in Christ.

Man as Dispossessed King
Summary of Man's wretched experience apart from God (surveyed in chapter 2-4) contrasted with his true happiness with God

Man's wretchedness apart from God	Man's idea of perfection (true good with God)
Death is coming soon; a reed, the weakest in nature	Immortality
Fleeting health and beauty; a mist	Permanent health and beauty
Restless, bored, diverted	Abiding rest
Indifferent; sensitive to minor things and insensitive to the greatest	Sanity
Gloom, depression, chagrin, resentment, despair	Joy
Full of natural error; reason a weak tool for perceiving truth	Certainty
No ethical standard; tyrannical; power determines what is just; hater of the truth about oneself	Justice
Fearful	Peace
Vanity, nullity of being (a vacuum)	Purposefulness, fullness of being/identity
Boasts in self	Boasts in God, in the cross of Christ
Small, inadequate, dependent, helpless	Great
Practitioner of all sorts of treachery	Virtuous
Concupiscence/over-desire/selfish passions	Satisfaction/temperance
Blind, proud, presumptuous	Wisdom
Lonely, isolated moribund being; committed to undue self-love	Loving community

5 MAN'S PARADOXICAL CONDITION: WRETCHED AND GREAT

"Man is literally split in two; he has an awareness of his own splendid uniqueness in that he sticks out of nature with a towering majesty, and yet he goes back into the ground a few feet in order to blindly and dumbly rot and disappear forever. It is a terrifying dilemma to be in and to have to live with."

– Ernest Becker (1973, *The Denial of Death*)

"The professional pessimist sees one half the picture, the professional optimist the other. The former calls the latter superficial and is in turn pronounced defeatist. Each possesses a distorted fragment of the Christian truth. The Bible's realism exceeds that of the worst cynic, for it knows what man has done to God. At the same time its hope surpasses the wildest utopian fantasy, for it has concrete experience of what this same God will do for man."

– Edmond La B. Cherbonnier, 1955

"Man is only a reed, the weakest in nature, but he is a thinking reed."

– Blaise Pascal, *Pensée* 200

In the past three chapters we heard from Pascal on Man's wretched condition without God, which includes (i) Man's unhappiness, entailing restlessness, apathy, and the terrible fact of his inescapable death; (ii) Man's being lost in the dark, with his error-prone faculties of knowing, entailing ignorance about the natural world, the supernatural world, and the meaning of his life; and (iii) Man's vanity and immorality, with an empty abyss in his heart and an excessive self-love, entailing pride, injustice, and subjugation of his reasoning to self-interested passions. Wretched is not all Man is, however; in fact Pascal suggests that as deep as Man's wretchedness sinks, his greatness exalts to an equal height. A major theme of the *Pensées* is Man's dual nature that is both very wretched and very great, and in this chapter we will explore Pascal's thoughts on this paradoxical condition and its implications.

Data on the Paradoxical Human Experience. To begin, let us consider some examples of the paradoxical human experience, as they relate to Man's knowledge, happiness, and morality.

Humans are capable of great ignorance and error. Until recently, scientists thought that vapors and humors were the essential elements of bodies, and that the earth was flat. But humans are also capable of attaining marvelous knowledge and applying it. People cracked the code of the human genome, understood physiology well enough to develop bone marrow transplantation techniques, and built Paris.

Humans are capable of profound despair, as evidenced by depression, addictions, suicide, and diversions. In *Pensée* 629 Pascal observes that "[Man is capable of] great and sudden variations, from boundless presumption to appalling dejection." But humans are also capable of great elation. Glowing satisfaction accompanies the birth of a child, a discovery, a meal shared with a friend.

Humans have willfully perpetrated atrocities such as genocides, the enslavement of the vulnerable poor, and the application of torture techniques so cruel that no other animal species could conceive of them. Such atrocities have been committed with enough historical regularity that we must conclude they are part of normal human behavior. But humans have also practiced hospitality to strangers, developed charities to provide food, shelter, and medicine for the poor, and at times have responded to cruelty with forgiveness and beneficence, such as through the Marshall Plan extended by the U.S. to Germany after World War II.

Pascal's point is not that some people are wretched and others are great; rather it is that *every* person is both wretched and great. To illustrate Pascal's point, let us consider, for each of the three areas, some individuals and groups who did both wretched and great things. The twentieth century mathematician Paul Erdös was astonishingly knowledgeable and astonishingly ignorant. As reported in *The Man Who Loved Only Numbers*, although Erdös published over 1000 papers and was the most prolific mathematician since Leonard Euler in the 1700s, Erdös did not know how to make toast or open a container of tomato juice! Second, each of us can reflect on our own periods of happy elation and unhappy dejection, and how suddenly at times we switch between these states. Third, examples abound of historical figures that were known to do both very good and very bad deeds. Pascal himself served the poor and upheld the truth in the face of danger, and struggled with an intellectual superiority complex. Thomas Jefferson and James Madison authored noble documents framing the U.S. democracy, and owned hundreds of slaves. Likewise John Newton was a cruel slave trader and a heroic abolitionist. Imperialist Protestant missionaries in 18th century New England not only set up missions that treated the Indians with kindness, helping provide education and other services, but also took the land. The Apostle Paul was complicit in Stephen's stoning to death, and he built up communities of faith, hope, and love. Many other biblical characters exhibit great moral depths and heights. Like Paul, Moses and David were murderers and men after God's own heart, rich in faith and courageous obedience. In fact only a few major biblical characters have life narratives that do not include at least one gaping moral flaw. Alexander Solzhenitsyn summarized the great and wretched moral state of every person:

> ...the line separating good and evil passes not through states, nor between classes, nor between political parties either – but right through every human heart. . . . This line shifts. Inside us, it oscillates with the years. And even within hearts overwhelmed with evil, one small bridgehead of good is retained. And even in the best of all hearts there remains... an uprooted small corner of evil. [*The Gulag Archipelago*, 1974, Part IV, chapter I]

What kind of being is this, capable of such dual depths: idiotic and brilliant, despairing and exalting, wicked and saintly? Who can explain its nature? Only Christianity, suggests Pascal; in fact a thesis of his *Pensées* is that of all philosophies and worldviews, only Christianity fully explains Man's paradoxical dual condition. Its explanatory power earns for it respect, suggests Pascal, making it compelling to investigate its claims. Furthermore, a reasonable evaluator must reject any worldview that is clearly inconsistent with the observed data on human behavior, and Pascal argues that Christianity passes this inspection with flying colors. Indeed, one of the most important and original contributions of the *Pensées* is their brilliant description of how Man's paradoxical dual condition and the Christian faith fit together like lock and key.

Outline of Chapter 5. This chapter is divided into five parts. In Part I we will look at Pascal's thoughts about what makes humankind great. In Part II we will tour *Pensées* that describe Man's dual condition. To Pascal we must accept the reality of our duality in order to understand human nature, as he summarizes in *Pensée* 131,

> ...unless we realize the duality of human nature we remain invincibly ignorant of the truth about ourselves.

In Part III we will explore Pascal's purpose in showing his listener his dual condition. To Pascal our awareness of this condition serves as powerful psychological and experiential evidence for the biblical account that humans are "dispossessed kings"– good in their origin, made by God and living happily with him; and bad in their subsequent self-centered rebellion and fall into banishment and corruption. Our experience of *feeling* like dispossessed kings is a clue suggesting that we *are* dispossessed kings.

In Part IV, we will explore Pascal's thesis that only Jesus Christ resolves the paradox of human greatness and wretchedness. Philosophers have uniformly failed to solve the riddle, Pascal suggests, and it is only when the person of Jesus Christ is admitted into the analysis that a solution appears. Lastly, in Part V we will consider practical implications of understanding our dual condition for living life well.

Part I. Marks of Greatness

We will consider two major proofs used by Pascal that Man is great: first that Man thinks and has consciousness, and second Man's wretchedness itself.

What Did Pascal Mean by "Greatness?" For Pascal, whether something is "great" depends on the order of reality under consideration (Pascal's theory of three orders will be addressed more fully in chapter 6). In the lowest physical/carnal order, greatness refers to an abundance of power, wealth, or might, as in the greatness of a king or military general, or a great mountain or tsunami. Man's carnal greatness is demonstrated by opulent palaces and military conquests. In the intellectual order, greatness refers to the ability to think and wonder, and is demonstrated by the practice of art and science. In the spiritual order, greatness refers to matters of the heart and will, and the quality of relationships with God and fellow creatures. Man's spiritual greatness is demonstrated by his awareness of moral duty, and by the freedom of his choice to fulfill it (e.g., as articulated by C.S. Lewis in *Mere Christianity*). Within each order, greatness can be expressed in good or bad ways; for example great military force can be used to protect or to kill, great minds can be used to solve problems or to perpetuate them, and spiritual greatness can be used to love or to hate.

Thinking Reed. With that introduction, let us consider Pascal's first proof of Man's greatness– that Man transcends the physical order through thought. In *Pensée* 200 Pascal famously characterizes Man as a thinking reed:

> Man is only a reed, the weakest in nature, but he is a thinking reed. There is no need for the whole universe to take up arms to crush him: a vapour, a drop of water is enough to kill him. But even if the universe were to crush him, man would still be nobler than his slayer, because he knows that he is dying and the advantage the universe has over him. The universe knows none of this...

Indeed, a mere pebble is enough to kill the strongest amongst us: "Cromwell was about to ravage the whole of Christendom; the royal family was lost and his own set for ever in power, but for a little grain of sand getting into his bladder..." [*Pensée* 750] Scientists today, with the benefit of 350 years of additional research, join Pascal in marveling at Man's juxtaposed attributes of extraordinary physical weakness ("the weakest in nature") and extraordinary intellectual strength. John Medina expresses awe at the surprising evolutionary course humans took to the top of the food chain, remarking, "It seems most improbable that such a physically weak species could take over the planet not by adding muscles to our skeletons but by adding neurons to our brains. But we did..." [Medina, 2008] Thus, long before scientists would confirm it, Pascal grasped a signature feature of Man– his colossal brain compared to his puny muscles– which separates him from all other species.

By defining Man as a thinking reed, Pascal observes that Man transcends his mortal physical biological existence through consciousness. Whereas the whole inanimate universe exists only in the physical order, Man also exists in the higher intellectual order– therefore through thought Man infinitely transcends the universe. This transcendence through thought includes Man's capacity for moral behavior– only the thinking reed ponders moral choices.

Man is Great Because He Knows His Ends. In *Pensée* 200 Pascal suggests that Man's knowledge that he will die makes him greater than all material bodies in the universe put together, because they know nothing of this. Man's vulnerability yet his higher order of nobility finds expression in philosopher Paul Ricoeur's description of life as "walking in and out of a narrative." Walking in-and-out represent the two ends of our story, birth and death. Man is wretched because he will be exiting the story, but is great because he is aware of his ends– plants and mere animals do not know their ends.

A woman with early Alzheimer's disease is wretched because her mental capacity is slipping, but she is also great, because she is aware she is slipping. In contrast a dying tree does not know about its demise; "A tree does not know it is wretched." [*Pensée* 114]

Pascal completes *Pensée* 200 by reinforcing the central position of thought for constituting Man's greatness:

> Thus all our dignity consists in thought. It is on thought that we must depend for our recovery, not on space and time, which we could never fill. Let us then strive to think well; that is the basic principle of morality.

Why is thinking well the basic principle of morality? First note that with "thinking well" Pascal did not mean merely reasoning well, he means both reasoning well and applying wisdom, which is partly acquired through the heart. Second, the crucial importance of thought for morality was well known to the ancients (Kreeft, 1993), and was also appreciated by America's founding fathers; for example Thomas Jefferson wrote of the necessity of education for a democracy to be able to promote the public good. Morality springs from our thought life, and thus only through thinking well will morally good behavior result. Peter Kreeft (1993) elaborates this point:

> Morality is first the regulation of our inner world and only secondarily the regulation of our outer world... All outer works are out-workings of inner works, both good and evil.

This principle was plainly taught by Jesus in the Sermon on the Mount, with his words to the scribes and Pharisees:

> For you cleanse the outside of the cup and dish, but inside they are full of extortion and self-indulgence. Blind Pharisee, first cleanse the inside of the cup and dish, then the outside of them may be clean

> also... For you are like whitewashed tombs which indeed appear beautiful outwardly, but inside are full of dead men's bones and all uncleanness. Even so you also outwardly appear righteous to men, but inside you are full of hypocrisy and lawlessness. [Matthew 23:25–28]

Professor Kreeft observes that the pattern of morality moving from inward-to-outward has been reversed by modern materialism, which "reduces morality to rules for regulating our outer world, visible society, because this outer world is the only one it believes in or cares about. This is like propping up a corpse, pushing it in the right direction and wondering why it doesn't work. It has no soul." In short, Pascal tells us that there are no intellectual short cuts to living morally– learning to think well is the basic pre-requisite.

Man is Great Because He Wonders. Man's greatness derived from thinking can also be seen in the fact that Man wonders. In his essay *Dogma and the Universe*, C.S. Lewis suggests that our capacity to awe or wonder makes us great:

> Men look on the starry heavens with reverence: monkeys do not. The silence of the eternal spaces terrified Pascal, but it was the greatness of Pascal that enabled them to do so.

Here Lewis cites Pascal's essay *Pensée* 199 (*the Disproportion of man*), wherein Pascal marvels at the vastness of the universe and the minuteness of microbes (addressed in chapter 3). Lewis' statement also recalls *Pensées* 113 and 200 on the same topic; for instance *Pensée* 113:

> *Thinking reed.* It is not in space and time that I must seek my human dignity, but in the ordering of my thought. It will do me no good to own land. Through space the universe grasps me and swallows me up like a speck; through thought I grasp it.

Man is Great Because He Worships. Man's greatness in thought includes his capacity to worship. Worship entails reflection and awe, and Terrence Cunio suggests that being a worshipper is one of Man's attributes that most distinguishes him from the animals. [Cunio, 1996] Pascal concurs that Man naturally worships– he cannot help but to worship– the only question is what he will worship:

> The mind naturally believes and the will naturally loves, so that when there are no true objects for them they necessarily become attached to false ones. [*Pensée* 661]

Thus, if one does not worship the Christian God, then he or she will worship idols, which can be almost anything. In *Pensée* 148 Pascal amusingly lists the following replacements for God that have been tried:

> ...the stars, the heavens, the earth, the elements, plants, cabbages, leeks, animals, insects, calves, serpents, fever, pestilence, war, famine, vices...

The point here is that Man's general capacity to worship, whatever the object, for great good or great ill, makes him great.

An illustration of Man's greatness in worship comes from the 2006 book *When Invisible Children Sing*, which tells the story of a Christian doctor (Chi Huang) who has boldly loved the street children in La Paz, Bolivia since 1997, which has included founding and operating orphanages. The book title stems from an event that took place in one of the street children's regular abodes, the sewer. The police had cornered them, and were about to beat them, as they often did. When the street children began singing hymns, something like scales fell from the eyes of the police, as this worshiping seemed to transform their perception of the children from vile animals to dignified human beings. The police turned away. In this event the greatness of the children shone through their worshiping, and the greatness of the police shone through their recognition of the children's dignity and their consequent turning away from their planned misdeed. Mere animals do not make moral turns.

Man is Great Because He is Wretched. A second major proof of Man's greatness wielded by Pascal is Man's wretchedness itself, as introduced in *Pensée* 114:

> Man's greatness comes from knowing he is wretched: A tree does not know it is wretched. Thus it is wretched to know that one is wretched, but there is greatness in knowing one is wretched.

I will describe four reasons why knowing one's wretchedness makes Man great:

1. Man is great because of his artistic capacity, specifically his artfulness to exquisitely describe his wretched condition;
2. Man is great because of his capacity to grow in character through suffering;
3. Man is great because of his magnificent accomplishments, many of which are fueled by a vile and prideful quest for self-glory; and
4. Man is great because of his capacity to repent, which is only possible because of sin.

1. Wretched Implies Great: Art. Art provides some insight into why there is greatness in knowing one's wretchedness. A piece of art may be considered great because it eloquently describes the human condition, that is, it has the quality of *knowing well* the wretched condition of Man. Examples include Greek tragedy, operas, Shakespeare, Dante's *Inferno*, and Picasso's *Guernica*. The ability of humans to deeply explore and express the intricacies of our wretchedness mark our greatness. A tree cannot compose *Don Giovanni*.

2. Wretched Implies Great: Human Suffering. A second reason why there is greatness in knowing one's wretchedness derives from human suffering. As pointed out by Peter Kreeft, though human suffering is a negative event in the physical world, it can be a positive event in the spiritual world. As noted above, many works of art and literature explore the good effects that come out of suffering. Consider Dostoyevsky's *Crime and Punishment*, in which the lead character, Raskolnikov, murders an old miser, in an attempt to become a Super Man who is not bound by conscience. The novel describes Raskolnikov's utter failure to stave away guilt, and his intense psychological and spiritual suffering that eventually leads to his confession of the crime. As he accepts punishment and repents in prison, Raskolnikov discovers peace and the healing grace-filled light of God. A lesser creature would not undergo such a transformation; a tiger is unaffected by eating its young.

3. Wretched Implies Great: Man's Quest for Glory. A third reason why Man's wretchedness makes him great derives from *Pensée* 470:

> The vilest feature of man is the quest for glory, but it is just this that most clearly shows his excellence.

Vileness here refers to the oldest sin, pride, which Adam committed in the garden when he tried to "make himself like unto God;" pride is the desire to replace God, to be the one to receive all praise and glory, to the exclusion of all others. Traditionally, Protestant Reformers agree with Pascal that pride is Man's vilest feature– Jonathan Edwards called pride the "lowest floor in Satan's house."

To appreciate Pascal's point that Man's proud quest for glory most clearly shows his excellence, consider that many great human achievements are motivated by the quest for glory. Athletes endure excruciating training striving for a gold medal; scientists work 100 hours a week striving for a Nobel Prize; kings build architectural masterpieces striving for acknowledgment of their power. When I travel through Europe the amazing buildings fill me with awe about what Man can accomplish. Man's tenacious and persevering will to excel– even for the vile motive of self-glory– demonstrates his greatness– a lesser being would have lesser aspirations. Beasts did not aspire to build the Roman Empire. Dogs and cats did not plan Louis the Fourteenth's palatial gardens.

Man's insatiable quest for glory is what we would expect if the biblical narrative is true that we were made in God's image but fell. For the Bible describes God's purpose as glorifying himself, and, looking around us, we can see that a (the?) signature characteristic of Man is his tenacious quest to glorify himself. Donald Trump's pursuit of riches and fame looks like a tarnished chip off of God's block– born to glorify but turned inward to self-glorying. Our hardwiring to pursue glory is a clue that we are indeed God's image bearers.

4. Wretched Implies Great: Repentance. A fourth reason why there is greatness in knowing one is wretched is that, by knowing one's sinful inclinations, one can choose to undertake the hard work to unlearn them. A lesser creature would be governed entirely by its animal passions; it would always do what its body felt like doing, without any awareness of moral dimensions to decision-making. A greater creature would see that her choices have moral consequences, and would possess the ability to resist inclinations and consider alternative courses. Therefore through his capacity to make moral turns Man transcends his animal desires.

Following Darwin, many modern thinkers disagree with this point, believing that humans are no greater than animals, are nothing but animals. For an example of this viewpoint, in 2004 I was in Gaborone, Botswana attending a conference on HIV research. I worked with the

Botswana-Harvard Partnership for several years on various research projects studying vaccines, treatments, and other interventions to prevent or treat HIV infection. The Botswana-Harvard Partnership hired a local Christian pastor to help with HIV prevention education and to work with Botswana communities. The pastor was teaching a version of the ABC HIV prevention program, that is the Abstinence, Be Faithful, and Wear a Condom message that was successful in preventing the spread of HIV in Uganda. Despite ABC's success, the pastor's message to communities was, "Abstinence is impossible– wearing a condom is the thing to do." This is apparently an example of a Christian infected with the modernist doctrine that Man is equal to an animal, with no ability to resist physical impulses. This pastor may have forgotten that Man is great, that through grace, he can recognize his sin and turn from it.

Greatness and Wretchedness Imply Each Other. We conclude Part I by observing Pascal's insistence that a fair examination of the human condition will find clear evidence that Man is both great and wretched:

> Since greatness and wretchedness can be concluded each from the other, some people have been more inclined to conclude that man is wretched for having used his greatness to prove it, while others have all the more cogently concluded he is great by basing their proof on wretchedness. Everything that could be said by one side as proof of greatness has only served as an argument for the others to conclude he is wretched, since the further one falls the more wretched one is, and vice versa. One has followed the other in an endless circle, for it is certain that as man's insight increases so he finds both wretchedness and greatness within himself. In a word man knows he is wretched. Thus he is wretched because he is so, but he is truly great because he knows it. [*Pensée* 122]

Part II. Dual Condition of Man: Great and Wretched

Now that we have explored some of Pascal's thoughts on Man's greatness, in Part II we turn to Pascal's clearest descriptions of Man's dual condition.

We begin with *Pensée* 131, in which Pascal summarizes what he saw as the stark contrast of Man's great condition with God and wretched condition without God.

> There are in faith two equally constant truths. One is that man in the state of his creation, or in the state of grace, is exalted above the whole of nature, made like unto God and sharing in his divinity. The other is that in the state of corruption and sin he has fallen from that first state and has become like the beasts...
> Whence it is clearly evident that man through grace is made like unto God and shares his divinity, and without grace he is treated like the beasts of the field.

This fragment makes clear that to Pascal, Man is extremely great in his origin– God made him as his dignified image-bearer, granted him dominion over the earth, and placed him in perfect fellowship with himself. And through grace Man is equally great. The fragment also makes clear that to Pascal, Man's falling out of fellowship with God was an extremely far fall- Man lost *all* his attributes that made him share God's divinity– he was now mortal, subject to a predator-prey existence, unable to reason reliably, unable to distinguish right from wrong, unable to worship properly. In a word, Man had become like the beasts. It hardly seems possible to draw the contrast more sharply than Pascal has– Man's greatness is infinite given that he can share in God's divinity, and his abased-ness is infinite given the infinite distance between God and the beasts of the field.

Man is Both Good and Bad. To Pascal, Man's good creation and bad fall imply that human nature is dually good-and-bad. Pascal suggests this in *Pensée* 616, which we also considered in the exploration of original sin in chapter 4:

> Concupiscence has become natural for us and has become a second nature. Thus there are two natures in us, one good, the other bad.

One way to recognize the reality of our dual nature is to reflect on our "civil wars within." For example the Apostle Paul writes candidly of the internal civil war between his good and bad natures:

> For I delight in the law of God according to the inward man. But I see another law in my members, warring against the law of my mind, and bringing me into captivity to the law of sin which is in my members. O

> wretched man that I am! Who will deliver me from this body of death? I thank God– through Jesus Christ our Lord! [Romans 7:22–25]

Pascal goes on to suggest that the duality of our nature makes it appropriate to both love and hate ourselves– love the good, original nature and hate the corrupt fallen one:

> Let man now judge his own worth, let him love himself, for there is within him a nature capable of good; but that is no reason to love the vileness within himself. Let him despise himself because this capacity remains unfulfilled; but that is no reason for him to despise this natural capacity. Let him both hate and love himself... [*Pensée* 119]

It may sound anachronistic to hate oneself, but Pascal's meaning here is orthodox Christianity, as was G.K. Chesterton's expression of the same idea, "One can hardly think too little of one's self. One can hardly think too much of one's soul." [*Orthodoxy*, chapter 6] This view can also be seen in the writings of Augustine and John Calvin, for example in their commentaries on David's verse, "Do I not hate them, O Lord, who hate you?" [Psalm 139: 21] Augustine interpreted David to mean, "I hated in them their iniquities, I loved Thy creation," while Calvin writes, "We are to observe... that the hatred of which the Psalmist speaks is directed to the sins rather than the persons of the wicked. We are, so far as in us lies, to study peace with all men; we are to seek the good of all..." To these authors God created humankind in his image, making us good and lovable in our essence– therefore we should love ourselves. But through the Fall humankind came to despise its Creator, choosing not to fulfill its capacity and intent for doing good in practice– therefore we should despise ourselves. In the words of Pascal's contemporary John Owens, "Be killing sin, or sin will be killing you." The seed of Original Sin is so powerful that unless we combat vigorously against it, it will surely produce a harvest of moral wretchedness.

Pascal suggests that grasping one's dual goodness-and-badness is a key for understanding the Christmas story and for embracing it:

> No other religion has proposed that we should hate ourselves. No other religion can therefore please those who hate themselves and seek a being who is really worthy of love. And if

> they had never [before] heard of the religion of a humiliated God, they would at once embrace it. [*Pensée* 220]

Is this really the Christmas message that moves people to sing "Joy to the World?" I think it is exactly that, for it states that a certain people-group hears good news in the story of a perfect God becoming human to be humiliated for the purpose of paying for their sins. This group is characterized both (1) by knowing their moral wretchedness and fighting to squelch its expression ("hating themselves"); and (2) by longing to be free from their wretched state to a state of goodness/happiness with a perfectly worthy God. Because they abhor their sins, they know that a God really worthy of love would abhor them all the more, and thus is cut off from them. For these, religions of a "non-humiliated God," whose God is like a stern perfectionist father that will associate with his child only if she perfectly tows the line– are useless. In asserting that God can be reached only through perfect obedience to moral commandments, such "works" religions are useless for this group that knows its moral wretchedness too well to believe they could ever achieve moral perfection on their own steam. In their hearts they know Martin Luther's lyric is true,

> "Did we in our own strength confide, Our striving would be losing,
> Were not the right Man on our side, The Man of God's own choosing,
> You ask who that may be? Christ Jesus, it is he;
> The Lord of Hosts his name, From age to age the same,
> And he must win the battle." [*A Mighty Fortress is Our God*]

Ahhh, now this religion is different, of a unique "humiliated God;" it opens a path to God that actually seems possible; rather than insultingly proposing that a perfect God can be reached without becoming good; or by naively proposing that a perfect God can be reached through their own efforts; it proposes that a humiliated God will do the work for them. A non-humiliated God either does not offer a remedy or offers one they are unable to take; a humiliated God offers a remedy and takes it himself on their behalf. For those realistic enough to perceive they can never resolve their wretchedness on their own steam, hope comes only from the religion of a humiliated God.

Chapter 14 of *The Screwtape Letters* helps distinguish harmful, inappropriate self-hatred from helpful, appropriate self-hatred. For paving his patient's road to hell, Screwtape suggests to Wormwood that he wants self-hatred to "be made the starting point for contempt of other selves, and thus for gloom, cynicism, and cruelty." On the other hand, C.S. Lewis suggests that God's purpose in the virtue of humility, which entails appropriate self-hatred, is to

> ...turn the man's attention away from self to Him, and to the man's neighbors. All the abjection and self-hatred are designed, in the long run, solely for this end.

Similarly, Dick Keyes suggests that appropriate self-denial entails hating that which would destroy you if it is expressed. [*True Heroisim*, 1995] This would include pouring contempt on one's pride (Isaac Watts). From C.S. Lewis and Dick Keyes we surmise a guideline for dividing helpful from harmful self-hatred– if it engenders spitefulness toward others, despair, or lack of hope, it is bad; if it squelches the expression of pride or destructive over-desires and turns our attention from self to God and neighbor, it is good.

This survey of Pascal's thought on Man's morality raises the age-old philosophical question of whether Man is basically good or bad?" Pascal's answer: a resounding "Good! But he has become ruined... not beyond restoration, however."

Pascal on What is Humility? Pascal's instruction to both love and hate myself clarifies for me the definition of humility. I have heard it spoken of in terms of groveling on the ground like an earthworm, but Jesus did not live out humility in this way. From Pascal, I surmise that humility simply means being a realist. Not a self-generated realism defined based on one's imagination and passions, but a realism that accepts both reasonable inferences from human experience and that God and his revelation are real. This realism perceives both our great dignity and worth derived at Creation and through our redemption, and our very real evil inclinations inherited at the Fall. As a realist, I should deplore and repent greatly of my sins, and I should exalt and praise God greatly for my dignified worth. Hating my sinful nature and loving my original redeemable nature is true to the facts and constitutes an authentic humility. Thus the image of a groveling earthworm is a half-true description of humility– it is half-false because the attributes that make me great are not found in an earthworm. I am a glorious earthworm, not a mere earthworm.

Essay on Greatness and Wretchedness: Pensée 149. Now let us turn to portions of Pascal's most fully developed *Pensée* on Man's greatness and wretchedness. *Pensée* 149 begins with God speaking:

> ...But you are no longer in the state in which I made you. I created man holy, innocent, perfect, I filled him with light and understanding, I showed him my glory and my wondrous works. Man's eye then beheld the majesty of God. He was not then in the darkness that now blinds his sight, nor subject to death and the miseries that afflict him.
>
> But he could not bear such great glory without falling into presumption. He wanted to make himself his own centre and do without my help. He withdrew from my rule, setting himself up as my equal in his desire to find happiness in himself, and I abandoned him to himself. The creatures who were subject to him I incited to revolt and made his enemies, so that today man has become like the beasts, and is so far apart from me that a barely glimmering idea of his author remains of all his dead and flickering knowledge. The senses, independent of reason and often its masters, have carried him off in pursuit of pleasure. All creatures either distress or tempt him, and dominate him either by forcibly subduing him or charming him with sweetness, which is a far more terrible and harmful yoke.
>
> That is the state in which men are today. They retain some feeble instinct from the happiness of their first nature, and are plunged into the wretchedness of their blindness and concupiscence, which has become their second nature...

In this *Pensée* Pascal suggests that humans are perfect in their origin, but fell from this state into almost perfect wretchedness. Such a great fall is like that of a great king who has been dispossessed. This brings us to Part III on Pascal's description of humankind as dispossessed kings.

Part III. Man as Dispossessed King

To begin Part III, we again consider *Pensée* 116:

> All these examples of wretchedness prove his greatness. It is the wretchedness of a great lord, the wretchedness of a dispossessed king.

Pascal expresses a similar thought in *Pensée* 117:

> Man's greatness is so obvious that it can even be deduced from his wretchedness, for what is nature in animals we call wretchedness in man, thus recognizing that, if his nature is today like that of the animals, he must have fallen from some better state which was once his own.

Here Pascal addresses what our awareness of our wretchedness tells us about our past. If we had always been wretched, then we would not feel anguish about it. But if we used to live happily in a paradise, then our current state of unhappiness would make us long to return to that blissful state. Therefore Pascal points to our awareness of our wretchedness as a clue to the reality that we used to be glorious kings, but we fell from that estate. This aching wretchedness we feel is experiential evidence for the biblical account of Man's origin in the Garden and his subsequent fall and expulsion from paradise.

G.K. Chesterton joins Pascal in suggesting that a general attribute of the human condition is a remembrance of the Fall. In *The Everlasting Man* (1925) Chesterton writes of ancient pagan peoples,

> These men were conscious of the Fall if they were conscious of nothing else; and the same is true of an heathen humanity. Those who have fallen may remember the fall, even when they forget the height.

To further support that we are dispossessed kings, consider Pascal's phrase in *Pensée* 117, "for what is nature in animals we call wretchedness in man..." When creatures in the animal kingdom die, we generally do not consider it scandalous or outrageous; it is just nature taking its course; but we *do* consider the death of a human outrageous. If we had not fallen from a high place, then we would not feel scandalized by death, rather we would simply accept it– but this is *not* the human experience. Rather, most people fight it with all they've got, suggesting we come from a place where death was not normal (Kreeft, 1993).

Pascal illustrates the dispossessed king principle in *Pensée* 117:

> Who indeed would think himself unhappy not to be a king except one who had been dispossessed?... Who would think himself unhappy if he had only one mouth and who would not if he had only one eye? It has probably never occurred to anyone to be

distressed at not having three eyes, but those who have none are inconsolable...

In this example Pascal applies the rule that we are only unhappy if we miss something we once had, we are only unhappy if we get less than we expect. A man with one mouth has no cause for unhappiness, since one mouth is expected, whereas a man with only one eye is unhappy because he has less than he should have, less than is normative to his nature. Similarly, the fact that a man thinks himself unhappy not to be a king proves that his normal state is to be a king. The fact that he finds himself unhappy shows he must have been dethroned. Our present unhappiness is a proof of our past paradise.

I have used the word "proof" here, and I believe this bold assertion can be defended. Peter Kreeft (1993) identifies two premises from which Pascal's conclusion logically follows.

Premise 1. No one would be unhappy not to be king unless he had once been king and been dethroned.

Premise 2. But man is unhappy not to be king. "All men complain."

Conclusion. Therefore man must once have been this king of happiness and has fallen from this state, that is, been dethroned.

The first premise is like saying no one regrets the absence of a third eye while some may regret the absence of a second. This strikes me as obviously true: Have you ever missed your third eye? The second premise seems to be verifiable empirically, as discussed at length in chapter 2 on diversions and indifference– humankind is manifestly restless and unhappy. The conclusion logically follows under the premises– therefore if one believes these he must swallow the conclusion. This is Pascal's brilliant proof-from-self-examination and experience of Man's happy origin and subsequent Fall. Like Pascal, Chesterton felt in his bones that human experience resonates with the Christian doctrine of Good Origin and Fall:

And my haunting instinct that somehow good was not merely a tool to be used, but a relic to be guarded, like the goods from Crusoe's ship– even that had been the wild whisper of something originally wise, for, according to Christianity, we were indeed the survivors of a wreck, the

> crew of a golden ship that had gone down before the beginning of the world. [*Orthodoxy*]

A related proof that Man has a happy and good origin comes from the observation that humankind possesses an idea of perfection. Throughout known history, humankind has striven for perfection– in architecture, art, mathematics, etc. From where did this idea of perfection come? Only if we beheld perfection in our original state would we now strive for it, Pascal suggests.

Pascal's View versus an Atheist View. To complete Part III, I will compare Pascal's view about our dual nature with that of the famous atheist philosopher Friedrich Nietzsche. Intriguingly, Nietzsche expresses a similar idea to Pascal's about the dual nature of Man, but with an opposite conclusion:

> Mankind is a rope fastened between animal and superman– a rope over an abyss. [*Thus Spoke Zarathustra*]

To both Nietzsche and Pascal, Man hangs precariously over an abyss, death may snatch him at any time. The first part of the dual condition of Man is the same for these philosophers, both assert an animal nature of Man. For Nietzsche, Man should struggle against the weakness of his humanity purely on his own effort. Man should pull himself up by his bootstraps, make himself tower above his station, and behave like a superman. Pascal also suggests Man should struggle against his animal condition, but in an opposite way, by listening to God and placing faith in him. Nietzsche scorned cries to a divine being to provide a way out of the mire; Pascal scorned presumptuous assertions that there could be no divine help. Nietzsche's conception of Man's dual nature is hopeless, because Man inevitably falls into the abyss; Pascal's conception is hopeful, because through God's grace Man may be rescued from the tightrope, redeemed to enjoy abundant life in the new Kingdom of God.

Because Nietzsche's conclusion of no way out is so depressing, I suspect that many upon reading him have sought refuge in God. Amusingly Pascal observes that some of his opponents of Christianity argued in such a feeble way (when asked to "describe the feeling and reasons which inspire their doubts about religion") that they made the faith look alluring in contrast: "If you go on arguing like that, you really will convert me." [*Pensée* 427] Christianity is attractive because it promises safe passage over the abyss.

Part IV. Jesus Christ Resolves the Greatness-Wretchedness Paradox

In Part IV, we turn to a thesis of the *Pensées*, that Jesus Christ resolves the paradoxical dual-condition of Man. Pascal summarizes this resolution in *Pensée* 192:

> Knowing God without knowing our own wretchedness makes for pride.
>
> Knowing our own wretchedness without knowing God makes for despair.
>
> Knowing Jesus Christ strikes the balance because he shows us both God and our wretchedness.

Christ's vocation as the incarnate God who came to redeem humanity simultaneously demonstrates the extreme greatness and the extreme wretchedness of humankind. To explore how, first consider how Jesus Christ shows us our greatness. The reason starts with the greatness of Christ. Greatness means being markedly superior in some attribute. As one who is uniquely perfect, Jesus demonstrates infinite superiority to all created things in attributes including creativity (making all things), power (reigning over all things forever), intellect and wisdom (governing and judging the world; Christ is full of truth), goodness (only God is good [Mark 10:18]; Christ is full of grace), and capacity to love (voluntarily dying for his enemies). As Christ's unique image-bearers, both in our origin and in our redemptive conformation to the likeness of Christ, [Romans 8:29] it follows immediately that Man is vastly superior to the whole created realm in all of these attributes– every attribute of Christ's greatness reflects on our greatness. Furthermore, Christ was born of a woman and "marries" the Church of humankind, establishing a relationship so intimate that even the angels are jealous. [1 Peter 1:12] This special fellowship includes prayer, which "God instituted to impart to his creatures the dignity of causality." [*Pensée* 930] What other created being is welcomed to influence the Godhead's decisions! Moreover, observation and reasoning (without referencing the Bible) demonstrate that human beings have exceptional qualities not found in other animals (e.g., our gargantuan brains); it does not take any religious faith to see that Man is amazing as a "thinking reed."

The greatest attribute of Man's greatness may be his beloved-ness. God loves us so much that he died to redeem us. Various biblical passages (e.g., John 17) describe redeemed humans as a supreme gift from God the Father to his beloved only Son. The Bible is replete with descriptions of God's treasuring of humans, for example in the parable of the lost sheep, wherein God the shepherd leaves the flock of 99 to find the one stray, and in the parable of the prodigal sons, wherein God the Father joyfully throws an extremely lavish party for his younger son out of boundless love that overlooks the son's disrespectful rebellion. Pascal writes in the fourteenth *Provincial Letter*, "She [the Church] considers all men not merely as men, but as made in the image of God she worships. She has a holy respect for each one of them, which makes them all worthy of veneration, as being redeemed at an infinite price to be made temples of the living God." We must be very great for God to declare us worth redeeming, and very great because our end is very great– to be holy and beautiful and true like Christ.

And how does Jesus Christ show us our wretchedness? If humankinds' greatness is demonstrated by Jesus' act of redemption, then its wretchedness is demonstrated by the same act, as the other side of the coin. For if humankind were not extremely wretched, then God would not have had to use an infinitely costly solution to redeem it. If humans were only mildly bad, then a mild solution would have sufficed– perhaps the sacrifice of a few pigeons. But only the substitutionary death of God himself was enough to pay for the mountains of sin that the human heart had compiled. In his Letter to Melanchthon, with hyperbole, Martin Luther asserts the infinite sacrifice of God,

> No sin will separate us from the Lamb, even though we commit fornication and murder a thousand times a day. Do you think that the purchase price that was paid for the redemption of our sins by so great a Lamb is too small? Pray boldly—you too are a mighty sinner.

Therefore, greatness and wretchedness are two sides of the same coin because the greatness of the salvation equals the wretchedness of the sin requiring the salvation. The messier the swimming pool, the greater the pool-cleaner is required to wash it– thus the great extent of Jesus' work to save us proves our wretchedness. And the more valuable a lost coin, the more effort is expended in recovering it– thus the great extent of Jesus' work to save us proves our greatness. Pascal wonderfully summarizes this in *Pensée* 352:

> Wretchedness induces despair. Pride induces presumption. The Incarnation shows man the greatness of his wretchedness through the greatness of the remedy required.

We Can Only Know Ourselves Through Jesus Christ. What is more, Pascal suggests, we can *only understand ourselves* through Jesus Christ:

> Not only do we only know God through Jesus Christ, but we only know ourselves through Jesus Christ; we only know life and death through Jesus Christ. Apart from Jesus Christ, we cannot know the meaning of our life or our death, of God or of ourselves... [*Pensée* 417]

Without Jesus Christ, Pascal purports, we are an impenetrable enigma. All worldviews that exclude Jesus Christ possess major blind spots about ourselves, where the "region of blindness" may vary across the worldviews. For example, Modernists are generally blind to their wretchedness apart from God, while Postmodernists are generally blind to the reality that God has broken into human history and has opened up a way for restoration. If we equate Jesus Christ to grace (as grace comes to us through Jesus Christ), then we can see Pascal's expression of the failure of Christ-less worldviews to know ourselves in *Pensée* 869:

> To make a man a saint, grace is certainly needed, and anyone who doubts this does not know what a saint, or a man, really is.

But through Jesus Christ, Pascal purports, we can see through the enigma– Jesus Christ makes sense of our paradoxical nature. Jesus Christ is uniquely positioned to do this, first of all, because he made us; only the architect and builder of a structure *really* understands its nature. Secondly, by living as a human being and experiencing every kind of suffering and desire that we could possibly experience, Jesus Christ understands all of our struggles and our abjection. Thirdly, it is Jesus Christ who shows us that the meaning of our life is to love God and neighbor– apart from this revelation we would be prone to concoct any meaning of life imaginable, even concupiscence. All the biblical voices on ethics are as from the one voice of Jesus Christ– apart from this revelation we have no way to know that love is better than indifference or hate. Fourthly, apart from Jesus Christ we are invincibly ignorant of the meaning of our death, and we are rightly terrified by it. But in his resurrection, Jesus Christ shows that rather than a final event, death is a transition from one type of perishable body to another type of imperishable body in a new era. Jesus Christ shows us everlasting new life.

In the book of Revelation an elder comforts the Apostle John with the good news that Jesus Christ, and only Jesus Christ, is able to solve the puzzle of the human enigma:

> Do not weep. Behold, the Lion of the tribe of Judah, the Root of David, has prevailed to open the scroll and to loose its seven seals. [Revelation 5:5]

As the lamb of God who opens the scroll, Jesus Christ, to Pascal, is the key that fits the human lock; Jesus Christ reveals the plan of God to redeem humanity from their dual great/wretched state to a lasting state in God's new kingdom that is only great.

In *The Screwtape Letters*, C.S. Lewis also suggests the necessity of knowing Jesus Christ for knowing oneself, as expressed in Screwtape's remark about Christians,

> When they are wholly His, they are more themselves than they ever were before.

The "dying to oneself" that is part of the Christian life refers only to the dying of one's false self, which labors to embellish an imaginary being [*Pensée* 421]. Christ shines light on the emptiness of a self-generated pursuit of happiness. Perceiving this vacuum in one's heart frees one to search for goodness and happiness where they really may be found. In Christ a person can develop his true self, the redeemed self that is full of Christ's attributes. In the end, it is Christ with us who shows us both our deep wretchedness and our deep beloved-ness, the two things we must know to make our way to true good.

> The Christians' God is a God who makes the soul aware that he is its sole good: that in him alone can it find peace; that only in loving him can it find joy: and who at the same time fills it with loathing for the obstacles which hold it back and prevent it from loving God with all its might. Self-love and concupiscence, which hold it back, are intolerable. This God makes the soul aware of

this underlying self-love which is destroying it, and which he alone can cure. [*Pensée* 460]

Part V. Applications to Living Well

Application 1. Spiritual Health Requires Knowing Both One's Greatness and One's Wretchedness. *Pensée* 121 addresses the danger of being unaware of either one's greatness or one's wretchedness:

> It is dangerous to explain too clearly to man how like he is to the animals without pointing out his greatness. It is also dangerous to make too much of his greatness without his vileness. It is still more dangerous to leave him in ignorance of both, but it is most valuable to represent both to him...
>
> Man must not be allowed to believe that he is equal either to animals or to angels, nor to be unaware of either, but he must know both.

Pascal lists two major errors– the first is to believe we are equal to the animals; the second is to believe we are equal to the angels. Kreeft (1993) describes these beliefs as the "two fundamental human heresies... animalism and angelism." Angelism includes Platonism, Gnosticism, and modernism, which under-appreciate Man's tie to the earth and his subjection to appetites, while animalism includes Marxism, Freudianism, and Darwinism, which under-appreciate Man's dignity in thought. Pascal stresses that for Man to find his way to happiness in God, he must know his condition as *both* animal and angel.

In particular, acknowledging oneself only as angel or only as animal can lead one astray into pride or despair. Pascal articulates these great dangers in *Pensée* 351:

> Christianity is strange; it bids man to recognize that he is vile, and even abominable, and bid him want to be like God. Without such a counterweight his exaltation would make him horribly vain or his abasement horribly abject.

Pascal reinforces his point with an anecdote:

> Someone told me one day that he felt full of joy and confidence when he had been to confession. Someone else told me that he was still afraid. My reaction was that one good man could be

> made by putting these two together, for each of them lacked something in not sharing the feelings of the other. The same thing happens in other connexions. [*Pensée* 712]

If the man is joyful and confident but not afraid (reverent), then he is presumptuous, but if he is afraid but not joyful, then he is despondent. Only the combination of joy, confidence, and reverence make a complete Christian.

These *Pensées* plus *Pensée* 130 constitute practical advice for how to be a good friend. Pascal suggests to bring down your brother if he is glorying in his greatness, and to bring him up if he is wallowing in his wretchedness:

> If he exalts himself, I humble him.
> If he humbles himself, I exalt him.
> And I go on contradicting him
> Until he understands
> That he is a monster that passes all understanding. [*Pensée* 130]

By calling a human being a "monster" Pascal means a misshapen being with parts out of proportion with the way they were meant to fit together; a composite being with very great and very wretched attributes that should not co-exist in a "normal" (non-monstrous) being. This monster looks like the Apostle Paul struggling in his internal civil war to do good and evil, [Romans 7:13–26] or like Saint Augustine who called his struggling of this kind a "monstrous state." [*Confessions*, Book 8, Chapter 9]

The errors of self-exaltation or self-dejection lead to pride or despair, which both draw us away from God– this is the reason for Pascal's advice. If my brother is boasting about his athletic or intellectual feats, I should remind him of his frailty– at any moment an aneurism could strike. If my brother is depressed or fearful, I should remind him of his great dignity and capacities. Furthermore, to Pascal, recognizing ourselves as monsters that pass all understanding is a pivotal move for us to find God. Acknowledging that we are unable to solve the riddle about ourselves encourages us to look for a solution outside of ourselves, in particular to Jesus Christ the only redeemer.

Pascal's advice to humble one's presumptuous friends mirrors the Old Testament story of the proud king Nebuchadnezzar. God humbled Nebuchadnezzar by stripping away his power and making him live literally as a beast eating grass in the fields. Once this seven-year humiliating experience rooted out the dispossessed king's presumption, God restored his power. After Nebuchadnezzar humbled himself, God exalted him.

Pascal's advice in *Pensée* 130 has the same purpose as John the Baptists' advice to "prepare the way of the Lord," that is, to clear away the obstacles to God's coming. The obstacle for the dejected is despair, and the obstacle for the proud is presumption. *Pensée* 130 echoes the prophet Isaiah's proclamation that "every valley shall be exalted and every mountain and hill brought low." [Isaiah 40:3–4]

Application 2: Beware of the Sacred-Secular Dualism. To address a particular danger of believing oneself an angel but not an animal, I will draw from Dick Keyes' lecture titled *All of Life Under the Lordship of Christ*. [2003 L'Abri Conference, Portland, Oregon] Keyes discussed the heretical worldview that he calls the "sacred-secular dualism." This worldview is closely related to Gnosticism, the ancient heresy that still lives, which taught that Jesus was not human, but was a spiritual phantom.

The worldview of sacred-secular dualism, seductive to Christians for hundreds of years, asserts that selected aspects of life labeled sacred are under the Lordship of Christ, while other aspects, labeled secular, are not. In particular, sacred-secular dualism asserts that God cares deeply about obviously sacred/spiritual things, like prayer, Bible study, missionary work, and evangelism, and expects his people to love these things and devote themselves to them; but on the other hand, God does not really care about so-called secular things, like politics, science, art, sexuality, and business, and therefore does not really care about how his people behave in these areas. Historically many Christian groups have swallowed this non-biblical idea, thereby sanctioning myriads of practices that dishonor God, in which Christians see no contradiction between their faith and, for example, engaging in corrupt business practices, treating the environment carelessly, lazily creating mediocre art, or living a promiscuous lifestyle or otherwise abusing the body. Descartes perceived no incompatibility with his Catholic faith (he declared his loyalty to the Jesuit faith throughout his life) and his practice to routinely dissect living dogs for the sake of medical science (stories tell of Descartes cutting beating hearts and sticking his finger in them until the animals expire, Grayling, 2005). After all, because God does not care about these low, worldly enterprises, why should I trouble myself with trying to honor God in these areas? Focusing on the majors like prayer and evangelism are what the Lord *really* wants from me, so my efforts should be concentrated there.

The Church at times has believed that material things, even the human body, are inherently evil; in fact this view has resulted in persecutions. The English pre-Reformer and Bible translator William Tyndale preached that God cares about all areas of life, as can be seen in his words,

> There is no work better than another to please God, to pour water, to wash dishes, to be a shoemaker or an apostle, all is one, to wash dishes and to preach, all is one, as touching the deed to please God.

These words were read as evidence at Tyndale's heresy trial at which he was sentenced to be burned at the stake. Following Tyndale, Martin Luther writes, "Washing diapers, rocking babies, and making beds are duties in the Spirit."

Consistent with Tyndale's and Luther's words, the Bible teaches that all of life is under the Lordship of Christ, both the obviously spiritual and the apparently secular. Psalm 24:1: "The earth is the Lord's, and everything in it." Romans 14:6: "He who eats, eats to the Lord, for he gives God thanks." Ephesians 6:7: "with goodwill doing service, as to the Lord, and not to men." Isaiah's beatific vision in 6:1–3:

> I saw the Lord sitting on a throne, and lifted up, and the train of His robe filled the temple. Above it stood seraphim; each one had six wings: with two he covered his face, with two he covered his feet, and with two he flew. And one cried to another and said: 'Holy, holy, holy is the Lord of hosts; The whole earth is full of his glory.'

The material, physical earth is filled with God's glory.

The conclusion from this example is that it is dangerous for believers to see some areas of life under the Lordship of Christ but not others– rather all areas reside there. Similarly Pascal stresses the danger in knowing some truths about ourselves but not others– in order to find God and live well, Man must know the whole truth, both his greatness and his vileness. (*Pensée* 121)

Application 3. Do Not Be a "One-Sided" Thinker. A third application is to beware of being a one-sided thinker, which can be defined as a person who thinks deeply about one side of Man's condition (his greatness or wretchedness) but neglects to think about the other side. In *Pensée* 613 Pascal writes,

> *Greatness, wretchedness.* The more enlightened we are the more greatness and vileness we discover in man...
> Philosophers:
> They surprise the ordinary run of men.
> Christians: they surprise the philosophers.

Many philosophers have delved deeply in one direction, some of which can be classified as optimists or pessimists. Famous optimists include Jean-Jacques Rousseau and Walt Whitman, and famous pessimists include Thomas Hobbes and Albert Camus. In addition, many Modernist and Postmodernist philosophers can roughly be classified as one-sided on greatness and wretchedness, respectively. Modernists plumb the heights of Man's greatness in thought but miss the frailty of his mind, whereas Postmodernists plumb the depths of Man's weakness in ignorance but miss the greatness of his thought.

For an example of a one-sided philosopher, consider the extremely influential Plato, who emphasized the immortality of the soul. To Platonists humans are made perfect and good in God's image. However Plato would not accept the Fall, sin, nor the Incarnation– to Plato it was inconceivable that God would become flesh and descend to live on earth in a human body. In denying these things, Plato would find the following words from the Apostle Paul incomprehensible:

> And being found in appearance as a man, [Jesus] humbled Himself and became obedient to the point of death, even the death of the cross. [Philippians 2:8]

Plato could not conceive of God making himself supremely wretched in order to redeem wretched Man; this is partly what Pascal means with the words, "Christians: they surprise the philosophers."

It is important to note that Pascal did not think these philosophers got it totally wrong– rather; they only got it half right! And this is deadly dangerous because it keeps one from seeking Jesus Christ. Pascal urges that the most enlightened thinkers study both the deep greatness and deep vileness of Man; in addition to Pascal these thinkers include the Apostle Paul, Augustine, Dostoevsky, C.S. Lewis, and G.K. Chesterton. Part of the greatness of great art derives from its success to give full (not one-sided) expression to Man's paradoxical nature– one example is Bach's use of point-counterpoint in his fugues.

In *Pensée* 430 Pascal further addresses the failure of philosophers to appreciate the heights and depths of Man's dual condition:

> No other [philosopher] has realized that man is the most excellent of creatures. Some, fully realizing how real his excellence is, have taken for cowardice and ingratitude men's natural feelings of abasement; while others, fully realizing how real this abasement is, have treated with haughty ridicule the feelings of greatness which are just as natural to man.
>
> `Lift up your eyes to God,' say some of them, 'look at him whom you resemble'... 'Hold your heads high, free men,' said Epictetus. And others say 'Cast down your eyes towards the ground, puny worm that you are, and look at the beasts whose companions you are.'
>
> What then is to become of Man? Will he be the equal of God or the beasts? What a terrifying distance! What then shall he be? Who cannot see from all this that man is lost, that he has fallen from his place, that he anxiously seeks it, and cannot find it again? And who then is to direct him there? The greatest men have failed.

Some criticize Christianity for ascribing to Man too much wretchedness, while others for ascribing too much greatness. These criticisms, however, are consistent with Christianity being true. Chesterton observes that if some find a man oddly thin, and others find him oddly fat, the truth may be that he is of normal size. [*Orthodoxy*]

One-Sided Heresies: Licentiousness and Legalism. Two major heresies that have dogged the Christian church for two thousand years, licentiousness and legalism, can be understood as the results of over-emphasizing Man's greatness or his wretchedness. The licentiousness camp over-emphasizes grace, while the legalist camp over-emphasizes law. Grace is essential, but by considering only grace, adherents to licentiousness overlook the role of the law to restrain Man's animal condition of concupiscence/over-desires. One effect of an unrestrained pursuit of over-desires is the erosion of gratitude: "We should thank God for beer and Burgundy by not drinking too much of them," writes Chesterton in *Orthodoxy*.

On the other hand, adherents to legalism acknowledge the appropriate role of law to help restrain sin, but in their zeal to strain out wretched deeds, overlook the role of grace as the only way to restore our original greatness. As such, licentiousness and legalism can be thought of as opposing one-sided heresies. "[The devil] always sends errors into the world in pairs– pairs of opposites," remarks C.S. Lewis. [*Mere Christianity*, Book 4, chapter 6] More generally, Pascal suggests that all heresies stem from accepting part of the truth but excluding the whole truth,

> The source of all heresies is the exclusion of certain of these truths... That is why the shortest way to prevent heresy is to teach all truths, and the surest way of refuting it is to proclaim them all. [*Pensée* 733]

In contrast to licentiousness and legalism, the Christian worldview emphasizes both grace and law; the Christian is called to love both. The Psalmist declares his love for God's law, "Oh, how I love Your law! It is my meditation all the day." [Psalm 119:47] John Newton, in his meditation on grace, acknowledges that grace engenders a fearful-yet-confident reverence for God's law,

> 'Twas grace that taught my heart to fear,
> And grace my fears reliev'd [*Amazing Grace*, verse 2]

Application 4. Danger for Political Parties to be One-Sided. *Pensée* 613 on the problem with one-sided thinking echoes my view on some of the stances of the major political parties in the U.S. In my view Republicans are right to stress the morality of protecting the life of unborn babies and Democrats are right to stress the morality of the care of children. But why are they not co-stressed– why are the unborn child and the born orphan not counted as members of the same vulnerable poor that Isaiah and the other prophets call people to care for? A party fully acknowledging Christian ethics would consider deeply *all* moral issues, neglecting none of them. It strikes me as impossible to find cogent reasons for prioritizing moral issue X and ignoring moral issue Y– all moral issues are important to God and thus all should be addressed fully. Jonathan Edwards suggests as much when he proposed that true virtue entails loving *all* that God loves, with no exceptions (*Dissertation Concerning the Nature of True Virtue,* 1765). In Edwards' day, this meant loving the Indians in New England in the face of resource and security concerns, a task that Edwards understood as integral to his duty to love God, while others, holding to *Manifest Destiny*, convinced themselves that true virtue could tolerate scorn for the Indians. To Edwards and Pascal it could not.

Pascal had strong words for those who consider only Man's greatness or only his wretchedness, or do not bother to think about either:

> I condemn equally those who choose to praise man, those who choose to condemn him, and those who choose to divert themselves, and I can only approve of those who seek with groans. [*Pensée* 405]

Application 5. Strength in Wretchedness. A fifth application emerges out of language used in one of the greatest confessions of the Christian faith, the Westminster Confession. Commissioned by the English Parliament in 1643, The Westminster Assembly, originally composed of 121 Episcopalian, Presbyterian, Independent, and Erastian clergy, plus ten lords and 20 commoners, completed this *Confession* in 1646, a few years before Pascal wrote the *Pensées*. The Assembly made a point similar to Pascal's on the necessity and usefulness for Christians to know their own wretchedness:

> The most wise, righteous, and gracious God doth oftentimes leave, for a season, His own children to... the corruption of their own hearts, ... to discover unto them the *hidden strength of corruption and deceitfulness of their hearts*, that they may be humbled; and, to raise them to a more close and constant dependence for their support upon Himself. [Chapter 5, Section 5]

The Westminster authors suggest that knowing the foulness of one's heart is of great value for humbling a believer and moving him to adhere more tightly to God. Jesus expresses a similar thought in the beatitudes, "Blessed are the poor in spirit, for theirs is the kingdom of heaven." [Matthew 5:3] Furthermore, Jesus tells a parable wherein God welcomes a tax collector who humbles himself by acknowledging he is an unworthy sinner, but rejects a Pharisee who exalts himself by asserting his confidence in his own righteousness. [Luke 18: 9-14] Humility includes an awareness of one's wretchedness, which is necessary for seeking and finding God. Just as the failure to know his wretchedness is Man's greatest weakness, so to know his weakness is one of his greatest strengths.

Application 6. Beyond Cynicism. For a sixth application, consider that many in our culture, Christians among them, unabashedly call themselves cynics. These hold deep suspicions about people and institutions, and pre-assume that these parties are incapable of doing good (Keyes, 2006). Pascal's first point on Man's dual condition, that he was made good and is redeemable by grace, warns cynics to not deny the redeemable original nature of every person. Pascal suggests that every human being is "capable of receiving grace which may enlighten them," and therefore we should humbly "believe that in a short time they may be filled with more faith than we are..." [*Pensée* 427]

Conclusion: Jesus Christ Embodies Greatness and Wretchedness. For Pascal Jesus Christ most clearly shows us our dual condition, as the one who embodies all that is great and all this is wretched in humankind:

> No man ever had such great glory, no man ever suffered greater ignominy. [*Pensée* 499]
>
> For by His Glory, Jesus Christ is all that is great, being God; and by His mortal life he is all that is poor and abject. [Letter to his sister Gilberte]

Jesus Christ is all that is great in the physical order, as the creator and sustainer of all matter (John 1). He is all that is great in the intellectual order, as the one who understands all things– he opens the scrolls and explains the meaning of human history. He is all that is great in the spiritual order, as the one in perfect/complete relationship with God the Father and the one who perfectly loves God and neighbor.

Jesus Christ is all that is poor and abject in the physical order, as he endured suffering, including hunger, torturous beatings ("... his appearance was so disfigured beyond that of any human being and his form marred beyond human likeness..." [Isaiah 52]), humiliation, and an ignominious death on a cross; he had no comeliness or achievements that would help his people overcome their political and military oppressors. [Isaiah 53] He is all that is poor and abject in the intellectual order, as he had no pride; he had no intellectual accomplishments such as degrees, publications or prestigious positions, his academic resume was empty. He came not to build a brilliant philosophical system, but to humble people and get them to take up their crosses; he counted intellectual wisdom foolishness, preferring the foolish way of death on a cross. [I Corinthians 2] Jesus Christ is all that is poor and abject in the spiritual order, as God counted him guilty for every human sin and fully punished him. The greatest abjection was God's abandonment of Jesus, even worse than Adam and Eve's abjection through God's abandonment at the Fall that constitutes humanities' deepest wretchedness. By becoming all that is poor and abject Jesus would restore his beloved to all that is rich and excellent. Jesus voluntarily became a "beast of the field" so that his beloved would become royal members of God's household.

***Pensée* of the Day: Number 192**

For the PoD I have selected the practical number 192:

> Knowing God without knowing our own wretchedness makes for pride.
> Knowing our own wretchedness without knowing God makes for despair.
> Knowing Jesus Christ strikes the balance because he shows us both God and our wretchedness.

Either pride or despair prevents a close relationship with God; the proud feel no need for him, while the gloomy may be too contemptuous, cynical, or cruel (as suggested by Screwtape in chapter 14 of *The Screwtape Letters*).

Synthesis Points of Chapter 5

1. Man's thought and Man's knowledge of his wretchedness show that he is great.
2. Roughly speaking, modernism appreciates Man's greatness but under-acknowledges his wretchedness, while postmodernism does the opposite. Neither worldview accounts for Man's paradoxical dual nature that exhibits both greatness and wretchedness. Any true worldview or religion must account for all the data about this misshapen, out of proportion "monster."

3. Our feeling of being un-fulfilled is a clue about our good Origin in paradise and our subsequent Fall into badness. We are "dispossessed kings."
4. Jesus Christ shows us both God and our wretchedness. Only Jesus Christ explains the human paradox, which makes Christianity "worthy of respect" (rationally plausible).
5. To avoid the pits of pride and despair, which each lead us away from God, it is necessary to know *both* one's wretchedness and ones' greatness.

6 WHY DOES GOD HIDE HIMSELF?

"I would rather discover one causal relation than be King of Persia."
– Democritus (430-380 BC)

"I thank You, Father, Lord of heaven and earth, that You have hidden these things from the wise and prudent and have revealed them to babes."
– Jesus, Matthew 11:25

"But there are some who are only capable of admiring carnal greatness, as if there were no such thing as greatness of the mind. And others who only admire greatness of the mind, as if there were not infinitely higher greatness in wisdom."
– Blaise Pascal, *Pensée* 308

Once I was talking with my 4-year old Goddaughter Emma, and had commented that God was in the room with us. Emma remarked: "Why can't I see God?" She was posing her first grand theological question: "Why is God hidden?" This question seems to get paid less attention than other monumental questions such as: "Why is evil in the world?" But I think it is equally important; throughout history people of diverse traditions and faiths have expressed sadness and perplexity at why God is hidden. For example the Psalmist laments:

But to You I have cried out, O Lord,
And in the morning my prayer comes before You,
Lord, why do You cast off my soul?
Why do you hide your face from me? [Psalm 88]

Furthermore many point to God's hiddenness as a major obstacle to belief. If there is a good God who created all people, with purpose to live forever in happy fellowship with himself, then it would seem to follow that God would make sure that everyone has clear knowledge of his existence. Why would this good God leave his created people in the dark? Thomas Morris articulates the problem of God's hiddenness:

> Why does God not act to show people clearly that He is? If there really were a God, wouldn't He do so? Conversely, doesn't the lack of action make it *rationally implausible* that God exists? Many philosophers have argued just this. [*Pascal and the Meaning of Life: Making Sense of it All*, 1992]

Pascal, as we will see, argues very differently. In fact Pascal proposes that not only does God's hiddenness not make his existence implausible, but it is a key piece of evidence for his reality! Furthermore, Pascal suggests that God's hiddenness is necessary for people to reach a happy relationship with him, and that achieving some understanding of why God hides is important for Christian growth.

Data and Assumptions about God's Hiddenness. To introduce you to Pascal's approach, consider the data, the facts. Some people are theists, some atheists, some agnostics. The data are that some perceive God's existence, and others do not.

Based on rational theology or scientism, many philosophers have purported that if God does exist, then he must show himself clearly. If this premise is accepted, then those who find God's presence unclear must conclude that God does not exist. Rationalists assume that if God is findable, then he can be found by reason alone, without the heart, and without passionate seeking. Many rationalistic atheists have relied on this premise in their arguments to disprove God. Others in the rationalistic camp deny the data– they claim that God is indeed shown clearly, and therefore exists.

Pascal departs from both these approaches, accepting the plain data that God's existence is ambiguous, but rejecting the rationalists' assumption that God can be found solely through reasoning. Because God's hiddenness is an observable fact, Pascal concludes that if God exists, then he must have hid himself from human knowledge. Any religion denying God's hiddenness, then, contradicts human experience. Moreover, Pascal puts forward a beautiful argument supporting that the true teachings of Christianity square precisely with the reality that God hides.

As Thomas Morris suggests, the key to understanding why God hides is to understand his purposes in doing so, and why hiding is necessary to achieve his objective to "conform people to the image of Christ." [Ephesians 1] In this chapter we will explore Pascal's thoughts on God's purpose in hiding himself.

Outline of Chapter 6. This chapter is divided into five parts. We will begin with brief background on the biblical account of God's hiddenness. Second we will look at Pascal's point that for a religion to be true it must offer a satisfactory explanation for the fact that God is not clearly seen by everyone. Pascal proposes that Christianity offers a uniquely compelling explanation, supporting its credibility. Third, we will explore Pascal's distinction between two different kinds of seekers, what he called the "temporal" and the "spiritual," who look for their good/treasure in different orders or realms of reality. Pascal shows that what they care about largely determines whether they can see God. Related to Part III, in Part IV we will explore *Pensées* on one of Pascal's most original and powerful ideas, his theory of orders. We will conclude with discussion about how it is practically helpful for Christians that God is hidden– in fact Pascal suggests it is necessary for us that God is hidden, otherwise we could never find him! I find Pascal's resolution of this paradox breathtaking; he compellingly answers my prior doubts about how God can be hidden and still be real.

Part I. Biblical Themes on God's Hiddenness

In Part I, I will summarize the many passages of the Bible suggesting that God is hidden. The Bible seems to present at least four themes on hiddenness.

God's Governance is Hidden. First, the Bible states that God's ways of governing creation are hidden. One example comes from Job 28:20–21:

> From where then does wisdom come? And where is the place of understanding? It is hidden from the eyes of the living, and concealed from the birds of the air.

For another example, in his prayer the prophet Habakkuk observes that God's power is hidden in heaven. [Habakkuk 3:4]

God's Plans for Humankind are Hidden. Second, the Bible states that God's plans for humankind are hidden. In his first letter to the Corinthians the Apostle Paul quotes Isaiah 64:4 and 65:17:

> Eye has not seen, nor ear heard, nor have entered into the heart of man the things which God has prepared for those who love him. [I Corinthians 2:9]

As we considered in chapter 5, in the book of Revelation the Apostle John describes a scroll, known only to the Lord and sealed with seven seals, which contains the secrets about how human history will unfold. John weeps when it appears that no one is able to open the scroll and interpret it. [Revelation 5] John may have wept because he longed to see God's purposes for the world accomplished, principally completing Man's transformation from its wretched state without God to its redeemed state as "kings and priests to our God," [Revelation 5:10] but he could not see assurance of this hoped-for future.

The Fall/Sin Impairs Human Knowledge of God. Third, and most importantly for Pascal's argument, the Bible describes God's hiding as a result of Man's disobedience. The prophet Isaiah describes this effect:

> But your iniquities have separated you from your God; and your sins have hidden His face from you, so that He will not hear. [Isaiah 59:2]

Also, Moses records God's prediction that the Israelites

> ...will forsake Me and break My covenant which I have made with them. Then My anger shall be aroused against them in that day, and I will forsake them, and I will hide My face from them... [Deuteronomy 31:16–17]

Furthermore the Hebrews believed that no man could see God and live. This incapacity derives not only from Man's unworthiness to see God, but also from Man's incapacity to endure the light of God's holiness, justice, and perfection. The prophet Habakkuk addresses God about this situation:

> You are of purer eyes than to behold evil, and cannot look on wickedness. [Habakkuk 1:13]

In the first half of *Pensée* 149 Pascal describes the Fall as a principal reason why God hides. Pascal leads up to this point by first observing that Man was created good, and at creation God was clearly known, not hidden:

> To make man happy the true religion must show him that a God exists whom we are bound to love; that our true bliss is to be in him, and our sole ill to be cut off from him. It must acknowledge that we are full of darkness which prevents us from knowing and loving him… It must teach us the cure for our helplessness and the means of obtaining the cure. Let us examine all the religions of the world on that point and let us see whether any but the Christian religion meets it…
>
> 'Men,' says God's wisdom, 'do not expect either truth or consolation from men. It is I who made you and I alone can teach you what you are.
>
> 'But you are no longer in the state in which I made you. I created man holy, innocent, perfect. I filled him with light and understanding, I showed him my glory and my wondrous works. Man's eyes then beheld the majesty of God. He was not then in the darkness that now blinds his sight, nor subject to death and the miseries that afflict him…

Pascal goes on in *Pensée* 149 to observe that what happened next led to God's hiding:

> 'But he could not bear such great glory without falling into presumption. He wanted to make himself his own centre and do without my help. He withdrew from my rule, setting himself up as my equal in his desire to find happiness in himself, and I abandoned him to himself. The creatures who were subject to him I incited to revolt and made his enemies, so that today man has become like the beasts, and is so far apart from me that a barely glimmering idea of his author alone remains of all his dead or flickering knowledge…
>
> 'That is the state in which men are today. They retain some feeble instinct from the happiness of their first nature, and are plunged into the wretchedness of their blindness and concupiscence, which has become their second nature.'

Because of the Fall, then, Man's second nature includes being blind to God. In Pascal's orthodox view, Original Sin and the Fall were the fundamental events that led to God's hiding himself, and the rejection of Original Sin by moderns partly explains their perplexity about God's hiddenness. Indeed, under a postulate that humankind is basically good in its present state, it is inexplicable why the good Creator would hide himself.

Some Perceive God and Others Do Not. Fourth, a biblical theme on hiddenness is that some people are able to see God and others cannot. Isaiah 6:9–10 seem to be key verses expressing this, as all four Gospels (e.g., Matthew 13:14, Mark 4:12, Luke 8:10 and John 12:40) record Jesus teaching from this passage, and the Apostle Paul quotes from these verses while teaching in a Roman prison. [Acts 28:26] Isaiah describes God's instructions for his prophetic message:

> And He said; Go, and tell this people:
> 'Keep on hearing, but do not understand;
> Keep on seeing, but do not perceive.'
> Make the heart of the people dull,
> and their ears heavy, and shut their eyes;
> Lest they see with their eyes,
> And hear with their ears,
> And understand with their heart,
> And return and be healed.

These verses suggest that part of Isaiah's ministry was to proclaim the reality that certain people with certain attitudes/conditions are not able to perceive God.

On the other hand, the Bible describes some people comprehending God's words. The Apostle John records Jesus speaking to the self-righteous Pharisees:

> He who is of God hears God's words; therefore you do not hear, because you are not of God. [John 8:47]

And Jesus answers the Jewish ruler Nicodemus:

> Most assuredly, I say to you, unless one is born again, he cannot see the kingdom of God. [John 3:3]

Verses like these suggest that people with a certain relationship with God can, and do, hear him. Pascal considered the attributes that are needed for hearing, which we will explore in this chapter.

Part II. True Religion Must Explain Why God Hides

We turn in Part II to find Pascal's starting point on God's hiddenness, *Pensée* 242:

> *That God wished to hide himself.* If there were only one religion, God would be clearly manifest. If there were no martyrs except in our religion, likewise.
>
> God being thus hidden, any religion that does not say that God is hidden is not true, and any religion which does not explain why does not instruct. Ours does all of this. *Verily thou art a God that hidest thyself*" [Isaiah 45:15].

Pascal suggests that Christianity is unique among religions, as the only one that teaches that God hides, and that provides an explanation for this fact. Pascal also proposes that God allowed many religions to exist as a means for hiding himself. As such, Pascal places the "problem of religious pluralism," that is, the question of, "Why would the Christian God confuse his created people by allowing many competing false religions?", as a subset of the problem of hiddenness. If we will accept Pascal's argument that Christianity explains why God is hidden, then as a corollary we will gain an answer to the question of why there is a plurality of religions.

Today a common stumbling block to Christian faith is the seeming arrogance and intolerance of Christ's claim that people can come to God only through himself. I have found Pascal's ideas extremely helpful for understanding how I may reasonably and humbly hold this position of exclusivity. This is one reason why I find Pascal's thoughts on hiddenness so exhilarating– he addresses head on one of the thorniest contemporary concerns about the Christian faith, and delivers a compelling and satisfying analysis.

Hiddenness as a Double-Edged Sword. On God's purpose in hiding, Pascal observes that the Bible narrates Jesus teaching in such a way that upon hearing him some were enlightened and comprehended it, while others were darkened and could not comprehend it. Thus God communicates to people in an obscure manner, with effect to blind some and enlighten others. Pascal starkly expresses this double-edged purpose of God's hiding in *Pensée* 235:

> Jesus came to blind those who have clear sight and to give sight to the blind; to heal the sick and let the healthy die; to call sinners to repentance and justify them, and leave the righteous to their sins; to fill the hungry with good things and to send the rich empty away.

This *Pensée* describes God *actively saving* sinners and *passively leaving* the self-righteous to their sins. To understand this *Pensée* it is critical to note the words "let" and "leave" chosen by Pascal to describe the means through which the self-righteous are condemned. In Pascal's Augustinian Christianity, all humanity is under condemnation by God. Some, through grace, are elected to redemption from this condemnation, while others are left in their condemned state. God's condemnation is described passively– they were already condemned and they remain in that state. To the contrary, God actively saves sinners, as conveyed in Pascal's phrase, "Jesus came to call sinners to repentance and justify them." Thus Pascal should not be mistaken as purporting "double predestination," whereby God actively elects some to heaven and actively elects others to hell. Instead, Pascal seemed to think, as Dick Keyes has suggested, that the Bible describes election and condemnation *asymmetrically*– God *actively* elects the redeemed as the means of salvation, and *passively* leaves or abandons people to their pre-existing sinful state as the means of condemnation. Specifically, as expressed in this *Pensée*, all who know they are sick and their need for God are actively saved by Jesus, and all who think they are well and do not need God are left to their sins.

Pascal similarly expresses God's double-edged intent to save the sick and leave the self-righteous condemned in *Pensée* 236:

> *Blind, enlighten.*
> There is enough light to enlighten the elect and enough obscurity to humiliate them. There is enough obscurity to blind the reprobate and enough light to condemn them and deprive them of excuse.

A symptom of blindness/obscurity for an atheist is bewilderment about how people, whom otherwise seem reasonable, can believe

Christianity. For example, Richard Dawkins remarks in *The God Delusion* (2006), "After amicable discussions with [prominent Christian British scientists including John Polkinghorne], both in public and in private, I remain baffled, not so much by their belief in a cosmic lawgiver of some kind, as by their belief in the details of the Christian religion: resurrection, forgiveness of sins and all."

Pascal elaborates *Pensée* 236 in *Pensée* 835:

> The prophecies, even the miracles and proofs of our religion, are not of such a kind that they can be said to be absolutely convincing, but they are at the same time such that it cannot be said to be unreasonable to believe in them. There is thus evidence and obscurity, to enlighten some and obfuscate others. But the evidence is such as to exceed, or at least equal, the evidence to the contrary, so that it cannot be reason that decides us against following it, and can therefore only be concupiscence and wickedness of heart. Thus, there is enough evidence to condemn and not enough to convince, so that it should be apparent that those who follow it are prompted to do so by grace and not by reason, and those who evade it are prompted by concupiscence and not by reason.

This *Pensée* begins to reveal Pascal's exhilarating idea about God's purpose in hiding, in that it allows all people prompted by grace to find God, but eliminates any other means of finding him. Only through grace, unmerited favor, is God found. Apart from grace, all are left in their fallen state of idolatry and wickedness of heart. If wicked people could find God merely by thinking well or working hard, without becoming truly sorry for their wickedness, then they could reach heaven in a proud state, with no sense of needing or depending on God. But this is a contradiction if we accept that heaven is constituted as Jesus Christ and the Apostles say it is– that all in God's kingdom want and need God. Thus God had to hide in order to bring people to free and true friendship with himself.

Connection of God's Hiddenness with Man's Greatness and Wretchedness. These thoughts on why God hides are closely connected to the thesis of the last chapter, that to know God one must know both one's greatness and wretchedness. Pascal draws this link directly in *Pensée* 444:

> But it is true at once that he hides from those who tempt him and that he reveals himself to those who seek him, because men are at once unworthy and capable of God: unworthy through their corruption, capable through their original nature.

Thus, humble seekers who acknowledge their wretchedness are capable of seeing him revealed, while proud non-seekers of God are incapable of seeing him revealed. The same words from Jesus or from a prophet reveal God to some people, and conceal him from others, depending on whether they seek or not.

Pascal expands on God's purpose in hiding himself in the last part of *Pensée* 149:

> God's will has been to redeem men and open the way of salvation to those who seek it, but men have shown themselves so unworthy that it is right for God to refuse to some, for their hardness of heart, what he grants to others by a mercy they have not earned.
>
> 'If he had wished to overcome the obstinacy of the most hardened, he could have done so by revealing himself to them so plainly that they could not doubt the truth of his essence, as he will appear on the last day with such thunder and lightning and such convulsions of nature that the dead will rise up and the blindest will see him. This is not the way he wished to appear when he came in mildness, because so many men had shown themselves unworthy of his clemency, that he wished to deprive them of the good they did not desire. It was therefore not right that he should appear in a manner manifestly divine and absolutely capable of convincing all men, but neither was it right that his coming should be so hidden that he could not be recognized by those who sincerely sought him. He wished to make himself perfectly recognizable to them. Thus wishing to appear openly to those who seek him with all their heart and hidden from those who shun him with all their heart, he has qualified our knowledge of him by giving signs which can be seen by those who seek him and not by those who do not.
>
> 'There is enough light for those who desire only to see, and enough darkness for those of a contrary disposition.'

In this *Pensée* Pascal expresses most clearly his understanding of God's purpose in wielding a double-edged sword– God wished to reveal himself to those who seek him and to conceal himself from those who shun him. It is the attitude, the disposition, which determines whether one can understand the signs that God provides. Pascal suggests that those whose hearts are fixed on treasures in heaven can understand the signs, while those whose hearts are fixed on treasures on earth, such as security or amassing money, fame, or power, cannot interpret the signs. These signs include prophecies, miracles, and nature, which Pascal discusses extensively in the *Pensées*.

Peter Kreeft (1993) suggests that God's respect for Man's free will is a key for appreciating the justice in God's providing "enough light" and "enough darkness":

> If he gave less [light], even the righteous would be unable to find him, and their will would be thwarted. If he gave more, even the wicked would find him, against their will. Thus he respects and fulfills the will of all.

C.S. Lewis expresses a similar thought in *The Great Divorce*:

> There are only two kinds of people in the end: those who say to God, 'Thy will be done,' and those to whom God says, in the end 'Thy will be done.'

Thus, those who want to find God, do, and those who do not care to seek God, do not. In *The Problem of Pain* (chapter on Hell), Lewis also expresses Pascal's idea that God deprives the non-seekers only of the good they do not desire.

For Christian believers who wish to persuade their non-believing friends to seek, the above *Pensées* provide practical advice on how to go about it– the priority should be on "making Christianity attractive," [*Pensée* 12] on demonstrating the loveliness of God (e.g., the mingling of beauty, truth, grace and love in Jesus, as expressed in stories about one's own life). Such demonstrations are of principal value for sparking seeking because they aim to move the heart, and the inexorable desire to be happy.

Part III. Temporal and Spiritual Jews

In Part III, we will expand on Pascal's comparison of the two kinds of treasure-hunters, those who seek God and treasures in heaven, and those who shun God and seek only their own selfish good, treasures on earth. Specifically we will explore Pascal's *Pensées* on two different kinds of Jews, who differ in what they look for in a Messiah who would fulfill the Old Testament prophecies.

In the New Testament, some Jews are described as rejecting Jesus' claim to be the Messiah, because Jesus did not fit their expectations for the prophesied Messiah. Pascal refers to these Jews as "carnal" or "temporal" Jews, because they were looking for the Messiah to come as a political king, who would free them from Roman bondage, and in a word, provide earthly blessings. In contrast, Pascal refers to Jews who recognized Jesus to be the Messiah as "spiritual Jews;" these looked for a spiritual king, who would free them from their sins, and to live fully in true spiritual worship of God. In some *Pensées* Pascal refers to "spiritual Jews" as "true Jews," and notes that true Jews and true Christians are the same thing; for example in *Pensée* 433:

> *To show that true Jews and true Christians have only one religion.*
>
> The religion of the Jews seem to consist essentially in the fatherhood of Abraham, circumcision, sacrifices, ceremonies, the Ark, the Temple, Jerusalem and finally the law and covenant of Moses.
>
> I say that it consisted in none of these things, but only in the love of God, and that God rejected all the other things...

Pascal may have had in mind the definition of a "true Jew" given by the Apostle Paul in his letter to the Romans, wherein Paul rebukes the Judaizers for not recognizing that the New Covenant in Christ had freed believers from following the external ceremonial law to which they were bound under the Old Covenant:

> The true Jew is not he who is such in externals, neither is the true circumcision the external mark in the flesh. The true Jew is he who is such inwardly, and the true circumcision is of the heart. [Romans 2:28–29]

To Pascal a true Jew is a person with a heart filled with God's grace and faith– this state does not derive from external appearances, customs, or systems.

The Temporal Jews' Expectation for the Messiah. Earl Palmer's 2005 Palm Sunday sermon on the Jews' interpretation of Jesus' triumphal entry into Jerusalem is helpful for understanding the temporal Jews. Reverend Palmer observed that Isaiah 53:1–6, if interpreted literally through temporal eyes, predicts that the Messiah will lead a successful revolt against the Romans. Palm branches were laid on the ground because the palm branch was the crest of the national Jewish hero Judas Macabees, who previously led a successful revolt. Therefore on Palm Sunday the crowds looked for the second coming of Judas Macabees, a military and political victor.

Dual Meanings of Scripture: Literal and Figurative. As Pascal notes in *Pensée* 287, at one level it was logical for the Jews to look for a "great temporal ruler," because on the surface the Old Testament does predict the coming of this kind of Messiah. To Pascal the prophecies and their fulfillment is the most important evidence for Christianity, and suggests that if the Bible did unambiguously predict a military Messiah, then Christianity must be false, because Christ was not a military king. For Christianity to be credible, then, it is necessary that the prophecies also contain a figurative meaning that predicts Christ as he actually came, in meekness as a spiritual king. In Pascal's words in *Pensée* 274, "Thus the whole question [about whether Christianity is true] is whether they [the Scriptures] have two meanings [literal and figurative]." If only the literal meaning is present, then the Bible is internally contradictory, the prophecies do not predict Jesus as Messiah, and therefore the most important proof of Jesus Christ is destroyed.

Pascal uses two main proofs that the Old Testament has both literal and figurative meaning: first, the Jewish tradition has always attributed a figurative level of meaning; and second, Saint Paul and Jesus Christ himself directly taught a figurative reading of the Old Testament. In turn I will summarize these two proofs.

Proof 1: The Jews Always Attributed a Figurative Meaning to the Scriptures. For Proof 1, I will consider four points, which draw on the book chapter *Pascal and Holy Writ* (Hammond, 2003) by David Wetsel, a Professor of French Literature at Arizona State University. First, the writings of Rabbis over the centuries show a consistent acknowledgment of a dual level of meaning. In *Pensée* 278 Pascal gives as an example the tradition of Rabbis to teach original sin and to teach their expectation that the Messiah would come to deliver the Jew's good nature from bad.

Second, Scripture openly declares itself to be speaking in enigmas or mysteries. Surely with verses such as Isaiah 6:9–10 in mind, Pascal writes:

> When we come upon an important letter, whose meaning is clear but where we are told that the meaning is veiled and obscure, that it is hidden so that seeing we shall not see and hearing we shall not hear, what else are we to think but that this is a cipher with a double meaning? [*Pensée* 260]

Thus, to Pascal, the most direct and plain interpretation of many biblical passages is that a dual meaning is intended.

Third, the prophets stated clearly that no one would understand their meaning and that their prophecies were veiled. As in *Pensée* 228:

> What do the prophets say about Jesus Christ? That he will plainly be God? No, but that he is a truly hidden God, that he will not be recognized, that people will not believe that it is he, that he will be a stumbling-block on which many will fall, etc. Let us then not be criticized for lack of clarity, since we openly profess it.

Here Pascal proposes that the fact that Christ's Messiah-ship is not obvious to all actually counts as evidence *for* the Christian claim, not against it. It was one of the formal intentions of the prophets to proclaim that the Messiah's coming would be obscure, and the fact that Jesus did come in obscurity is consistent with fulfillment of the prophecy of the hidden Messiah. [Isaiah 6:10]

Fourth, if the Old Testament is read totally literally, then many flat contradictions within it can be found. Pascal lists contradictions in *Pensée* 263, including that in Genesis 49:10 Jacob predicted that "the sceptre shall not be taken away from Judea," whereas the prophet Hosea predicted that Israel will find herself "with neither king nor prince." [Hosea 3:4] A literal reading cannot reconcile these two predictions, whereas a figurative reading of Jacobs' prediction, fulfilled in Jesus Christ, reconciles them. Pascal insists that intellectual integrity must be preserved when studying the Bible:

> To understand the meaning of an author, one must be able to reconcile all contradictory passages. Thus to understand Scripture, a meaning must be found which reconciles all contradictory passages. [*Pensée* 257]

Pascal was convinced that only Jesus Christ makes the whole Bible coherent, concluding *Pensée* 257 with the words: "In Christ all contradictions are reconciled."

Taken together, these points form Pascal's argument that a straightforward reading of the Scriptures, interpreted fairly in the light and style in which they are presented, would lead one to expect multiple meanings. Only an unfair, manipulated interpretation would conclude that a literal interpretation alone is admissible. Importantly, this first proof that Scripture has both literal and figurative meaning is based on the Old Testament alone, so that it is fair to expect the Jews to look for figurative fulfillments of prophecy. This helps explain Jesus' indignation at the Pharisees and Scribes for their blindness to various passages of the Old Testament, despite their priding themselves on their mastery of the Scriptures. For example, the Apostle John records Jesus rebuking some Jews who were trying to kill him for healing a lame man on the Sabbath:

> For if you believed Moses, you would believe Me, for he wrote about Me. [John 5:46]

Proof 2: The New Testament Directly Teaches a Figurative Meaning. While the first proof that the Old Testament has a figurative meaning allows Pascal to establish this result based solely on the Old Testament, Pascal and his like-minded contemporaries at Port-Royal took as the most definitive proof the New Testament events and teachings of the Apostle Paul and Jesus Christ. The New Testament records many statements from Jesus that seem to be intentionally cryptic. For example, consider the sign that Jesus gives the Pharisees, "Destroy this temple, and in three days I will raise it up." [John 2:19] At the time, those present assumed Jesus was talking about the physical temple in Jerusalem, but after Jesus' resurrection his disciples understood that Jesus was referring to the death and resurrection of his body. Thus, Jesus intended his puzzling statement to be misunderstood by the temporally minded and understood by the spiritually minded.

For a second example, the Romans hung the sign "King of the Jews" over Jesus' cross. To the temporal Jews that pressed for Jesus' death, this statement was interpreted as false, for to them it was clear that Jesus was not king of the Jews. This temporally-minded vantage point is represented by one of the thieves on the cross next to Jesus, who mocked him, saying, "If you are the Christ, save yourself and us." [Luke 23:39] The spiritually-minded vantage point is represented by the other thief on the cross, who recognized Jesus' spiritual kingdom, "Lord, remember me when You come into Your kingdom." [Luke 23:42] Therefore the two thieves represent those without and with eyes to see, those with temporal and spiritual eyes.

For a third example, consider Jesus' conversation with Peter and John on the road to Emmaus after rising from the dead. Pascal cites this event (*Pensée* 253) as narrated by Luke:

> And beginning at Moses and all the prophets, he expounded unto them in all the Scriptures the things concerning himself. [Luke 24:27]

Professor Wetsel proposes that both Pascal and Pascal's spiritual director Sacy regarded this testimony as the most definitive proof of the figurative meaning of the Old Testament. Furthermore, in other places in the Gospels Jesus indicates that he knew that the Old Testament prophecies "must be fulfilled in me." [Luke 22: 37] Therefore, those who reject the figurative interpretation of the Old Testament also reject Jesus Christ as the Messiah.

In the Jesuit-Jansenist controversy, the Jesuits charged the Jansenists with not interpreting the Old Testament literally enough, placing the Jansenists in hot water. Pascal and the Jansenists believed this accusation was misguided because the Jesuits were failing to accept the appropriateness of a figurative interpretation of many scriptures. In the preface to his 1699 book *The Psalms of David,* Sacy pleads the Jansenists' case, arguing that a level-headed analysis must conclude that the Scriptures have a dual meaning:

> We beg those who are shocked to see us add the spiritual to the literal meanings [of the Old Testament] to remember that we are only following the example of all the Holy Fathers... of St. Paul... and of Jesus Christ himself, who so advantageously used these kinds of spiritual explications.

Moreover, Professor Wetsel proposes that Sacy viewed the Bible's use of figurative meaning as unique:

> Sacy insists that what distinguishes the Bible's use of metaphor from that of any other book is that its figures are organized into a completely coherent system, into an organized level of meaning:

> 'Nothing is more useful when attempting to penetrate the meaning of an author than to know what his purpose is. The purpose of the Old Testament is to represent Jesus Christ, but Jesus Christ hidden under the veil of Figures and under the obscurities of the prophets. The purpose of the New Testament is to show forth Jesus Christ plainly, and to show that he is the truth of Figures and the accomplishment of the Prophecies. Thus the two Testaments mirror and explain one another. The New Testament is hidden in the Old, and the Old is manifested in the New.'

In fact, based on *Pensées* including number 255, Wetsel proposes that Pascal's ultimate argument for the truth of the Christian religion rests on the observation that the "manner" of the coming of the Messiah must be interpreted figuratively– thus God's hiddenness is a key to unlocking Christian truth. Moreover, Pascal suggests that the figurative prophecies of the Old Testament are great gifts of grace, because they enable those who seek with all their heart to perceive the true religion hidden in history.

Example: Literal versus Figurative Interpretation of "Enemies." As a specific example of an Old Testament prophecy that has been interpreted literally or figuratively by the temporally and spiritually minded, consider the promise, carried by Moses, David, and Isaiah among others, that the Messiah will come to deliver the Jews from their enemies. In *Pensée* 502 Pascal observes that,

> the righteous took [the word enemy] to mean their passions [their intellectual pride and sensual desires which lead them away from God] and the carnal people took it to mean the Babylonians, and so these terms were only obscure for the unrighteous.

That is, temporal Jews looked for victory over political enemies, while spiritual Jews looked for victory over their own sins. (See also *Pensée* 269.)

Consider the prophet Isaiah's words about the kind of victory the Messiah would bring:

> But He was wounded for our transgressions, He was bruised for our iniquities; the chastisement for our peace was upon Him, And by His stripes we are healed. All we like sheep have gone astray; We have

turned, every one, to his own way; And the Lord has laid on Him the iniquity of us all. [Isaiah 53:5–6]

To Pascal, spiritual Jews interpret such verses as implying the Messiah would deliver the people from their sins, but temporal Jews cannot comprehend this meaning– they can only understand delivery from political enemies. Pascal elaborates this idea in *Pensées* 256, 257, 269, 270, 502 and elsewhere.

Supporting Pascal's interpretation, the Bible is replete with statements that God will win a victory to defeat the enemy of our sins. The prophet Isaiah speaks to God, "You cast all my sins behind your back," [Isaiah 38:17] while God himself declares, "I am He who blots out your transgressions for my sake, and I will not remember your sins." [Isaiah 43:25] The prophet Micah declares, "You will cast all our sins into the depths of the sea," [Micah 7:19] and David sings, "as far as the east is from the west, so far does he remove our transgressions from us." [Psalm 103:12] Furthermore, David names his iniquities as the besieging army from which he asks for deliverance:

> For innumerable evils have surrounded me;
> My iniquities have overtaken me, so that I am not able to look up;
> They are more than the hairs of my head;
> Therefore my heart fails me. [Psalm 40:12]

Who is Our Chief Enemy? In *Pensées* exemplified by numbers 269 and 270, Pascal considers, Who is our chief adversary? *Pensée* 269 begins:

> There are some who see clearly that man has no other enemy but concupiscence, which turns him away from God, and not [human] enemies, no other good but God, and not a rich land.

Pascal expresses a similar thought in *Pensée* 270:

> After Christ's death St. Paul came to teach them [the Jews] that all these things [the fulfillment of prophecy] happened figuratively... that the enemies of men were not the Babylonians but their passions.

This line of thinking suggests that it may be more important to fight our sins than to fight our political enemies. This raises a challenge to us as post 9–11 Americans: what do we consider our chief enemy? Is it terrorists, or is it our own selfish desires and indifference? If we focus on defeating the temporal, physical enemy, do we risk taking our eye off the ball of defeating our spiritual enemy, with potentially infinite cost that we remain forever in our wretched state? Pascal suggests we consider our own sins as our chief enemy to fight; this is what he meant by declaring we must hate ourselves– we must wage war against our sinful inclinations. Our sinful inclinations un-combated are what really prevent us from a good relationship with God and neighbor, and these relationships are our true good– not physical Canaan.

Jesus' Historical Obscurity. Defenders of the Christian faith have traditionally tried to make the most of rare references to Jesus in first-century history books written by Josephus and the Romans. They suppose that the more importance ascribed to Jesus by contemporary historians, the more plausible that Jesus was truly the promised Messiah and is truly God. As pointed out by Professor Wetsel, however, Pascal believed the opposite, proposing that the historical obscurity of Jesus is a sign that he truly is the Messiah! As Pascal writes in *Pensée* 499,

> What other comparatively obscure historical figure ever wrought such dramatic changes in the history of the world?

Because of the dual meaning of scripture, Pascal suggests, we should expect Jesus to be obscure in historical accounts written from a literal/temporal perspective. But in the spiritual realm, we should expect great impact– and this precisely squares with history.

Part IV. Pascal's Theory of Orders

Pascal's theory of orders, one of his most prominent themes spliced through the *Pensées*, is important for understanding his thoughts on why Jesus can be perceived by some but not others.

In past chapters we touched on Pascal's distinction of three orders (or realms) of reality: the carnal order, the intellectual order, and the spiritual order. The carnal order consists of material things like physical strength, physical beauty, athletic or military achievements, and wealth. The carnally great include kings, the rich, and military generals, as well as sports stars and super-models. The intellectual order consists of reasoning, the world of ideas, the pursuit of truth; intellectual greats include Nobel Prize winners and mathematical savants. The spiritual order is about the will, heart, love and wisdom; the spiritually great are those whose principal business is loving God and neighbor.

Some People Live for One Order Only. Pascal observes that some people find their purpose, their end, their reason for living, exclusively in one of these orders. Alexander the Great found his purpose in conquering the world, in acquiring land; likewise some rich CEOs find their purpose in accumulating companies and yachts. Some devoted scientists like Archimedes live only for pursuing knowledge. In chapter 5 we noted that the great mathematician Paul Erdös lived so exclusively for solving math problems that he never learned how to make toast. Mother Theresa cared only for the spiritual order, being concerned wholly with inclining her heart to listen to God, and conforming her will obediently to God's.

The 2004 film *Sideways* illustrates the point that some people find their meaning in life virtually entirely within one order. In this movie two old college buddies spend a week touring California wine-country before Jack gets married to a beautiful woman. Jack lives entirely in the order of the physical; all he cares about is satisfying his animal desire for sex. Miles, on the other hand, lives almost totally in the order of the intellect– he is a writer who cares about the subtleties of wine and language, and is totally uncomfortable in the carnal realm. There is a poignant moment in the film that reveals their different spheres of existence. At a diner, Jack is angling to commit adultery with a frumpy looking waitress. When Jack informs Miles of his intention, Miles expresses great astonishment– why would Jack want to do this? Jack's response: "You understand movies, literature, wine– but you don't understand my plight." How true, his plight was living exclusively in the order of the body, a slave to this order, with an inability to appreciate higher pleasures of the mind or heart– a "plight" indeed. Miles could not understand this plight because he did not live for carnal pleasures. In contrast to both Jack and Miles, Mother Theresa cared nothing for physical beauty, comfort, or pleasures, nor for the subtleties of wine or high intellectual wit, but only about loving God and neighbor.

Some Today Only Care About Goods in the Carnal or Intellectual Order. In our day, many care only for treasure in the carnal order, finding their meaning and purpose in property, retirement portfolios, automobiles, toys, athletic achievements, good looks. Such moderns that live for material security and toys have been called new Victorians (Keyes,

1998). Alternatively many today care only for treasure in the intellectual order, occupied with proving themselves smarter than others. Pascal called out the vanity of scholars who foolishly

> ...sweat away in their studies to prove to scholars that they have solved some hitherto insoluble problem in algebra. [*Pensée* 136]

Essay on the Theory of Orders: Pensée 308. Pascal emphasizes the mutual exclusivity of the goods/treasures that are sought within the different orders. A great achievement in one order will be completely uninteresting for someone living within another order. Napoleon's conquests did not impress physicists absorbed with understanding the properties of light. Paul Erdös' proof of 10,000 theorems gained for him no reputation among football fans. Mother Theresa's sustained love for the poor was quite irrelevant for those trying to get ahead. Pascal describes this in *Pensée* 308, which contains the fullest description of Pascal's theory of orders.

> The infinite distance between body and mind symbolizes the infinitely more infinite distance between mind and charity, for charity is supernatural.
>
> All the splendour of greatness lacks luster for those engaged in pursuits of the mind.
>
> The greatness of intellectual people is not visible to kings, rich men, captains, who are all great in a carnal sense.
>
> The greatness of wisdom, which is nothing if it does not come from God, is not visible to carnal or intellectual people. They are three orders differing in kind.
>
> Great geniuses have their power, their splendour, their greatness, their victory and their lustre, and do not need carnal greatness, which has no relevance for them. They are recognized not with the eyes but with the mind, and that is enough.
>
> Saints have their power, their splendour, their victory, their lustre, and do not need either carnal or intellectual greatness, which has no relevance for them, for it neither adds nor takes away anything. They are recognized by God and the angels, and not by bodies or by curious minds. God is enough for them.
>
> Archimedes in obscurity would still be revered. He fought no battles visible to the eyes, but enriched every mind with his discoveries. How splendidly he shone in the minds of men!

> Jesus without wealth or any outward show of knowledge has his own order of holiness. He made no discoveries; he did not reign, but he was humble, patient, thrice holy to God, terrible to devils, and without sin. With what great pomp and marvelously magnificent array he came in the eyes of the heart, which perceive wisdom!
>
> It would have been pointless for Archimedes to play the prince in his mathematical books, prince though he was.
>
> It would have been pointless for Our Lord Jesus Christ to come as a king with splendour in his reign of holiness, but he truly came in splendour in his own order...

This *Pensée* has a direct application for distinguishing temporal and spiritual Jews. Temporal Jews operate in the carnal order, and as such look for a Messiah to be great in the political and military arena, to overthrow Rome. Thus when Jesus scored no political victories, first century temporal Jews were unimpressed. They were blind to Jesus' greatness because it did not reside in their realm of concern. On the other hand, because spiritual Jews operate in the spiritual order, they see Jesus with "eyes of the heart," perceiving him as the Messiah who dazzles with great splendor.

The response of different parties to the raising of Lazarus from the dead illustrates two kinds of witnesses who looked on with carnal or spiritual eyes. After Jesus raised Lazarus following four days in the tomb, many Jews believed in Jesus, and many others persisted in disbelief. [John 11] The Chief Priest Caiphus' reaction to this great miracle suggests he only had eyes to see within the carnal order:

> If we left Him [Jesus] alone like this, everyone will believe in Him, and the Romans will come and take away both our place and nation. [John 11:48]

Caiphus' utmost concern was for land and nation, for carnal goods; because he cared little or not for a spiritual kingdom he could not be moved by the momentous miracle. Only if one cares to see God's spiritual kingdom, wants to see it, can it be seen.

Pointing to the reaction of the Jewish leaders to Lazarus' raising from the dead as an example, Dick Keyes (2006) observes that, "evidence can never compel belief, because evidence is always interpreted." Even though no one who witnessed Lazarus' raising seems to have disputed whether it happened, and it happened right in front of the religious leaders eyes, they could not allow this evidence to convince them that Jesus was God's Son, because of their self-interest to maintain their power. Thus one's interpretation, shaped by the hoped for good (e.g., "place and nation"), can win the day over plain evidence. This human attribute for self-interest to trump evidence echoes our discussion in chapters 3 and 4 on the weakness of Man's reasoning compared to myriad competing factors.

Temporal and Spiritual Jews Today. Surely at all times in history there have been some people with dispositions that fit Pascal's description of temporal Jews, and others of spiritual Jews. One arena illustrating this is the Israel-Palestine conflict. In modern times, the temporally minded interpret the formation of the Israeli state in 1946 as a fulfillment of biblical prophecies that the Jewish nation will be delivered to a rich land. These interpret this event as primary in God's plan for redeeming Israel, and include American Christians who suggest that Israel's right to land must be defended at all costs, even if it means not practicing hospitality to their foreign neighbors. In contrast, the primary concern of the spiritually minded is to extend love and grace to the other. Through spiritual eyes Jews would consider a Palestinian child equally valuable to a Jewish child and vice versa, each willing to bend on the matter of land if it would mean preserving the lives of their neighbors' children.

By suggesting that the Christian life is principally about winning material blessings on earth, adherents to the health and wealth gospel also fit Pascal's definition of temporal Jews. Like deism, the theology of health and wealth downplays suffering, neglecting the Scriptures that suggest value in suffering for cultivating spiritual growth, and missing Jesus' explicit statements that Christians should not expect to forego suffering. A temporal Jew may be devastated by cancer because it takes away his chief good (physical health and material security), while a spiritual Jew may experience joy in the midst of suffering to the extent that it cultivates his chief good of knowing God. A temporal Jew may shun knowledge of his own frailty, while a spiritual Jew accepts it and is open to growth through it. Furthermore, the same individual may look through temporal eyeglasses at some times and through spiritual eyeglasses at others. Indeed every Christian may experience this dual vision, as the impact of the Fall is too thorough for a fallen creature to *never* hold a temporal perspective. But through growing in grace the acuity of a Christian's spiritual eyesight may increase over time.

Tyranny/Disorder. Pascal also emphasizes that tyranny and disorder will result if a person uses the means appropriate for obtaining an end residing within one order to try and achieve an end that resides in a different order. For a first example, consider the disproportionate funding for preventive versus therapeutic medical research in the United States. Reason and ethics would suggest choosing to spend money to minimize the total amount of morbidity and mortality. But the reality is that vastly disproportionate funds are spent to develop therapies rather than prevention tools. The reason? Many care more about private wealth than public health– there is more money to be made on therapeutic drugs that must be taken every day than on preventive vaccines, which only need to be taken once. So it is a desire for private profits, not for an intelligent and ethical outcome, that plays a heavy role in determining what research gets done. This constitutes tyranny in using carnal means where intellectual and spiritual means are appropriate.

For a second example of disorder, which stems from the misapplication of purely intellectual means, consider atheist intellectualists who propose that science and logic alone should be used in debates about abortion, end-of-life issues, stem-cell issues, etc. Pascal's theory suggests that this is a misapplication of tools– science and logic are appropriate for answering how questions, how do things work, but why questions are beyond their reach. Values determine answers to questions about whether certain actions are right or wrong, and values stem from a conception of the meaning and purpose of life. To Pascal questions of meaning are appropriately addressed within the spiritual order, and true meaning comes only from listening to God.

For a third example, the Old Testament prophets proclaim it is tyrannical to pursue peace through back room bargaining. For example Isaiah incessantly points out the futility of the Jewish peoples' attempts at peace through cutting corrupt deals with neighboring nations. Calling out the disorder of this approach, Isaiah likens it to "threshing cumin with a threshing sledge," [Isaiah 28:27] which to their culturally agrarian ears must have sounded as inappropriate as "cutting steak with a butter-knife." Isaiah suggests that the only appropriate, non-tyrannical way to attain real peace is to listen to God and to trust in him to bring about the deliverance.

Hierarchy of the Three Orders. Continuing *Pensée* 308, Pascal suggests the three orders form a hierarchy of increasing dimension of greatness, value, and importance:

> All bodies, the firmament, the stars, the earth and its kingdoms are not worth the least of minds, for it knows them all and itself too, while bodies know nothing.
>
> All bodies together and all minds together and all their products are not worth the least impulse of charity. This is of an infinitely superior order...

As one moves from the first order to the second, and from the second to the third, infinitely more greatness becomes available. This is illustrated by likening the carnal order to a point, the intellectual order to a line, and the spiritual order to a plane. A point contributes no measure or substance to a line– all the carnal greatness in the world does not contribute one ounce of intellectual greatness. Similarly, a line contributes no measure or substance to a plane– all the carnal and intellectual greatness in the world does not contribute one ounce of spiritual greatness.

To Perceive God, One Must Not Exclude the Order of the Heart. For seekers, the spiritual order is of greatest importance because the heart is the critical organ for attaining friendship with God. Efforts purely through carnal or intellectual means will fail. This is why neither carnal temporal Jews nor rationalistic philosophers can find God. From a purely scientific perspective, the appropriate way to evaluate if God exists is to think logically and to look for him diligently– can we see him, hear him, smell him? From this perspective, if God cannot be found through the senses, then he must not be there. The rules of the scientist for finding truth are sense data and logical reasoning. But God may not be found in this way, because the scientific seeker may be proud.

Within the spiritual order, in contrast, the assurance about God's reality has to do with "inward grace," the invisible substance that informs people that God is and loves them. Through such grace one can recognize that one's true good and end lies in being conformed unto Christ– from spiritual eyes it meets expectations that Jesus Christ only showed his splendor in the order that matters for attaining this end. Because my deepest needs are cures for my badness, unhappiness, and mortality, I could care less whether Jesus would lead an army or prove Einstein's theorems. The necessity of seeking within the spiritual order explains why Pascal was so upset with Descartes and other Enlightenment thinkers who proposed that humanity could make great progress through carnal and intellectual means alone. Yet by excluding the order of the heart, this sort of progress could never include movement toward friendship with God or with people different from ourselves. Descartes neglected the highest faculty, the heart, making the Enlightenment a darkness in spiritual matters.

Within the carnal and intellectual orders, human effort is the normal means for achieving greatness, for example in sports or computer science. But within the spiritual order, human effort is not enough for advancement. Rather, revelation and movement from God is primary. This distinction is illustrated by Jesus' encounter with the Jewish ruler Nicodemus. Nicodemus seemed to live primarily within the carnal and intellectual realms, with primary concern to behave fastidiously as a highly respected teacher of the Jewish law. However, when Nicodemus came to Jesus at night, curious to learn about this man who was performing miraculous signs, Jesus replied:

> I tell you the truth, no one can see the kingdom of God unless he is born again. [John 3:3]

That is, an event performed by God is needed, which has nothing to do with the carnal or intellectual strivings of men. Because of Nicodemus' perspective, he was bewildered by Jesus' answer– it did not fit into the orders of being that he was accustomed to living in.

Saint Augustine, great in both knowledge (in the intellectual order) and wisdom (in the spiritual order), recognized that wisdom was of infinitely greater value than intellectual knowledge. He expresses this wonderfully in *The Confessions*:

> Lord God of truth, is any man pleasing to you for knowing such things? Surely a man is unhappy even if he knows all these things but does not know you; and that man is happy who knows you even though he knows nothing of them. And that man who knows both you and them is not the happier for them but only on account of you. [*The Confessions*, Chapter 5]

Augustine shares Pascal's thought that all the intellectual knowledge in the world is less valuable than heart knowledge of God; a massive accumulation of lines does not contribute any area to a plane. It is better to be ignorant and perceive God with the heart than to be an intellectual colossus but not perceive God.

Love is Supreme. Pascal concludes *Pensée* 308 by expressing the supreme worth of true charity:

> Out of all bodies together we could not succeed in creating one little thought. It is impossible, and of a different order. Out of all bodies and minds we could not extract one impulse of true charity. It is impossible, and of a different, supernatural order.

This fragment is immensely practical, suggesting that we regularly diagnose our lives to see if we are living for the order of the body and the mind at the expense of loving God and people. Am I so focused on my own physical comfort, health, and entertainment that I am distracted from building community with my neighbors? Am I so focused on getting my work done that I forget to be kind to my co-workers? In classifying true charity as belonging to the highest order, Pascal surely had in mind the Apostle Paul's words in his first letter to the Corinthians:

> And although I have the gift of prophecy, and understand all mysteries and knowledge, and though I have all faith, so that I could move mountains, but have not love, I am nothing. And though I bestow all my goods to feed the poor, and though I give my body to be burned, but have not love, it profits me nothing. [I Corinthians 13:2–3]

Furthermore, Paul writes about Christ's love surpassing knowledge [Ephesians 3:19] and transcending intellectual understanding. [Philippians 4:7]

Faith Through All Three Orders. While Pascal stresses the importance of living well in the spiritual order, we should not mistake him to be advising us to be concerned only with this activity as a separated pursuit, and thus to be unconcerned with living well in the carnal and intellectual orders. This separation would commit the error of sacred-secular dualism discussed in chapter 2. The point, line, and plane metaphor for the body, mind, and heart illustrate this error. As points are contained within lines and lines are contained within planes; so actions of the body and mind are contained within the spiritual order– for the body and mind are involved in submitting, in behaving courageously, in suffering with dignity, in loving one's neighbor, and in other activities associated with the heart. As such, a practical point from Pascal's theory of orders is that belief in God requires attention and effort in all three orders. A complete approach to faith entails thinking, bowing, and opening oneself to revelation:

> There are three ways to believe: reason, habit, inspiration. Christianity, which alone has reason, does not admit as its true children those who believe without inspiration. It is not that it excludes reason and habit, quite the contrary, but we must open our mind to the proofs, confirm ourselves in it through habit, while offering ourselves through humiliations [humbleness] to inspiration, which alone can produce the real and salutary effect. *Lest the Cross of Christ be made of none effect.* [I Corinthians 1:17] [*Pensée* 808]

Part V. Usefulness of God's Hiddenness for Believers

In Parts II and III of this chapter, we considered Pascal's thesis that the true teaching of Christianity fits squarely with human experience that God is hidden, and this concordance is an important mark of the truth of Christianity. In Part IV we began to address the practical impact of Pascal's thought for Christian seeking and living. We now turn full attention to the usefulness of God's hiddenness for believers. For this we need to return to the question of God's purpose in only revealing himself to those with the appropriate disposition to seek him. Pascal addresses this question in *Pensée* 446:

> If there were no obscurity man would not feel his corruption: if there were no light man could not hope for a cure. Thus it is not only right but useful for us that God should be partly concealed and partly revealed, since it is equally dangerous for man to know God without knowing his own wretchedness as to know his wretchedness without knowing God.

By "know God," I think Pascal means knowing that we are great because we are made by God, in his image, and thus have great dignity and capacity for excellence. The danger for a person who knows he is great, but not that he is also corrupt, is puffed up pride, and the danger for a person who knows his baseness, but not that there is a loving redeemer, is despair. In either case, it is not possible to find God– a self-reliant prideful man will not know his need for God, so that the offer of a redeemer is irrelevant, and a despairing man is unable to recognize God's reaching out to him with an offer of redemption. It is useful for us that God is obscure, then, because it helps us learn both of the two central truths that every Christian must know– one's need for God and that God offers a cure. If too much or too little light were provided, then we would know only one of these truths, and thus could not find God. Thus God's being hidden is necessary for us to find him– what a wonderful paradox Pascal observes!

Pascal elaborates this concept in *Pensée* 234:

> God wishes to move the will rather than the mind. Perfect clarity would help the mind and harm the will.
>
> Humble their pride.

Though Jesus Christ is infinitely great in the carnal and intellectual orders, he chose to display his greatness only in the spiritual order. He could have dazzled his onlookers with displays of strength and scientific genius, but he did not. Pascal observes the reason: for God to meet his objective to transform people to be like Christ, God wishes to move the will rather than the mind. Inspiration [through demonstrations of the beauty of God's moral excellence, love, and truth] and humiliation [humbleness] are the engines for this task, for which intellectual knowledge in itself has no locomotive power. In fact, in this *Pensée* Pascal warns that accumulating sheer intellectual knowledge about God tends to take us farther away from finding him, because it will make us proud. "How smart I am for discovering these truths that other, lesser, minds cannot grasp," the intellectual exclaims in his heart. This proud attitude encourages one to trust only in himself, rather than in God. Therefore it is good for us that the mysteries of God are impenetrable, as it helps us to acknowledge our limitations, and to incline us to a station of humility.

C.S. Lewis suggests it is a truism that the proud cannot know God:

> In God you come up against something which is in every respect immeasurably superior to yourself. Unless you know God as that– and, therefore, know yourself as nothing in comparison– you do not know God at all. As long as you are proud you cannot know God. A proud man is always looking down on things and people; and, of course, as long as you are looking down, you cannot see something that is above you. [*Mere Christianity*, Book 3, chapter 8]

Pascal goes on in *Pensée* 255 to note that God wished to make

> ...the Messiah recognizable to the good and unrecognizable to the wicked... For an understanding of the promised good depends on the heart, which calls good that which it loves.

Therefore it is treasuring God's true promises– not our own wished-for ends– that enable people to recognize Jesus as the Messiah.

Necessity of Humility for Knowing God. Pascal summarizes the necessity of humility for attaining knowledge of God in *Pensée* 378:

> True conversion consists in self-annihilation before the universal being whom we have so often vexed and who is perfectly entitled to destroy us at any moment, in recognizing that we can do nothing without him and that we have deserved nothing but his disfavor. It consists in knowing that there is an irreconcilable opposition between God and us, and that without a mediator there can be no exchange.

I believe Pascal's intent with this strong language was to move us to a position of humility, the only stance from which the Mediator can be received. These words reflect countless biblical admonitions from patriarchs, judges, prophets, apostles, and kings, including in Proverbs 3:34, "God opposes the proud and gives grace to the humble," and in Matthew 11:25 (and Luke 10:21), which records Jesus' prayer:

I thank you Father, Lord of heaven and earth, that You have hidden these things from the wise and prudent and have revealed them to babes.

In *The Confessions* Saint Augustine repeatedly referenced these verses when describing his journey to faith in Christ.

Things Invisible Are of Greatest Value. A final lesson I will draw is that things invisible are of greatest value. Various biblical passages suggest this, for example the author of Hebrews defines faith as "the evidence of things not seen" [Hebrews 11:1] and the Apostle Paul observes that he and fellow Christians "fix our eyes not on what is seen, but on what is unseen. For what is seen is temporary, but what is unseen is eternal." [2

Corinthians 4:18] The Bible also holds up invisible inner qualities as possessing great value, for example Peter proposes that,

> Your beauty should not come from outward adornment... Instead it should be that of your inner self, the unfading beauty of a gentle and quiet spirit, which is of great worth in God's sight. [I Peter 3:3–4]

Consistent with these verses, Pascal proposes that God uses visible gifts and visible signs to teach us about invisible gifts and invisible holiness that are of a higher order of value than the visible (the visible can be likened to points and lines, and the invisible to a plane, possessing a greater dimension of value). Pascal lists some of these visible signs and gifts in *Pensée* 275:

> Wishing to show that he could create a people holy with an invisible holiness and fill them with eternal glory, God created visible things. As nature is an image of grace, he created in natural gifts what he was to do in gifts of grace, so that men should judge him able to create invisible things from seeing created visible ones.

Here Pascal suggests that God's works in nature are signposts to help us understand the works of holiness that God will create and shape in the hearts of believers. Pascal suggests that God's historical work to save the people from the Flood, cause Israel to be born of Abraham, deliver them from out of Egypt, and lead them to a rich land, is an image of the delivery from sins that God will provide. The visible reality is the people being led to a rich land; the invisible reality is the people being redeemed from their sins and filled with invisible holiness and with eternal glory. In *Pensée* 275 Pascal makes clear his view that this invisible reality is of greater importance than the visible:

> God's objective was not to save them from the Flood and cause a whole people to be born of Abraham just to lead us into a rich land.

On the invisible meaning of physical miracles, Pascal cites Mark 2:10, which reports Jesus raising a paralytic from the dead:

But that you may know that the Son of Man has power on earth to forgive sins... I say to you, arise, take up your bed, and go to your house.

John Medina once commented that he views the miracles reported in the Gospels as "magic tricks" that point to deeper invisible miracles. The forgiveness of a sinner, the creation of a holy person, the infusion of eternal glory, these are the great invisible miracles that Jesus came to perform– the magic tricks were tutors to these invisible events. "Where is Thy God? (Psalm 42:3) Miracles reveal him, like a flash of lightning." [*Pensée* 878]

The temporally minded, Pascal suggests, are unable to read the visible signs as pointers to the invisible realities:

> ...for those deprived of faith and grace... all they see is obscurity and darkness. [*Pensée* 787]

Thus, unlike the spiritually minded Jonathan Edwards, who in his daily walks in New England could see in natural beauty pointers to spiritual realities of God's gracious love to his creatures, the temporally minded can only see in nature temporal physical beauty.

In fact, Pascal suggests that trying to prove God to skeptics from the works of nature is often counterproductive. To provide them with no greater proof than "the course of the moon and the planets" will give them "cause to think that the proofs of our religion are indeed feeble," and "nothing is more likely to bring it into contempt in their eyes." [*Pensée* 781] Moreover Pascal remarks in *Pensée* 463,

> It is a remarkable fact that no canonical author has ever used nature to prove God. They all try to make people believe in him. David, Solomon, etc., never said: 'There is no such thing as a vacuum, therefore God exists.' They must have been cleverer than the cleverest of their successors, all of whom have used proofs from nature. This is very noteworthy.

For believers, on the other hand, Pascal suggests that proofs from nature are helpful, because the living faith in their hearts makes them "see at once that everything which exists is entirely the work of the God they worship." Pascal reasoned that proofs from nature are feeble for unbelievers because such proofs *assume that God's works are intended to clearly blaze his divinity to all, regardless of their disposition*. Because God declared to hide himself, it is illogical to expect him to shine forth like the noonday sun. Thus, to Pascal the temporally minded are unable to read the clues in nature, and he would not have pursued the Intelligent Design approach to apologetics.

Can Only Know God Through Jesus Christ. Pascal's theology was Christo-centric, and I will close this chapter with two *Pensées* expressing his belief that God's veil of hiddenness is penetrated only through Jesus Christ. The last word from Pascal on why God is hidden is that God is revealed only through Jesus Christ.

> *God through Jesus Christ.* We know God only through Jesus Christ. Without this mediator all communication with God is broken off. Through Jesus we know God. All those who have claimed to know God and prove his existence without Jesus Christ have only had futile proofs to offer. But to prove Christ we have the prophecies which are solid and palpable proofs. By being fulfilled and proved true by the event, these prophecies show that these truths are certain and thus prove that Jesus is divine. In him and through him, therefore, we know God. Apart from that, without Scripture, without original sin, without the necessary mediator, who was promised and came, it is impossible to prove absolutely that God exists, or to teach sound doctrine and sound morality. But through and in Christ we can prove God's existence, and teach both doctrine and morality. Therefore Jesus is the true God of men.
>
> But at the same time we know our own wretchedness, because this God is nothing less than our redeemer from wretchedness. Thus we know God properly only by knowing our own iniquities.
>
> Those who have known God without knowing their own wretchedness have not glorified him but themselves. [*Pensée* 189]

> All those who seek God apart from Christ, and who go no further than nature, either find no light to satisfy them or come to devise a means of knowing and serving God without a mediator, thus falling into either atheism or deism, two things almost equally abhorrent to Christianity.
>
> But for Christ the world would not go on existing, for it would either have to be destroyed or be a kind of hell.

> If the world existed in order to teach man about God, his divinity would shine out on every hand in a way that could not be gainsaid: but as it only exists through Christ, for Christ, and to teach men about their corruption and redemption, everything in it blazes with proofs of these two truths. What can be seen on earth indicates neither the total absence, nor the manifest presence of divinity, but the presence of a hidden God. Everything bears this stamp...
>
> He must not see nothing at all, nor must he see enough to think that he possesses God, but he must see enough to know that he has lost him. For, to know that one has lost something one must see and not see: such precisely is the state of nature...[*Pensée* 449]

Being Grateful for What God Has Revealed. I find that I sometimes complain about why God does not make himself more plainly present and knowable to me. In *Pensée* 394, Pascal shows me how to turn my complaint into gratitude, reminding me I should be thankful for what God does reveal, rather than grumble about what he does not:

> Instead of complaining that God has hidden himself, you will give him thanks for revealing himself as much as he has, and you will thank him too for not revealing himself to wise men full of pride and unworthy of knowing so holy a God.

***Pensée* of the Day: Number 149**

The PoD sums up Pascal's central point that God is revealed to people who seek him with humility and with their hearts, whereas God is concealed to those who find their good and treasure in places other than God.

> There is enough light for those who desire only to see, and enough darkness for those of a contrary disposition.

This *Pensée* contains the biblical theme, expressed in both testaments, that God is found by all who seek him. For example, in the Old Testament Moses proclaims this promise to the Israelites:

But from there you will seek the Lord your God, and you will find Him if you seek Him with all your heart and with all your soul. [Deuteronomy 4:39]

And, in the New Testament Jesus proclaims it to all people:

For everyone who asks receives, and he who seeks finds, and to him who knocks it will be opened. [Matthew 7:8, Sermon on the Mount]

Synthesis Points of Chapter 6

1. Since data show God is hidden, a true religion must proclaim God's hiddenness and explain why. Pascal proposes Christianity does just this, a mark of its truthfulness.
2. God's revelation about himself is intentionally obscure, emitting enough light for seekers to find him and enough darkness for the indifferent and proud to not find him.
3. One's disposition determines whether God can be seen or not. God is revealed only to the humble who know their own wretchedness.
4. Pascal's theory of orders helps explain why some perceive Jesus Christ as the Messiah and God and others do not. Those who chiefly treasure worldly goods (material wealth, physical security, intellectual prestige) will not recognize him, while those who chiefly treasure spiritual goods (moral excellence, freedom from sin, freedom to serve and love) will recognize him.

7 THE WAGER

"The Christian ideal has not been tried and found wanting; it has been found difficult and left untried."
– G.K. Chesterton

"He is no fool who gives what he cannot keep to gain what he cannot lose."
– Jim Elliot

"We must resort to habit once the mind has seen where the truth lies, in order to steep and stain ourselves in that belief."
– Blaise Pascal, *Pensée* 821

Several commentators on the Wager think that Pascal would have placed it at the turning point of his case for the Christian faith. Dr. Krailsheimer (1980) suggests it would have been at the "hinge of the Apology… when the believer is ready to give Christianity a trial." If correct, Pascal intended his famous Wager argument for people whose ears were still ringing from his series of anthropological and other reasons about why Christianity was "worthy of respect," and are now open to exploring it This disposition of Pascal's interlocutor will turn out to be important for answering some common critiques of the Wager.

Outline of Chapter 7. This chapter is divided into four parts. In Part I we will go through the major parts of Pascal's Wager, leaving the last part, with its practical implications, to Part III. Critics have challenged the assumptions of the Wager, purporting that its conclusion is invalidated if certain assumptions are shown false. However, as developed in Part II, I believe it can be shown that the Wager argument is valid under realistic assumptions, supporting its robustness. In Part III we will address Pascal's purpose in the Wager, and its take-home point, which may be quite different from caricatures of it that you may have heard. I find Pascal's conclusion of the Wager surprising, constituting highly practical advice for how to go about seeking God and cultivating the reception of faith. The Wager has been subjected to storms of criticism, and in Part IV I will defend it against several major points of attack. Through studying many criticisms I have become convinced that the Wager stands up well.

With his Wager argument, Pascal appealed to his friends who had not had religious experiences that compelled them to believe in God, nor had they become convinced by traditional apologetics or by reason that God is, or is not. The Wager is for skeptical and open unbelievers. It is not a proof about God's existence; rather it is an argument that it is for the good/in the best interest of every person to pursue belief in God. It is a prudential argument, appealing to a gambler's hope to get a large return for as small a stake as possible, very different from most arguments in religion that try to demonstrate that beliefs are true or false.

Part I. Pascal's Wager: Rationality Compels Betting on God

Before considering Pascal's Wager *Pensée*, we begin with the miniature Wager, *Pensée* 387:

> *Order.* I should be much more afraid of being mistaken and then finding out that Christianity is true than of being mistaken in believing it to be true.

Pascal observes that every person makes a choice to believe or to disbelieve Christianity. Pascal's interlocutor, being biblically literate, would know the basic stakes and payoffs of this choice. In particular, he would know that Christianity promises perfectly happy life for believers and condemnation for unbelievers, and that salvation from condemnation happens only through faith in Jesus Christ. Pascal's listener would know John 14:6, which records Jesus saying, "No one comes to the Father but through me." Pascal considers the two possible mistakes– not believing Christianity if it is true, and believing it if it is false. He expresses greater fear at making the first mistake, because it would lead to condemnation, and loss of eternal happiness, whereas the second mistake would have a far milder consequence.

Let us now consider Pascal's Wager, *Pensée* 418, wherein Pascal explores in detail the stakes and payoffs of the choice. Pascal headed this fragment "infinity-nothing," fitting to its first line:

> The finite is annihilated in the presence of the infinite and becomes pure nothingness. So it is with our mind before God...

As a mathematician, with his opening sentence Pascal would have a numerical illustration in mind. For example, dividing a finite number by infinity leaves zero, annihilating the number.

Pascal begins the Wager by observing the "infinite" disproportion of Man's mind compared to God's. Because God is infinite and Man is finite, Man is inherently extremely limited in his capacity to understand God, and Man's reasoning alone cannot understand God's nature or his will. By establishing up front Man's lack of knowledge, Pascal suggests it is reasonable to be skeptical about if or who God is. This move is critical for the Wager's effectiveness, as Pascal's argument to come will be compelling only for the un-entrenched skeptic; it will not work for those who have decidedly closed their mind to the possibility of God. In addition, Pascal's argument will not require prior faith in God to accept it–it will require only honest skepticism and natural reason. Pascal makes this clear at the end of the Wager's introduction:

> Let us now speak according to our natural lights.
>
> If there is a God, he is infinitely beyond our comprehension, since, being indivisible without limits, he bears no relation to us. We are therefore incapable of knowing either what he is or whether he is. That being so, who would dare to attempt to an answer to the question? Certainly not we, who bear no relation to him.
>
> Who then will condemn Christians for being unable to give rational grounds for their belief, professing as they do a religion for which they cannot give rational grounds?...
>
> Let us then examine this point, and let us say: 'Either God is or he is not.' But to which view shall we be inclined? Reason cannot decide this question. Infinite chaos separates us. At the far end of this infinite distance a coin is being spun which will come down heads or tails. How will you wager? Reason cannot make you choose either, reason cannot prove either wrong...

Here is the wager, with the two possible bets having different payoffs. Pascal points out the fact of two possible realities, either the Christian God is true or he is not, and asks his interlocutor, "How will you wager?" The two bets and the two realities compose four possibilities: the Christian God is and I believe him; is and I do not believe him; is not and I believe him; and is not and I do not believe him.

Reason Cannot Decide the Better Bet. In the Wager's introduction, Pascal stresses that reason is unable to decide the better bet; his phrase "infinite chaos separates us" reinforces his point on the infinite distance between the mind of Man and God. Pascal believed reasoning, logic, and science cannot prove either theism or atheism, nor Christianity in particular. For persons who feel totally convinced based on reason, the Wager is superfluous; its power is for skeptics who recognize that their reasoning alone cannot finally decide the question.

One Must Wager. Pascal goes on:

> Do not then condemn as wrong those who have made a choice, for you know nothing about it. 'No, but I will condemn them not for having made this particular choice, but any choice, for, although the one who calls heads and the other are equally at fault, the fact is that they are both at fault: the right thing is not to wager at all.'

Here the interlocutor raises a third option besides theism and atheism– agnosticism– and proclaims it right to be agnostic, as an honest skeptic. Pascal replies:

> Yes, but you must wager. There is no choice, you are already committed.

That is, it is impossible to avoid wagering. The reason is that it is not possible to stay neutral forever. At death, an agnostic will have passively decided to bet against God. Pascal's answer that one must wager applies to many decisions in life. If I linger in indecision about whether to buy a house, someone else will buy it; if I wait too long to have biological children, my "hold off" will become "no." Someday I may develop arthritis, closing the window of opportunity to take up the guitar. We must wager because of our inevitable death that may strike at any moment, as Pascal vividly reminds us in *Pensée* 154: "...it is certain that we shall not be here for long, and uncertain whether we shall be here even one hour."

Peter Kreeft (1993) points to Pascal's ruling out agnosticism as the most critical part of the Wager. The reason is that outright atheism is unpopular and rare, whereas staying on the fence is popular and common. This is what many of the diverted and indifferent do.

Moreover, from his experience teaching philosophy to thousands of college students, Kreeft reports that once indifferent people are jolted from their neutral position onto the battlefield of theism versus atheism, most agree with the Wager.

Douglas Groothuis (2003) observes that the importance of wagering depends on whether Christianity is true. If Christianity is false, then not to wager is a fine decision, because it avoids making an error, and there is no penalty. But if Christianity is true, then not wagering has the same result as betting wrongly– infinite loss. Indeed, to Pascal wagering is urgent because, if one dies "without worshiping the true principle," [*Pensée* 158] then one is forever lost. William James concurs, calling the choice for or against God "momentous," because the stakes are high, the opportunity is unique, and the choice is irreversible (James, 1956).

Next, Pascal introduces the stakes of the gamble:

> Which will you choose then? Let us see: since a choice must be made, let us see which offers you the least interest. You have two things to lose: the true and the good; and two things to stake: your reason and your will, your knowledge and your happiness; and your nature has two things to avoid: error and wretchedness.

The two stakes are truth and happiness. The gambler wants to be both right and happy; recall Pascal's claim that every act of every person is done in the pursuit of happiness. [*Pensée* 148] The opposite of the two goals of attaining truth and happiness are expressed negatively as the two things to avoid, error and wretchedness.

The Stake of Happiness. Pascal continues the Wager:

> Since you must necessarily choose, your reason is no more affronted by choosing one rather than the other. That is one point cleared up. But your happiness? Let us weigh up the gain and the loss involved in calling heads that God exists. Let us assess the two cases: If you win, you win everything, if you lose you lose nothing.

Pascal repeats his point that reason is impotent to decide the bet, because it cannot prove the truth of theism or atheism. This moves the debate to the domain of happiness, to the question of which bet will bring more happiness? Christianity promises eternal happiness to those who believe; thus if you win, you win everything. But if atheism is true, then there is no eternity, no Heaven or Hell, only annihilation at death. Thus even if one bets wrongly on God, he loses nothing, because without eternity the reward is nothing. Against this point many have argued that there are finite rewards and losses if atheism is true, and I will discuss these fine points later. However, Pascal's assertion "if you lose you lose nothing" makes sense in light of the Wager's title, infinity-nothing, and its opening line, "The finite is annihilated in the presence of the infinite and becomes pure nothingness." A finite life span is infinitesimal and negligible compared to eternity; 83 years divided by an infinite number of years is zero.

Pascal next invokes decision theory and mathematical expectation to 'prove' it is rational to wager:

> Do not hesitate then; wager that he does exist. 'That is wonderful. Yes, I must wager, but perhaps I am wagering too much.' Let us see; since there is an equal chance of gain and loss, if you stood to win only two lives for one you could still wager, but supposing you stood to win three?
>
> You would have to play (since you must necessarily play) and it would be unwise of you, once you are obliged to play, not to risk your life in order to win three lives at a game in which there is an equal chance of losing and winning... But here there is an infinity of infinitely happy life to be won, one chance of winning against a finite number of chances of losing, and what you are staking is finite. That leaves no choice; wherever there is infinity, and where there are not infinite chances of losing against that of winning, there is no room for hesitation, you must give everything. And thus, since you are obliged to play; you must be renouncing reason if you hoard your life rather than risk it for an infinite gain, just as likely to occur as a loss amounting to nothing...
>
> Thus our argument carries infinite weight, when the stakes are finite in a game where there are even chances of winning and losing and an infinite prize to be won.
>
> This is conclusive and if men are capable of any truth this is it.

Example of a Compelling Bet. For an analogy with Pascal's argument that rationality demands betting on God, suppose you bet one dollar on a Seattle Mariners baseball game, and if the M's win, then you receive one billion dollars. Now, even in the M's worst year, when they play the best team, their chance of winning is still at least 5%, so that the potential reward dwarfs the small stake. The risk of one dollar is negligible in the hopes of such a large prize. But this prize Pascal speaks of is infinitely better than one billion dollars, it is an "infinity of infinitely happy life," that is, both infinite in quantity, everlasting, and infinite in quality, holiness, goodness, and happy fellowship with God and neighbor.

Decision Theory. Pascal is recognized as the Father of the field of probability, and his Wager argument is developed in the framework of decision theory, a discipline within probability. In fact, the Wager is original and distinctive for its role in founding decision theory. Ian Hacking (1975) describes it as "the first well-understood contribution to decision theory." I will now describe the Wager using this decision theoretic framework, which I hope will clarify Pascal's argument.

In a decision problem, the state of reality, and the decision of an agent, determine an outcome for the agent. Each possible outcome is assigned a utility, which represents the value the agent places on the outcome. The utility values can be arranged in a matrix, in which the columns represent the possible states of reality, and the rows represent the various decisions the agent can make.

The agent making the decision may not know the current state of reality, but can assign a probability value to each state. Then the agent can calculate the expected utility of each decision by a simple formula: sum over all states the state probability times the utility of that decision in that state. This is the standard formula for mathematical expectation encountered in Statistics & Probability 101. The decision with the highest expected utility is the most rational decision, the best decision, given these probabilities and utilities.

For a simple example, consider a game of flipping a fair coin. The two possible states of reality are that the coin will come up heads or tails, and the two possible decisions are to bet on heads or to bet on tails. Because the coin is fair, the probability of heads equals the probability of tails, one-half. Suppose the utilities on heads and tails are as shown in the decision matrix below. One dollar is staked, and if the wrong bet is made, the dollar is lost– thus the utility is –1 in both cells for the wrong bet. If you bet heads and the coin turns up heads, you win $2, and if you bet tails and the coin turns up tails, you win $1. The expected utility for betting heads is computed as $\frac{1}{2} \times 2 + \frac{1}{2} \times (-1) = \frac{1}{2}$, 50 cents, whereas the expected utility for betting tails is $\frac{1}{2} \times (-1) + \frac{1}{2} \times 1 = 0$. Because the utility is greater for betting on heads, a rational better must bet heads. In this example heads is a better bet because there is greater utility, i.e. payoff, assigned to the state of heads compared to tails.

	Coin Comes Up	
	Heads	Tails
Bet on Heads	Uhh = 2	Uht = –1
Bet on Tails	Uth = –1	Utt = 1

The Wager Decision Matrix. With this background, Pascal's Wager can be formulated as a decision matrix. The two possible realities are that the Christian God is true, or not. The actions are to believe, or not believe, in this God.

	State of Reality	
	God Exists	God Does Not Exist
Believe	Ube = ?	Ubne = ?
Do Not Believe	Unbe = ?	Unbne = ?

Once we specify the utilities Ube, Ubne , Unbe, Unbne , and the probability that the Christian God is true, p, the expected utilities for each action are given by the formulas

$$\text{Expected Utility for Betting on God} = \text{Ube}\times p + \text{Ubne}\times(1-p),$$
$$\text{Expected Utility for Betting Against God} = \text{Unbe}\times p + \text{Unbne}\times(1-p).$$

To calculate the expected utilities, we need to fill in the utilities of the matrix. Pascal's phrase "if you win, you win everything" puts Ube = infinity– an infinite reward. His phrase "if you lose you lose nothing" implies Ubne = 0. Pascal's phrase "The finite is annihilated in the presence of the infinite and becomes pure nothingness" explains why he sets Ubne = 0 instead of some nonzero and finite number. Under the assumption that there is positive probability that the Christian God is true ($p > 0$), the expected utility of betting on God is infinity plus zero, which equals infinity.

Now let us consider the utility of betting against God if God is true. In this case everything is lost. So we may put negative infinity for Unbe. Lastly, what is the utility of betting against God and being right? It is not totally clear what utility Pascal would assign here. However, it is clear that Pascal would not have assigned infinite utility, simply because if atheism is true then at death a person is annihilated– therefore any rewards are restricted to the finite lifespan and thus the utility is finite. Based on Pascal's reference to the finite becoming pure nothingness compared to infinity, my guess is that Pascal would have put Unbne = 0, but even if we assign Unbne = 1, or any finite value, it will make no difference to the expected utility. In fact, the expected utility in betting against God is negative infinity plus a finite value, which equals negative infinity! Thus we have

Expected Utility for Betting on God =
infinity×p + 0×(1–p) = infinity (perfect bliss)

Expected Utility for Betting Against God =
–infinity×p + Unbne ×(1–p) = –infinity (perfect anti-bliss)

The difference in the two expected utilities, infinite bliss for betting on God and infinite anti-bliss for betting against him, implies a rational person must bet on God (under decision theory). And it is not a close call– the expected utility is unimaginably greater for betting on God than for betting against him; this explains Pascal's statement "this argument carries infinite weight."

	State of Reality	
	God Exists	God Does Not Exist
Believe	Ube = infinity	Ubne = 0
Do Not Believe	Unbe = –infinity	Unbne = 0

Part II. The Wager Argument is Valid Under a Broad Range of Assumptions

This brings us to Part II, in which we will examine the assumptions of the Wager and see if it withstands scrutiny. I will make the following main points: 1) The Wager is robust to assumptions about utilities; 2) The Wager is robust to assumptions about risk tolerances; and 3) Reason cannot refute the key assumption of the Wager that the Christian God exists with probability greater than zero.

The Wager is Robust to Assumptions About Utilities. To begin the examination, we will evaluate the assumptions Pascal made about each of the four utilities Ube, Ubne , Unbe, Unbne . Pascal put Ube = infinity, which asserts that if Christianity is true, then there is infinite reward in believing Christ. This assumption is crucial for the Wager's conclusion, and is easily defended, for if biblical Christianity is true, then clear teachings of the Bible must be reliable, and the Bible states unequivocally that those who believe in Christ receive eternal reward (e.g., John 3:16). I have never heard a serious challenge about Pascal's assumption that Ube = infinity.

The values for Ubne , Unbe, and Unbne have been debated, and I will put forward a case that the Wager's conclusion still holds under much looser assumptions about these utilities than considered above. In fact, its conclusion still holds under the following objections.

First, some say that if the Christian God is false, then there is a cost to believing him. Pascal states that the truth is staked, and it seems right to count the loss of the truth as a cost. In addition, a person betting on a false God is wasting time and money attending worship services, praying and tithing, and may be needlessly forgoing pleasures. I am sympathetic to this point of view and think it fair to allow Ubne to be a finite negative number.

Second, the flip side of this point is that, if atheism is true, then there are finite rewards for not betting on God. In this scenario the bettor wins the reward of being right, as well as the freedom to pursue happy life without false guilt and arbitrary moral boundaries. Therefore the utility Unbne may be taken to be a finite positive number.

Thomas Morris (1992) suggests some additional costs of holding the Christian and atheist worldviews. Both positions sound presumptuous, because they claim to be absolutely true. Consequently, both sides invite ill treatment. This cost may be palpable in our current culture, as many interpret truth relativistically, and blame those who hold absolute positions as the cause of much human suffering.

Atheists have additional costs including having no source for meaning, dignity, and help for dealing with death. That is, atheism lacks the psychological advantages of believing in a loving and helping God. A mature atheist might reply that he has managed to develop his own source of comfort; however Pascal would not buy it, holding that an annihilationist worldview cannot possibly provide real comfort for the abyss of death. The prospect of annihilation is terrifying to most people– recall Pascal's vivid images, including this new one:

> The last act is bloody, however fine the rest of the play. They throw earth over your head and it is finished forever. [*Pensée* 165]

Morris considers another psychological edge of the Christian bet versus the atheist bet. If a Christian wins the bet, then after death, he will have the satisfaction of discovering he was right– in heaven he will enjoy consciousness and gains the truth. And if he loses the bet, because of annihilation he will never discover his error! Vice versa, if the atheist wins the bet, then he will never know it, because of the extinction of his consciousness at death. But if he loses, then he will experience the injury of a decisive disproof, since he retains consciousness in hell. Therefore there is an asymmetry regarding possible satisfaction in knowing the outcome– the Christian cannot be dissatisfied and the atheist cannot be satisfied. In Morris' words the Christian has a "final no-dissatisfaction guarantee" and the atheist has a "final no-satisfaction guarantee."

On the third utility Unbe, some say that if the Christian God is true, then there is no penalty for not believing him, that is Unbe = 0. I think this position is almost impossible to defend, because again, if the Christian God is true, then clear teachings of the Bible are trustworthy, and in many places Jesus teaches explicitly about hell, describing it with phrases such as "everlasting torment." The most straightforward reading of Scripture would conclude an infinitely bad utility Unbe = –infinity. However, for the rare Christian who disagrees that the Bible describes everlasting hell for unbelievers (much less rare in the post-Descartes era) and disagrees that losing heaven is an infinite loss, it is fitting to assign Unbe a finite negative number, or even a number as high as zero.

Summing up on robustness to utilities, under different perspectives the utilities Ubne , Unbe, and Unbne may take values different than supposed in the original Wager argument, which potentially work against the Wager's conclusion. Specifically, let us grant the atheist a finite cost for betting on God if he is false (–infinity < Ubne < 0), a finite reward for betting against God if he is false (0 < Unbne < infinity), and even that there is no cost for not betting on God if he is true (Unbe = 0). These concessions are generous, arguably pushing the assumptions as far in the atheist's favor as possible while staying within the bounds of logic. The point is this– even under these worst-case assumptions, the expected utility for betting on God is greater than the expected utility for betting against God– infinity compared to a finite number! This follows because the reward in Christianity is still infinity and the costs or rewards in favor of the atheist are finite. Therefore the Wager's conclusion is robust to loosened assumptions about the assigned utilities, supporting Pascal's statement (quite literally) that his Wager argument "carries infinite weight."

The Wager is Robust to Different Risk Tolerances. By basing rational betting on expected utility, Pascal implicitly assumes the bettor is risk tolerant. That is, the Wager assumes that a rational person would bet $100 at the chance of winning a million dollars if there is a fair chance of winning. This is indeed the case for a risk-friendly bettor most concerned about maximizing winnings. But a risk-averse bettor, whose primary concern is to minimize losses, might keep the $100 under his mattress. How does the Wager apply to the risk-averse?

To address this question, first note that if the utility Unbne for not betting on the true Christian God is negative infinity (as Pascal suggests), then the Wager applies equally well to the risk-averse. In fact, the more risk-averse a person is, the more he may be compelled to bet on God, as "fire insurance" against the ultimate loss of residing in hell! Furthermore, in the parable of the talents Jesus suggests that God expects his servants to accept risks in investing their talents– the master rewards the servant who works to double his talents, but rejects the unprofitable servant who buries his talent in the ground [Matthew 25:14–30] – hence "avoiding risk" can be quite risky! Therefore, if one allows for the existence of hell, then the Wager holds for any level of risk-tolerance.

Under a Christian theology that excludes hell and supposes the loss of heaven is only finite, the penalty for failing to bet on the true God is a finite negative number. In this case, whether it is compelling for the risk-averse to wager on God depends on the utilities Ubne and Unbe. If the utility for betting on God if he is false is greater than the utility for not betting on God if he is true (i.e., Ubne > Unbe), then he should still wager. As discussed above, this assumption is highly plausible, because if Christianity is true, then not betting on God forgoes infinite and everlasting joy, meaning, peace, happiness, etc.; whereas betting on God if he is false forgoes certain pleasures including instant gratification, and involves the loss of the truth, money, time, etc. While serious, these latter losses are of a lower order of importance than the infinite losses incurred for the atheist, because they last only for a person's finite life-span. Nevertheless, some persons with a peculiar psychology may yet believe Unbe < Ubne , and under this assumption plus a theology that holds heaven is finite and hell does not exist, then indeed the Wager fails for the risk-averse. However, because Christian doctrine must be accepted as true if the Christian God is true, this scenario may be impossible. Therefore the issue of risk heterogeneity does not pose a serious obstruction to the Wager.

The Wager Requires a Positive Probability that God Exists ($p > 0$). Third, many have pointed out that the Wager relies crucially on the assumption that there is positive probability that God exists. For if this probability is zero, then the expected utility of betting on God is calculated as zero times infinity, whose value is indeterminate. In this case decision theory is uninformative about whether it is rational to bet on God.

A rare sub-group of atheists, so-called "strong atheists," are so convinced of atheism that they do assign zero probability, and for these the Wager argument does not work. However, most atheists, including famous proponents such as Bertrand Russell, are not so bold– they may conclude that it seems "very unlikely" that God exists, but will admit, as Russell did in his book *Why I am not a Christian* (1957), that no one can prove that God is not. If Pascal's interlocutor accepts positive probability that God exists, however, he may still object that if this probability is very low, then it may not be worth wagering even with an infinite prize to win. If the available evidence strongly favors atheism, then it may be more honest to bet on atheism, and perhaps finite happiness can be won. Thus for some skeptics, what is really needed for Pascal's Wager to be convincing is that Christianity be "rationally plausible"– true with a reasonably high chance– not just remotely possible (Groothuis, 2003).

Pascal Argues that $p \geq ½$. In the *Pensées* Pascal considers in detail many clues and evidences for Christianity, and argues vigorously that, although Christianity cannot be proved, it is rationally plausible. In fact, in *Pensée* 835 Pascal explicitly states his view that an honest look at the clues and evidence suggest at least a 50% chance that God is true:

> The prophecies, even the miracles and proofs of our religion, are not of such a kind that they can be said to be absolutely convincing, but they are at the same time such that it cannot be said to be unreasonable to believe in them. There is thus evidence and obscurity, to enlighten some and obfuscate others. But the evidence is such as to exceed, or at least equal, the evidence to the contrary, so that it cannot be reason that decides

us against following it, and therefore can only be concupiscence and wickedness of heart.

C.S. Lewis is an example of a committed atheist who, despite not wishing to believe Christianity, found himself persuaded by reason (in Lewis' case from reading G.K. Chesterton) that the evidence for Christianity exceeds the evidence against it.

Pascal's Case for Rational Plausibility (p >> 0). However, one may simply disagree with Pascal on this point, and indeed many atheist critics have objected that the probability of theism is very low. In reading several of these critiques, it is striking that frequently the critic seems to think that Pascal is asking the seeker to bet on God solely based on the decision theoretic argument; to believe solely for the chance of an infinite prize, without invoking their reason in the decision. Douglas Groothuis points out that this reading of Pascal's Wager hinges on weighing heavily the following phrase from the prologue: "Reason cannot decide this question. Infinite chaos separates us." Taken in isolation, this statement can make it seem that Pascal is proposing a non-rational Kierkegaardian leap of faith.

However, this "blind leap of faith" objection loses its basis when we consider that the Wager is one component within Pascal's comprehensive apologetic project. As we have noted the Wager likely would have followed the first part of the *Pensées*, which was designed to establish the rational plausibility of Christianity. If indeed the Wager were placed at the end of the first part, then an interlocutor still engaged at this point will have already accepted Christianity's rational plausibility, otherwise he would have abandoned the dialogue! Therefore, this common critique suffers from an isolated analysis of *Pensée* 418, which fails to place it in the context of the whole *Pensées*. In fact, in the Wager *Pensée* itself Pascal acknowledges that there is evidence supporting Christianity's rational plausibility. To his interlocutor's question, "But is there really no way of seeing what the cards are?" Pascal replies, "Yes. Scripture and the rest, etc;" and near the end of the Wager, Pascal notes that "reason impels you to believe." Once the context is accounted for many criticisms of the Wager are weakened or eliminated.

Relaxing the Assumption that p > > 0. Now I will explore the fine point about whether the assumption that p >> 0 (i.e., that p is not infinitesimally small) can be relaxed such that the Wager argument is still valid. This subsection may be safely skipped if you have an allergic reaction to mathematics. I will suggest that Pascal's Wager anticipates later mathematical work on cardinality and infinitesimals, and that, by combining Pascal's definition of mathematical expectation with this later work, the Wager can be shown to be valid even if p is assumed infinitesimally small (heuristically, an *infinitesimal* is a number greater than zero that is so small that it is smaller than any positive number). In his statement "Even though there were an infinite number of chances, of which only one were in your favor," Pascal seems to address the case of an infinitesimal p. This p can be likened to one divided by the cardinality (i.e., number of elements) of the set of counting numbers, $1/\aleph(C)$.

Later in the same sentence, Pascal proposes that, "...you would be acting wrongly" in refusing to stake your life in such a game "if there were an infinity of infinitely happy life to be won." The fact that Pascal describes the number of chances of God not existing as "infinite," using this word once, but describes the reward for betting on the true God as an "infinity of infinitely happy life," suggests we can liken the utility for betting on the true God to the cardinality of a set of numbers that is larger than the set of whole numbers, for example the cardinality of the real numbers, $\aleph(R)$. The expected utility then equals $\aleph(R)/\aleph(C)$, which, as Georg Cantor proved in 1891, equals infinity! Given Pascal's mathematical genius, I speculate that in this argument Pascal anticipates Cantor's work; for example Cantor's theorem establishes that the set of all subsets of counting numbers is uncountably infinite, which implies the existence of an infinity of infinities. Under this interpretation, even if Pascal's interlocutor is very conservative, in supposing that the probability that God exists is infinitesimally small, then based on decision theory and Cantor's theorem it is still rationally compelling to bet on God!

This argument is based on likening the reciprocal probability that God exists to an infinite number that is smaller than another infinite number that measures the degree of happy life that is promised. It can be justified by the Bible's description of heaven as being infinite in both the quality of happiness and in the duration of this blissful state. Hence infinity of infinitely happy life to be won aptly describes the Bible's promised reward. The seventh stanza of *Amazing Grace* expresses this infinity of infinities:

When we've been there ten thousand years,
Bright shining as the sun,

We've no less days to sing God's praise
Than when we'd first begun.

Part III. Purpose of Pascal's Wager: Induce a Spiritual Experiment

In Part III we will explore the warm heart of the Wager, the passionate purpose for which Pascal wrote it, to inspire people to seek God through a spiritual experiment. We pick up where we left off in the Wager *Pensée* 418. By this point Pascal's listener has accepted Pascal's argument that, for the sake of happiness, he must wager. But he objects:

> 'Yes, but my hands are tied and my lips are sealed; I am being forced to wager and I am not free; I am being held fast and I am so made that I cannot believe. What do you want me to do then?'

Even though Pascal's interlocutor now sees he would be wise to bet on God, he cannot make himself believe. As we will see, Pascal agrees that belief is not under direct voluntary control, and all of the commentators I have read on the Wager concur. Belief is not something that can be drummed up, it can only happen as a response to evidence; to believe something it must seem true to a person. To illustrate this, suppose a million dollar prize is offered to you if you believe there is a white rhinoceros in your living room. No matter how much you would like the money, you will not be able to believe it, because neither your senses nor any other faculty suggest to you that it can be reality.

Purpose of Pascal's Wager: Induce a Spiritual Experiment. In response to his interlocutors' question of what can he do to believe, Pascal answers:

> 'That is true, but at least get it into your head that, if you are unable to believe, it is because of your passions, since reason impels you to believe and yet you cannot do so. Concentrate then not on convincing yourself with multiplying proofs of God's existence but by diminishing your passions.'

These passions Pascal speaks of include pride, lust, fear, greed, and it is the habitual engagement in them, Pascal proposes, is what really holds the objector back from faith in God (recall Pascal suggests concupiscence has become Man's second nature). I suspect Pascal had in mind Saint

Augustine's journey of faith. In his spiritual autobiography, Augustine describes at length how even though in his head he was certain that Christianity was true, he felt paralyzed to engage in a life of service and love for God, because he found his habits of lust, vanity, and lying in his work as a teacher of rhetoric as overpowering chains holding him back. He finally broke free from these chains when his eyes fell on Romans 13:13–14:

> Let us walk properly, as in the day, not in revelry and drunkenness, not in lewdness and lust, not in strife and envy. But put on the Lord Jesus Christ, and make no provision for the flesh, to fulfill its lusts. [*The Confessions*, Book 8, Chapter 12].

Pascal elaborates his recommendation to diminish one's passions as a path to making oneself receptive to faith in *Pensée* 816:

> 'I should soon have given up a life of pleasure,' they say, 'if I had faith.' But I tell you: 'You would soon have faith if you gave up a life of pleasure. Now it is up to you to begin. If I could give you faith, I would. But I cannot, nor can I test the truth of what you say, but you can easily give up your pleasure and test whether I am telling the truth.' [*Pensée* 816]

Here Pascal acknowledges that no one can make someone believe, only God generates faith. Nevertheless, people can help remove barriers to seeking and believing, especially the addictions that blind (Kreeft, 1993). Notice the two suggested experiments. Whereas the interlocutor proposes that if he had faith, then he would give up pleasures, Pascal proposes the opposite– if his interlocutor gives up pleasures, then he will discover faith. The first experiment is impossible, Pascal observes, because the condition of faith is not in the control of the investigator. But the second experiment can be conducted– irrespective of a man's beliefs, he can change his behavior as the experimental condition. Recall that Pascal is engaging his friends who share his value and interest in performing experiments– thus Pascal is appealing to his interlocutor's worldview that embraces experimentation as an appropriate means for discovering truth. Pascal challenges his friend to consider whether he really believes in experimentation, or at bottom he betrays his own worldview. To be coherent, you should be willing to try this experiment, Pascal presses. And the sub-current of this *Pensée* carries Pascal's rebuff of his friend's excuse that his reason holds him back from seeking. It is your heart that is unwilling to engage, and not the reason– this lack of will stems from moral issues– too lazy, too addicted to pleasure, too proud (*Pensée* 835).

Returning to the Wager *Pensée* Number 418, Pascal continues his reply, suggesting that to find God his interlocutor must add to the discipline of 'diminishing his passions' the discipline of 'acting as if he believes:'

> 'You want to find faith and you do not know the road. You want to be cured of unbelief and you ask for the remedy: learn from those who were once bound like you and who now wager all they have. These are people who know the road you wish to follow, who have been cured of the affliction of which you wish to be cured: follow the way that they began. They behaved just as if they did believe, taking holy water, having masses said, and so on.'

I believe here we have the heart of the Wager, Pascal's intention in it– he wished to move people to begin a spiritual experiment, to try out the Christian faith, not abstractly in the mind alone, but in body and action.

As part of his recommended spiritual experiment, Pascal advises his listener to imitate Christians who have found their way, to look to them as models. If Pascal's model Augustine can be cured of the afflictions of his passions after more than a decade of struggling, then so can you, Pascal suggests. In his books *True Heroism* (1995) and *Beyond Identity* (1998), Dick Keyes observes the importance of models in shaping human actions, for instance writing:

> Many people have no conscious philosophy of life, but have models– heroes and heroines– that define them to the extent that they see the world through the model's eyes... Our models exert tremendous control over our lives, often more than our morals do. [*Beyond Identity*, pages 107 and 110].

Pascal's Advice: Imitate Other Christians. Keyes (1998) also observes that biblical writers call believers to imitate the faith of those who imitate Christ. The Apostle Paul calls the Christians in Corinth to "Be imitators of me as I am of Christ," [1 Corinthians 11:1] and the author of Hebrews asks believers to "Remember your leaders, those who spoke to you the word of God; consider the outcome of their life and imitate their faith." [Hebrews 13:7] Furthermore Paul urges the Colossians, "Do not lie to one another, seeing that you have put off the old nature with its practices and have put on the new nature, which is being renewed in knowledge after the image of the creator." [Colossians 3:9–10]

In the Wager *Pensée* and in *Pensée* 816 we can see Pascal's advice to his friend to act like a believer, to go through the motions as if he believed. Peter Kreeft (1993) refers to this approach to faith-development as "growing faith by planting good works." Though this is backwards from the normal sequence, Pascal proposes it has practical power. Love your neighbors, sign up to volunteer, put yourself in a small group Bible study, do more dishes around the house; these activities can germinate faith. Kreeft describes the effect of such an experiment in these terms:

> Love of God in action or love of neighbor in action will release the irrational chains that bind us, will open our eyes and enable us to believe. For they will diminish selfish passions, which are the chains that bind us and blind us like an addiction.

And C.S. Lewis suggests that love in action is the first step; it may be only later that we also feel love:

> Do not waste time bothering whether you 'love' your neighbor; act as if you did. As soon as we do this we find one of the great secrets. When you are behaving as if you loved someone, you will presently come to love him. [*Mere Christianity*, Book 3, chapter 9]

Lewis also observes that acting as if you believe is a "good kind of pretending," because "very often the only way to get a quality in reality is to start behaving as if you had it already." "That is why children's games are so important," suggests Lewis, because "all the time, they are hardening their muscles and sharpening their wits, so that the pretence of being grown-up helps them to grow up in earnest." [*Mere Christianity*, Book 4, chapter 7]

Incidentally, undergoing Pascal's experiment can help one to accept the Wager's key assumption that the probability that God exists exceeds zero. Giving up living only for oneself and initiating active love of neighbor can lead one to discover the plausibility of God. It is only pride and entrenched-ness, a refusal to seek, which allows one to conclude with certainty, as strong atheists do, that the probability of God's existence must be zero.

Pascal's Advice: Act as if You Believe. On a similar thought train, Thomas Morris worked to correct the mistaken impression of some that Pascal's Wager aims to spark immediate belief in God. Instead, in Morris' words,

> He intended it only to issue in a certain form of behavior, which would erode obstacles to belief, obstacles to be found in our emotions, attitudes, passions, and habitual ways of thinking and acting. He believed that religious behavior and religious thought would, at least over the long run, open the way to religious insight... Pascalian wagering is best viewed as a determined attempt to cultivate those capacities on the part of people who, because of the great values involved, are gambling their lives, hoping for success.

Morris also helpfully suggests that it should not seem odd to us that investment is required before all of the evidence is in, because this is the norm in many areas of life. One chooses a college major unsure that it will durably capture her interest; one chooses a spouse unsure that he will be a good parent; one moves across the country unsure that life will be better there. In other areas of life we are willing to seek after a good while holding doubt, why not in the area of seeking God?

Returning to the Wager *Pensée*, Pascal next suggests that behaving as if you believe "will make you believe quite naturally, and will make you more docile." This may sound like Pascal is recommending blindly and dumbly accepting changes in one's beliefs, but I do not think this was Pascal's intent. Rather, I suggest Pascal meant two things with the word docile. The first is teachability, openness, receptiveness– the opposite of entrenched-ness. Being teachable is a virtue and is necessary for growth, in religion or in any other area, and in *Pensée* 816 Pascal proposes that the only way to be receptive is to diminish ones passions. Douglas Groothuis (2003) defends Pascal against the charge of recommending self-inflicted brainwashing as a way to belief:

> Pascal's recommendation of religious practices does not necessarily involve brainwashing, but rather a vulnerability to persuasion through various religious practices that may serve to temper the passions and

thus open one to certain claims not otherwise convincing and to experiences not otherwise possible.

In other words, Pascal suggests conducting a legitimate hypothesis test, not a thoughtless mechanical exercise.

Second, I think with the word docile Pascal points to the importance of human 'organs' other than the mind for cultivating faith– the body (i.e., the habituating 'machine') and the heart are of primary importance. Recall in *Pensée* 821 Pascal insists that habit has a greater influence on beliefs and actions than reason:

> For we must make no mistake about ourselves: we are as much automaton as mind... Proofs only convince the mind; habit provides the strongest proofs and those that are most believed. It inclines the automaton, which leads the mind unconsciously along with it.

The Hungarian philosopher of science Michael Polanyi's concept of tacit knowledge helps explain the vital role of habit for developing a depth of understanding in some area (*The Tacit Dimension*, 1967). For example, Polanyi suggests that the only way for a person to become a master violinmaker is for her to watch and imitate another master violinmaker– it will not happen through reading books about violin making. Expertise is transmitted by physical imitation, through honing a physical habit. Master saxophonist Sonny Rollins observes that when practicing a composition, he learns everything about its structure and form, but when performing, he forgets all that, and "tries to let the music play me... this produces my best work." [Interview on National Public Radio, April 27, 2007] Likewise, habitually going to church, habitually reflecting on Bible passages, etc., can "make you believe quite naturally." Aristotle went so far as to consider habit to be a central attribute of human identity:

> We are what we repeatedly do. Excellence then is not an act but a habit.

Pascal emphasizes that the heart, like habit, also plays a greater role in cultivating faith than reason. In fact, to Pascal the heart is the essential organ– the receiver and dwelling-place of faith.

> That is why those to whom God has given religious faith by moving their hearts are very fortunate, and feel quite legitimately convinced, but to those who do not have it we can only give such faith through reasoning, until God gives it by moving their heart, without which faith is only human and useless for salvation. [*Pensée* 110]

Purpose of Pascal's Wager: Induce a Spiritual Experiment. Pascal goes on in the last section of the Wager *Pensée*:

> 'Now what harm will come to you from choosing this course? You will be faithful, honest, humble, grateful, full of good works, a sincere, true friend... It is true you will not enjoy noxious pleasures, glory and good living, but will you not have others?
>
> 'I tell you that you will gain even in this life, and that at every step you take along this road you will see that your gain is so certain and your risk so negligible that in the end you will realize that you have wagered on something certain and infinite for which you have paid nothing.'
>
> 'How these words fill me with rapture and delight!'

Pascal suggests there are additional utilities added to Ube for correctly betting on the Christian God, which serves as further encouragement for wagering– even in this life there are rewards. This is the "already" part of the "already-not yet" tension of the kingdom of God– Jesus and the Apostle Paul taught that Christ's new kingdom began with Jesus' life on earth, but it has not yet been completed/perfected. Christians experience joy and peace now, as adopted sons and daughters into Christ's loving family, yet they continue to struggle against sin and evil that still holds power in the world. They are not yet completely freed from sinfulness to goodness. Pascal observes this already-not yet reality in *Pensée* 917:

> The Christian's hope of possessing an infinite good is mingled with actual enjoyment as well as with fear, for, unlike people hoping for a kingdom of which they will have no part because they are subjects, Christians hope for holiness, and to be freed from unrighteousness, and some part of this is already theirs.

Some data on human experience support the rewards for Christians that are already theirs. For one example, a centerpiece of the Christian faith is the practice of forgiveness, and this practice apparently has health benefits. A Harvard Women's Health Watch study (2005) found that forgiveness– defined by doctors as letting go of anger or resentment-reduced stress, improved heart health, strengthened relationships, reduced pain, and increased happiness. More generally, New Testament authors proclaim the abundant Christian life that bursts with fruit of the Spirit including peace, joy, and mirth. [Galatians 5:22–23]

Pascal concludes the Wager *Pensée* with a personal postscript, letting his friend know that he has been praying for him, and hoping good for him:

> 'If my words please you and seem cogent, you must know that they come from a man who went down upon his knees before and after to pray this infinite and indivisible being, to whom he submits his own, that he might bring your being also to submit to him for your own good and for his glory.'

Here Pascal reveals his beneficent motivation in composing the Wager. Pascal ardently hoped his interlocutor, too, will come to believe and share in his rapture and delight.

Conclusion of Part III. To conclude Part III, I would like to emphasize that to understand Pascal's Wager it is important to recognize that Pascal's intent was not to instantly convert his listener, but rather to move him to begin a spiritual experiment. Many critics miss this crucial point, and because they see that it is psychologically impossible to believe something just because it offers pie in the sky and partial pie on earth, they dismiss the Wager. Their critique knocks down a straw man, however, as nowhere in the *Pensées* does Pascal recommend believing dumbly or making a blind leap of faith; rather Pascal acknowledges that accepting the rational plausibility of the Christian religion is a pre-requisite for wagering. Moreover Pascal dedicated the second part of the *Pensées* to provide clues and evidence for rationale plausibility, which we will discuss in chapter 8.

Part IV. Responding to Criticisms of The Wager

In *On Pascal* Douglas Groothuis suggests that in order to ground the Wager, Pascal needs the "rough plausibility of what he has argued concerning the intellectual respectability of Christianity." Jon Elster also suggests the need for Pascal to establish the "real possibility" of

Christianity (*The Cambridge Companion to Pascal*, 2003). Groothuis and Elster point out, rightly I believe, that even if a course of action has infinite utility for gaining bliss or avoiding misery, it must be a real possibility to be worth betting on– not merely conceivable.

To illustrate this point, let's say I am told by a fortune teller that there is a bogey man living in my bedroom closet, who will murder me this evening unless I pay the fortune teller $49.99 for magical protection. Although the stakes are very high, I will not give the man a dime, because I do not believe the scenario is a real possibility. Betting on something when there appears to be no chance of winning is at the expense of one's intellectual rectitude.

This brings us to the first critique of the Wager that we will address, that Pascal failed to provide a rational criterion for deciding whether God is a real possibility versus merely conceivable.

Critique 1: Pascal Provided no Rational Criterion for God's Real Possibility. Professor Elster criticized the Wager for not providing an explicit rational criterion (a "causal model") for deciding whether Christianity is a real possibility. Without such a criterion, Elster argues, it is reasonable to conclude that the probability that God exists is indeterminate. If this probability is taken to be zero, then, as we have seen, the Wager is not compelling.

A particular version of this critique asks whether Pascal provided a rational criterion for deciding plausibility of life after death. For many today an afterlife does not seem like a real possibility. Articulating this position in *Why I Am Not a Christian*, Bertrand Russell notes that neuroscientists had shown that consciousness depends on the physical equipment of neurons and other material things. Without proper functioning of the physical apparatus, consciousness does not happen. At death, the neural apparatus dies, and the direct logical conclusion, Russell suggests, is that consciousness dies. To Russell, then, the afterlife is not a logical possibility.

One reply to Russell is that miracles are possible– if the God of the Bible is real, then he is able to preserve a person after death even if the physical apparatus of consciousness dies. Russell himself did not absolutely rule out such miracles, although he considered them to be only remotely possible, failing a rational plausibility criterion. Pascal might retort that Man's capacity for reasoning is too weak to provide solid ground for concluding remote possibility: "It is not possible to have reasonable grounds for not believing in miracles." [*Pensée* 568] However, rather than answering the critique, *Pensée* 568 turns it around, suggesting that the atheist does not provide an explicit rational criterion for the annihilationist position.

Response to Critique 1: Pascal Provided Rational Criteria in the Pensées for Christianity Being a Real Possibility. I agree with Elster that the Wager argument would be bolstered by explicit criteria for judging the rational plausibility of Christianity, and that Pascal did not provide explicit criteria in the Wager fragment itself. However, when considering the *Pensées* as a whole, it becomes evident that Pascal appreciated the necessity of establishing real possibility, and in fact devoted major portions of the *Pensées* to describing explicit criteria.

Pascal emphasized the fulfillment of prophecies and miracles as signs that make Christianity plausible, as we will expand upon in chapter 8. The many *Pensées* on miracles indicate that Pascal would not believe unless there was some evidence that Jesus could do supernatural things, such as preserve consciousness after death. Miracles by Jesus are a proof-of-concept, if you will, that he is able to do the things he claims to do– ranging from raising people from the dead to forgiving their sins. In addition, Pascal probed the history of the Jewish people as evidence for the truthfulness of Christianity. And Pascal's signature argument for rationale plausibility is the unique success of the Christian model to accurately explain the complex data about the paradoxical human condition.

Response to Critique 1: Real Possibility is Felt as Well as Thought. While Pascal recognized the need to establish plausibility criteria, he suggests that apologists err when they center on developing such criteria (as most apologists do). A more effective approach addresses Man holistically, accounting for his feelings, fears, fancies, frailties, etc., in addition to his thought. Recall Pascal's awesome demonstration that most people are influenced more by their passions and imaginations than by their reason. Further recall Pascal's expression of the feebleness of proofs of God from nature, and the necessity of God's revelation– a lightning bolt– to reach people. Moreover, in his work on why God hides, Pascal suggests that most people will never come to assured knowledge of God from intellectual study and empirical observation alone. As such an apologetic approach that seeks primarily to develop a rational criterion for knowing that God is a real possibility is incompatible with Pascal's kind of apologetics, which stress that, on its own, human reason is incapable of finding God.

Indeed, Pascal's strategy for bringing his interlocutor to see that God is a real possibility is based on the demonstration that Christianity is in better synchronicity with the human experience than any other worldview. Pascal brings scores of vivid pictures to his viewer, each one conveying a flash of Christian resonance with an aspect of human experience. These artful blazes wield a powerful cumulative effect, leading many to be convinced, in both mind and heart, that it is not ridiculous to think that God might really be. In addition, I suspect that many of the critics not only fail to appreciate that Pascal dealt with the real possibility question extensively elsewhere in the *Pensées*, but also incorrectly elevate the question of rational plausibility to a place of pivotal importance in the whole Wager. Such critics, influenced by the Enlightenment worldview, may fail to recognize Pascal's intention in making rational plausibility the background, but not the focus of the Wager. Rather, the Wager appeals to Man's basic desire to be happy, which, Pascal purports, has far greater influence on a man than his reasoning. Pascal's goal was not to prove a theorem about the real possibility of God, but rather to set people on fire to seek God.

Critique 2: Pascal Contradicts Himself by Believing Both in Predestination and in Free Will to Choose to Believe/Wager. Another critique from Professor Elster has to do with the apparent incongruence between Pascal's belief in predestination, and the Wager's pitch to the skeptic that he should make the effort to seek after God. That is, if it is God's election "before we were born" that decides whether a person will ultimately develop faith, then what is the use in telling someone they should make efforts to find God? This point is a common critique against the doctrine of predestination, which Christians have been answering since before the time of Augustine.

Dick Keyes provides insight into how election and human responsibility can coexist. Keyes observes that the Bible has much to say about both God's sovereignty and Man's responsibility, but does not provide an explanation for how they co-exist. Keyes uses the metaphor of parallel lines– the Bible presents these truths side by side, as two tracks. Many have tried to devise a way to make the lines intersect, but we should be wary to do so, Keyes suggests, because the Bible describes it as a mysterious paradox that cannot be resolved by human reasoning. Attempts to make the lines meet inevitably constitute oversimplifications and lead to a different gospel than biblical Christianity– thus it is better to humbly accept the mystery than to force a fully explanatory, but incorrect, model.

Pascal likely would have liked an alternative metaphor from Reverend Leonard Verduin, "Truth is elliptical; it always has two foci." An ellipse is a conic section, the subject of Pascal's first publication at age 17; a publication that made Descartes acknowledge Pascal's genius. One can draw an ellipse by putting a marker in a loop of string that surrounds two push-pins; moving the marker draws an oval that tends toward a circle as the push-pins become closer. Thus, an ellipse is defined by two fixed points (i.e., foci), as the set of points in a plane such that every point has the same sum of distances to the two foci. The two foci represent the two Biblical truths of God's sovereignty and human responsibility. For every 'point' in the Bible, the distance to one of these truths may be shorter, seemingly supporting it more than the other, but the sum of the two distances is constant. As such the Bible is like an ellipse that is defined by and encompasses two balanced truths. In the eighteenth *Provincial Letter* Pascal expresses his belief in the co-truths of God's sovereignty and Man's responsibility, "Yet this infallibility of God's operation [to touch man by his mercy and make him do what he wants] in no way impairs Man's natural liberty, through the secret and wonderful ways in which God effects this change, so excellently explained by St. Augustine, and which dispel all the imaginary contradictions conceived by the enemies of efficacious grace to exist between the sovereign power of grace over free will and the ability of free will to resist grace."

This response answers Professor Elster's critique, because Pascal certainly had in mind both the many Scriptures that speak of God's election of believers and the many Scriptures urging people to vigorously seek God, and Pascal made great use of paradox in his apologetics. Moreover, as we considered in chapters 3 and 4, Pascal was acutely aware of reason's arrogant inclination to generate a presumptuous and overreaching solution to a difficult problem. Therefore I suspect that Pascal had deep insight into how election and human effort can stand together, and it would be fascinating to examine what his body of writings contribute to this discussion.

Furthermore, the Bible not only describes people seeking God as the means to finding faith, it describes God seeking people to generate their faith. The Gospels depict God going after the lost sheep and looking for the lost coin (e.g., Luke 15); the Apostle John reports Jesus standing at the door and knocking; (Revelation 3:20) and the whole Bible narrates God's persistent seeking of people to turn their hearts back to him. Throughout the Bible God's plan for creating and sustaining faith is described as a relational process that depends both on God's seeking people and on their response.

Critique 3: Many Gods Objection. Perhaps the most common and challenging critique of the Wager is the so-called many gods objection. Marilyn vos Savant, who is reported (on the internet) to have the highest IQ in the world, summarizes the Wager argument as simply saying that one should believe in the religion that offers the most rewards. Thus, the many gods objection is that the Wager argument can be used to justify any religion that makes wonderful promises, which make it unpersuasive for betting on the Christian religion in particular. For example, Diderot in the 1700s raised this charge, commenting, "An Imam [an Islamic leader, akin to a Christian priest] could reason just as well this way."

Islam makes for an instructive comparator to Christianity for responding to the many gods objection, because Islam shares with Christianity several attributes relevant to the Wager. Islam claims to be the unique true religion, it asserts that all who do not embrace Islam end up forever in hell, and it asserts that through their religion Muslims can achieve eternal paradise. The Wager argument seems to largely go through for the Islam faith, since a risk-benefit analysis, which considers the infinite negative utility of mistakenly failing to bet on Islam and the infinite positive utility of betting on Islam, suggests that a person, for the sake of happiness, should bet on Islam.

However, there are three differences between Christianity and Islam that I suggest make the Wager a stronger argument for Christianity. The first difference is that Islam does not offer heaven for all believers– it holds no assurance of salvation for anyone. All the Muslim is told in the Koran is that if he works very hard to be a righteous and obedient Muslim then he may receive the reward of paradise, but no promise is made. This contrasts starkly with Christianity that qualifies people for heaven based on grace and faith (not works), and the Bible is replete with assurances about secure salvation. This greater assurance of bliss implies greater utility for betting on Christianity. The second difference, suggested by Pascal in *Pensée* 149, is that the heaven promised by the Koran belongs to a lower order of bliss than the heaven promised by the Bible– whereas Islam's heaven merely continues the same blessings experienced on earth, Christianity's heaven entails a higher order of bliss than now experienced, "Eye has not seen, nor ear heard, nor have entered into the heart of man, the things which God has prepared for those who love Him." [Isaiah 64:4, quoted by Paul in I Corinthians 2:9]." The third difference is that Christianity and Islam have different degrees of evidence supporting whether they are really possible. People will disagree on their relative plausibility, of course; however, Pascal provides sketches of thoughts arguing that the rational plausibility of Christianity is much higher. For example, Pascal argues that Mohammed was inferior to Jesus Christ as a religious leader, since Mohammed did no miracles, did not prophecy, and was not prophesied about.

Response to Many Gods Objection: Some World Religions Have Greater Expected Utilities Than Others. Beyond Islam, how does the Wager play for other religions? To set the context for addressing this question, consider that the major religions of the world can be divided into ones that have infinite or finite reward-punishment systems. Islam, Christianity, and Mormonism are "infinity religions," whereas Unitarianism, Judaism, Hinduism (world's third largest religion after Christianity and Islam), and most versions of Buddhism (world's fourth largest religion) are "finity religions," with neither an everlasting heaven nor an everlasting hell. For example Hinduism and most versions of Buddhism are finity religions– although they offer ultimate enlightenment (nirvana), this enlightenment is hardly eternal joy. The nirvana state typically constitutes a freeing from all desires and attachments, and an attending permanent escape from the reincarnation cycle. Thus a person achieving such enlightenment does not enjoy positive everlasting bliss, but only the absence of desire. In addition, some religions, including Mormonism, Sikhism (world's fifth largest religion) and Jainism (world's tenth largest religion), have an everlasting heaven but not an everlasting hell.

With this background, we first note that the Wager argument implies that only religions offering an infinite reward are rationally compelling to explore. Based on comparative expected utility it is not compelling to seek after religions that do not offer lasting happiness, as it would be equally rational to remain in one's agnostic condition. Secondly, we note that the Wager implies that religions with reincarnation are less compelling than religions without reincarnation. Reincarnation allows second, third, and millionth chances; if a Hindu or Buddhist bets on the wrong religion, then in their next lifetime they will have a chance to ante-up again. In contrast Christianity and Islam teach that people only have one life– one chance to wager– thus the stakes are far greater in these religions, making it far more urgent to bet on Christianity or Islam. Thirdly, we note that the Wager implies that religions with everlasting heaven and everlasting hell are more compelling than religions with everlasting heaven but not everlasting hell. This follows based on comparative utility because the latter religions have an infinitely smaller penalty for not believing in them. Therefore, of the world's major religions, only Islam and Christianity merge as rationally compelling to explore based on the Wager.

Response to Many Gods Objection and Real Possibility. Beyond world religions, what if I make up my own boutique religion, say based on rooting for the Seattle Mariners baseball team, which promises a doubly blissful heaven than either Christianity or Islam for believers and a doubly terrible hell? Doesn't the Wager imply that I am rationally compelled to bet on this new religion? Marilyn vos Savant suggests this is exactly the Wager's conclusion. However, based on our previous discussion, the problem with this analysis is that the element of real possibility is needed to make it rationally compelling to bet on a religion offering excellent rewards. Professor Elster states the issue well:

> For the Wager to be persuasive... Pascal has to establish that among religions that assign infinitely large rewards to believers, Christianity is the only one to possess real possibility.

While I agree that for Pascal's overall case for Christianity to be persuasive he needs to establish that only Christianity is really possible, I do not think Pascal needs to establish this to compel wagering. Rather, to justify launching a spiritual experiment of seeking, it is enough to establish that Christianity is not contrary to reason and is no less rationally credible than alternative infinity-religions. Indeed, at the end of the Wager Pascal affirms that once a person seeks God and discovers faith in him, the evidence for Christianity becomes more and more certain– and this weight of evidence cumulates *after* initiating serious seeking, not before.

Critique 4: The Wager Appeals Only to Self-Interest. Many, most notably William James, have objected to the Wager because it appeals to base self-interest– to a desire to avoid hell and to opportunistically land a pleasant estate– whereas true faith requires deep and sincere commitment. Tim Keller has phrased this critique as, "We should gamble because it is right, not to buy fire insurance." A person with this objection may be more persuaded by an adapted version of the Wager, suggested by Peter Kreeft (1993), which re-casts the Wager by substituting the motive of happiness for the "righteous" motive of doing justice. The mathematical logic of the Wager is unchanged. Moreover, a person with the fire-insurance objection is already half way won as a seeker, because he cares about (is not indifferent about) being right. If he also perceives his own wretchedness, then he will perceive himself as a dispossessed king– possessing an idea of truth and justice but experiencing it to be elusive in practice. And as we have seen, those who know they are dispossessed kings are on the threshold of seeking.

A second reply to James' objection is that Jesus took Pascal's approach in giving unsure people incentives to seek a fuller assurance of their faith (Groothuis, 2003). Frequently Jesus encouraged persistent seeking of God, promising that it will be rewarded– the door will be opened to those who knock. [Matthew 7:7–8]

A third reply to James' objection is that not all self-interest in one's happiness is morally wrong. Taking care of oneself is never discouraged by Jesus; rather his withering criticism is for those who only care for themselves and harm others. In prodding people to seek God, Jesus acknowledges that seeking will bring a good to the seeker:

> What good will it be for you to gain the whole world, yet forfeit your soul? Or what can you give in exchange for your soul? [Matthew 16:25–26]

Furthermore, in his letters to various churches the Apostle Paul explicitly shares that he is praying "for their good;" for example in his letter to the Colossians Paul writes of his ceaseless prayers for their well-being, that for their good they will be delivered from the power of darkness into Christ's kingdom. [Colossians 1:14] Finally, Pascal's proposed spiritual experiment begins with diminishing ones' selfish passions, to enable the search for God. As such, Pascal addresses the "self-interest" of his listener only to get him to see that what he really needs is diminishing his selfish interests. Seeing the conclusion of the Wager as a springboard for this experiment insulates it from the criticism that the Wager is a selfish argument. Indeed, given the emphasis Pascal placed in the *Pensées* and in his life on the importance of sincere and diligent faith and committed service to God, the critique that the Wager is selfish fails to appreciate the context of the Wager and its author. The Wager is a starting point to cultivating faith, not the end.

To those who say they choose not to wager because wagering flows from base self-interest, we can question whether this is the real barrier holding them back. Could the real obstacle flow from the profound influence of the 'masters of suspicion' in the 19th and early 20th centuries (including Karl Marx, Nietzsche, and Freud), who asserted that religious people believe God out of shameful motivations? (Keyes, 2006) For example, Freud endeavored to dissuade people of their religious beliefs by getting them to feel ashamed of their motives for belief, which include a childish grasping to assuage one's fear of death. Despite the fact that Freud did not back up his assertions with credible scientific data or plausible assumptions, his ideas are still widely believed. (Robinson, 2005) As such, if we feel embarrassed to seek God, it may simply be due to an infection with Freud's suspicion– being (invisibly) exposed to it since birth– and have nothing to do with an alleged affront to our nobility. This is supported by the paucity of self-interest critiques of the Wager prior to Freud. Who shall we then listen to more closely, Freud, who tells us to be ashamed to seek, or Pascal, who tells us to be ashamed not to? I am more compelled by the better scientist, writer, and friend.

In sum, the critiques of the Wager I have seen are valid only if constructed in a context different than Pascal's. Often critics argue like logician philosophers, as Descartes might argue, but as we have seen Pascal found the dry approach of philosophers unhelpful for ordinary people struggling with diversions, indifference, and selfish passions. Pascal wrote to gamblers, not to philosophers, to warm their hearts and minds to take an interest in seeking God. When this purpose to get people moving and acting as if they believe is appreciated, the criticisms melt away (as Chesterton expressed in the epigraph beginning this chapter).

Conclusion of the Wager. The conclusion I draw from the Wager is that it is rationally compelling to vigorously explore all religions with infinite reward/punishment systems that strike one as rationally plausible, where vigorous exploration entails modifying one's behavior on the religions own terms. The list of existing religions that fit these criteria will be very short for most people; in fact in Pascal's France there were essentially only two options– Christianity or atheism. Today the only two major infinity-religion options are Christianity and Islam. The stakes and utilities are high enough that I believe the Wager still has legs to move people to take Pascal's advice to give Christianity a try.

***Pensée* of the Day: Number 418**

The PoD is a fragment from the Wager *Pensée* 418, in which Pascal encourages us to risk our lives in following Christ:

> And thus, since you are obliged to play, you must be renouncing reason if you hoard your life rather than risk it for an infinite gain.

Synthesis Points of Chapter 7

1. Pascal wrote the Wager ("infinity-nothing") to skeptical, open unbelievers who were not convinced by reason or by traditional arguments that the Christian God is true.
2. Pascal's Wager appeals to a person's desire for happiness. The expected happiness for betting on God is infinity compared to negative infinity for betting against God. By decision theory it is rationally compelling to bet on God.
3. Pascal acknowledged that one cannot "make oneself believe." The take-home point of the Wager is to begin a spiritual experiment, to diminish one's selfish passions/over-desires, look to Christian models, and "act as if you believe." Cultivating Christian habits can grow faith.
4. Pascal's Wager withstands criticisms, which usually take the Wager out of its context (the whole *Pensées*) or fail to appreciate Pascal's purpose in the Wager to prompt a spiritual experiment.

8 THE CURE: UNIQUENESS OF CHRISTIANITY AND CLUES FOR ITS TRUTH

"I would not believe but for the miracles."
– Saint Augustine, *The Confessions*

"An artisan speaking of riches, a lawyer speaking of war, or kingship, etc., but the rich man can well speak of riches, the king can speak indifferently of some great gift he has just bestowed, and God can well speak of God."
– Blaise Pascal, *Pensée* 303

In the previous chapter I stressed that Pascal did not expect his interlocutor to wager blindly. Recall Pascal's overall plan for his apologetic project to "make [Christianity] attractive, make good men wish it were true, and then show that it is." [*Pensée* 12] Half of Pascal's planned apology would be written to 'show that it is true,' and in this chapter we will explore what evidence Pascal drew upon to make this case.

Whereas Pascal's approach uses traditional evidence for Christianity, two factors make it distinctive. First, he makes great use of paradox, frequently putting forth two opposing points that seem irreconcilable, and then introducing Jesus Christ as the key that resolves the conundrum. Second, by aiming arrows at the heart and the psychological mind as well as the reasoning mind, Pascal departs from dry systematic theology that endeavors to logically prove that the Christian religion is true. It is only after the heavy work of making his listener wish Christianity were true that Pascal delivers the evidence, and then with art and emotion that help him *feel* its truth. *Pensée* 7 gives a window into Pascal's approach:

> Faith is different from proof. One is human and the other a gift of God. *The just shall live by faith* [Romans 1:17]. This is the faith that God himself puts into our hearts, often using proof as the instrument.

The last sentence reveals Pascal's primary objective– to make hearts conducive to receiving faith from God, relegating proof to a mere instrument. Pascal submitted his craft of persuasion to his own aphorism, "The heart has its reasons of which reason knows nothing." [*Pensée* 423]

Outline of Chapter 8. In Part I, we will consider Pascal's *Pensées* on the uniqueness of Christianity. To Pascal the whole Christian religion falls like a house of cards if Jesus Christ did not actually rise from the dead, and in Part II we will consider Pascal's thoughts on the credibility of the historical resurrection. In Part III we will survey Pascal's *Pensées* on three classical pillars of evidence for the Christian faith– miracles, prophecies, and the amazing Jewish people. In Part IV I will discuss Pascal's comparison of the evidence for Christianity versus for other religions, and in Part V, I will discuss Pascal's answers to some common objections of current-day atheists to the truthfulness of Christianity.

Part I. Uniqueness of Christianity

In our times the dominant interpretation of religious pluralism presupposes that no one can reasonably claim a particular religion to be the only true one. I hear from many that only a fundamentalist or a fool can believe this, yet this is what I believe. On occasion I have doubted, wondering on what grounds I can be so exclusive. At a minimum, Christianity had better be distinctive; otherwise I cannot believe it over other religions. Pascal has helped me see the stunning uniqueness of the Christian faith, which buoys my belief in it.

In a certain sense, Pascal includes Judaism with Christianity as one unique religion, writing "true Jews and true Christians have only one religion." [*Pensée* 453] Thus to Pascal the unique attributes of the Christian faith are equivalently unique to true Judaism, where "true Jews and true Christians" are characterized by their "worship of a Messiah who makes them love God," as opposed to carnal Jews and carnal Christians "who believe that the Messiah has dispensed them from loving God." [*Pensée* 286]

Essay Introducing the Uniqueness of Christianity: Pensée 149. With his heading "Beginning" for *Pensée* 149, one can guess that Pascal meant to introduce his case for uniqueness with this essay.

Beginning, after explaining incomprehensibility.

Man's greatness and wretchedness are so evident that the true religion must necessarily teach us that there is in man some great principle of greatness and some great principle of wretchedness.

It must account for such amazing contradictions.

To make man happy it must show him that a God exists whom we are bound to love; that our true bliss is to be in him, and our sole ill to be cut off from him. It must acknowledge that we are full of darkness that prevents us from knowing and loving him, and so, with our duty obliging us to love God and our concupiscence leading us astray, we are full of unrighteousness.

It must account to us for the way in which we thus go against God and our own good. It must teach us the cure for our helplessness and the means of obtaining the cure. Let us examine all the religions of the world on that point and let us see whether any but the Christian religion meets it.

Do the philosophers, who offer nothing else for our good but the good that is within us? Have they found the cure for our ills? Is it curing man's presumption to set him up as God's equal? Have those who put us on the level of the beasts, have the Moslems, who offer nothing else for our good than earthly pleasures, even in eternity, brought us the cure for our concupiscence?

What religion, then, will teach us how to cure pride and concupiscence? What religion, in short, will teach us our true good, our duties, the weaknesses which lead us astray, the cause of these weaknesses, the treatment that can cure them, and the means of obtaining such treatment? All the other religions have failed to do so. Let us see what the wisdom of God will do.

Points of Uniqueness of Christianity. Pascal listed five fragments under the heading Uniqueness of Christianity, which we will explore in turn:

1. Christianity explains human experience
2. Christianity is love-centered
3. Christianity is both the deepest philosophy and is understood by children
4. Christianity completes/perfects a human being
5. Christianity is wonderful/astonishing

Uniqueness Point 1: Christianity Explains Human Experience. Pascal's first point is that only Christianity understands Man's nature, in particular his dual nature of being both very great and very wretched. No other religion diagnoses Man's paradoxical condition:

> (After hearing the whole nature of man.) For a religion to be true it must have known our nature; it must have known its greatness and smallness, and the reason for both. What other religion but Christianity has known this? [*Pensée* 215]

By this point in the dialog Pascal has presented his interlocutor with his whole arsenal of portraits of Man's strange condition. For a religion to be credible, its statements about what is human nature must be consistent with these portraits– a true model must accurately fit the observed data.

Uniqueness Point 2: Christianity is Love-Centered. Pascal's second point is that only for the Christian religion is love at its center. Pascal summarizes this in *Pensée* 270:

> The sole object of Scripture is charity.

Here Pascal reflects Augustine's teaching that if the meaning of a Scriptural passage is unclear, then the safest course is to interpret it in terms of God's love. When in doubt, assume charity is in view– it is a more dangerous error to miss an intention of charity than to incorrectly ascribe charity. By overlooking charity the Church has often gone astray, such as when it used biblical texts to justify enslavement and to convert people coercively. Against such anti-charity all of the biblical prophets persistently proclaim that God's people must love the vulnerable poor. The sole object of Scripture is to bring about love of God and neighbor, Pascal purports.

As an implication, a unique teaching of Christianity is to turn the other cheek, to absorb sin rather than to retaliate, to love one's enemy. For example, Luke describes the beating and jailing of Paul and Silas by a Roman magistrate. [Acts chapter 16] This severe punishment was unjust, being without cause, and was illegal, being that Paul and Silas were Roman citizens. An earthquake released all the inmates from their chains. The jailer was sleeping, providing opportunity for the prisoners to escape. However, Paul and Silas knew that the jailer would commit suicide if the prisoners departed, and they waited for him to awake. Despite the jailer's membership in the group that had just cruelly mistreated them, Paul and Silas repaid him with love– a unique Christian love that extends even to the perpetrator. In fact Christian love extends to everyone– everyone is counted as a neighbor. "But I say: we ought to embrace the whole human race without exception in a single feeling of love; here there is no distinction between barbarian and Greek, worthy and unworthy, friend and enemy, since all should be contemplated in God, not in themselves." [John Calvin] Tim Keller points out that all religions and worldviews have a fundamental, and Christianity's fundamental is to love one's enemies (as chiefly demonstrated in Christ's infinite love of his enemies).

In addition, Christianity is uniquely love-centered because it imparts blessing through belief in God's unconditional love as opposed to through earning God's favors through good deeds. All other religions impart blessing through a moral law-based "if-then" process– if I follow this or that commandment, then I receive this or that blessing. For example, following the Pharisees religion of self-righteousness, the elder brother in the prodigal son parable seeks God's blessings through works, striving to control his father through his good moral behavior (see Tim Keller's The Prodigal God [2009]). Such a 'self-salvation project' is the opposite to belief in God to do the saving; hence the infinite difference between belief and religious moralism. Indeed, belief is altogether different because it is free from if-then moralism. It is so unusual that atheists find it stupefying that Christianity is based on belief, for example, commenting on the Wager, Richard Dawkins (2006) expresses surprise at Pascal's notion that faith is what matters:

> But why, in any case, do we so readily accept the idea that the one thing you must do if you want to please God is *believe* in him? What's so special about believing?

Thus even atheists find Christianity unique for departing from rewarding people based on belief rather than good behavior.

Tied to imparting blessing through faith not works, grace is a central quality of Christian love that makes it unique. Gracious love is practiced when one voluntarily expends one's life to bless people that do not deserve it, with God the premier practioner. To underscore the infinite price God voluntarily paid to bless humanity, and hence the infinite gracious love of God, consider the tabulated list at the end of Chapter 4, on the wretched attributes of man as dispossessed king apart from god, and the corresponding glorious attributes of man as restored king. In a word, Jesus Christ was the infinitely happy king in heaven, with all of the glorious attributes perfectly expressed, and voluntary became dispossessed, "emptying himself of his glory" [Philippians 2:7], to embody several of the wretched attributes. Jesus gave up immortality for death, beauty for beastliness marred beyond human likeness (Isaiah 53), glorious reputation for ignominiousness, abiding rest for weariness and agitation (sweating blood in the garden of Gethsemane), joy for despair, a perfectly just society for a cruel and unjust one, perfect friendships (within the trinity) for loneliness and abandonment (his friends disowned him at his hour of trial, and his Father turned away at his death). By giving up infinite happiness in exchange for infinite wretchedness, the descent of Jesus Christ was greater than any human's. Jesus became the perfectly dispossessed king so that we may be restored to be happy kings.

Pensée 214 succinctly expresses both of Pascal's first two points on the uniqueness of Christianity:

> The sign of the true religion must be that it obliges men to love God. That is quite right, yet while none enjoined it, ours has done so.
>
> It must also have understood about concupiscence and weakness; ours has done so.
>
> It must have provided the remedies; one is prayer. No other religion has asked God to make us love and follow him.

Thus whereas other religions are human-driven, based on strivings to reach God, Christianity is God-driven, based on God's reaching down to make saints. Judeo-Christianity is unique for its insistence that knowing God is a God-initiated process, a gift from God.

Uniqueness Point 3: Christianity is Both the Deepest Philosophy and is Understood by Children. For his third point of uniqueness, Pascal observes that the wisdom of Christianity is as deep as wisdom can be, yet is remarkably simple:

> This religion taught its children what men had managed to know only at their most enlightened. [*Pensée* 229]

> Jesus said great things so simply that he seems not to have thought about them, and yet so clearly that it is obvious what he

> thought about them. Such clarity together with such simplicity is wonderful. [*Pensée* 309]

Jesus never wrote a theological or philosophical treatise; he spoke with simple everyday metaphors that ordinary people could understand. Yet his words have inspired endless probing of their deep wisdom. Such profundity, clarity and simplicity juxtaposed together in the same words comprise a clue that Jesus is very special. Earl Palmer illustrates this by relaying Karl Barth's response to a question about how would he sum up his massive body of intricate theological work? Dr. Barth said he could indeed summarize it simply, with a lyric from a Child's song: "Jesus loves me this I know, for the Bible tells me so." Christianity is both simple and wise.

In *Pensée* 842 Pascal amplifies his third uniqueness point:

> Our religion is wise and foolish: wise, because it is the most learned and most strongly based on miracles, prophecies, etc., foolish, because it is not all this which makes people belong to it. This is good enough reason for condemning those who do not belong, but not for making those who do belong believe. What makes them believe is the Cross. *Lest the Cross of Christ should be made of none effect* (I Corinthians 1:17).

Perhaps drawing from the book of Hebrews (Chapter 11) and the Apostle Paul's first letter to the Corinthians (Chapter 1), in *Pensée* 291 Pascal expands his thoughts on the paradox of Christianity's wisdom and foolishness:

> This religion is so great in miracles, in men holy, pure and irreproachable, in scholars, great witnesses and martyrs, established kings – David – Isaiah, a prince of the blood; so great in knowledge, after displaying all its miracles and all its wisdom, rejects it all and says that it offers neither wisdom nor signs, but only the Cross and folly.
>
> For those who by this wisdom and these signs have deserved your trust, and who have proved their character, declare to you that none of this can change us and make us capable of knowing and loving God, except the virtue contained in the folly of the Cross, without wisdom or signs, and not the signs without this virtue.

Furthermore, in *Pensée* 381 Pascal describes how non-intellectuals can believe. For these, for example the illiterate, proofs of Christianity can be felt inwardly in their hearts, with no need for arguments. Non-intellectuals can feel in their bones the key points that they were made by God, they desire to love God, they cannot reach God on their own effort, and it is their duty to love God. Feeling these truths, plus hearing it said that God made himself a human being in order to unite himself to us, is enough to make many believe:

> Those who believe without having read the Testaments do so because their inward disposition is truly holy and what they hear about our religion matches it. They feel that a God made them, they only want to love God, they only want to hate themselves. They feel that they are not strong enough to do this by themselves, that they are incapable of going to God, and that if God does not come to them that they are incapable of communicating with him at all. They hear it said in our religion that we must only love God and only hate ourselves, but that, since we are all corrupt and incapable of reaching God, God made himself man in order to unite himself with us. It takes no more than this to convince men whose hearts are thus disposed and who have such an understanding of their duty and incapacity. [*Pensée* 381]

Given that intellectuals and the literate have been the minority in world history, it is likely that the majority of Christians have believed in this direct way without requiring logical argument. In a word, Christianity can be understood by children.

Uniqueness Point 4: Christianity Completes/Perfects a Human Being. Fourth, Pascal suggests that only Christianity can make people complete/perfect:

> No one is so happy as a true Christian, or so reasonable, virtuous, and lovable. [*Pensée* 357]

> In [Christ] is all our virtue and all our happiness. [*Pensée* 416]

Only Christ's friendship can make one joyful in the midst of suffering, reasonable and virtuous in the face of pressures to bow to self-interest, and good and kind enough to be lovable.

Uniqueness Point 5: Christianity is Wonderful/Astonishing. Fifth, Christianity is wonderful, generating awe.

> There is no denying it; one must admit that there is something astonishing about Christianity. 'It is because you were born in it,' they will say. Far from it; I stiffen myself against it for that very reason, for fear of being corrupted by prejudice. But, though I was born in it, I cannot help finding it astonishing. [*Pensée* 817]

Additional Uniqueness Point: Original Sin. We now consider other *Pensées* wherein Pascal points to unique attributes of Christianity, without explicitly listing them as such. In *Pensée* 421 Pascal observes that among all philosophies and religions, only Christianity teaches the doctrine of original sin:

> No religion except ours has taught that man is born sinful, no philosophical sect has said so, so none has told the truth...

Pascal suggests that Original Sin has enormous explanatory power, so much so that we can understand nothing about ourselves without it:

> It is, however, an astounding thing that the mystery furthest from our ken, that of the transmission of sin, should be something without which we can have no knowledge of ourselves.
>
> Without doubt nothing is more shocking to our reason than to say that the sin of the first man has implicated in its guilt men so far from the original sin that they seem incapable of sharing it. This flow of guilt does not seem merely impossible to us, but indeed most unjust. What could be more contrary to the rules of our miserable justice than the eternal damnation of a child, incapable of will, for an act in which he seems to have so little part that it was actually committed 6,000 years before he existed? Certainly nothing jolts us more rudely than this doctrine, and yet, but for this mystery, the most incomprehensible of all, we remain incomprehensible to ourselves. The knot of our condition was twisted and turned in the abyss, so that it is harder to conceive of man without this mystery than for man to conceive of it himself. [*Pensée* 131]

Indeed, even great non-Christian thinkers, such as the Argentine master of the short-story, Jorge Luis Borges, intuit something of the truth of this mystery. Borges writes in *The Form of the Sword* (*Ficciones*, 1956),

> What one man does is something done, in some measure, by all men. For that reason a disobedience committed in a garden contaminates the human race; for that reason it is not unjust that the crucifixion of a single Jew suffices to save it.

The grand positive flip side of Christianity's unique belief in Original Sin is its unique promise of a gracious remedy. As in *Pensée* 222:

> Carnal Jews and heathen have their miseries, and so have Christians. There is no redeemer for the heathen, for they do not even hope for one. There is no redeemer for the [carnal] Jews; they hope for him in vain. Only for the Christians is there a redeemer.

Marilynne Robinson observes that while on the surface the doctrine that all people sin seems severe and to lead to meanness among people, a second glance shows it to foster kindliness better than more optimistic doctrines like perfectionism.

> The belief that we are all sinners gives us excellent grounds for forgiveness and self-forgiveness, and is kindlier than any expectation that we might be saints, even while it affirms the standards all of us fail to attain.
>
> A Puritan confronted by failure and ambivalence could find his faith justified by the experience, could feel that the world had answered his expectations. We have replaced this and other religious visions with an unsystematic, uncritical and in fact unconscious perfectionism, which may have taken root among us while Stalinism still seemed full of promise, and to have been refreshed by the palmy days of National Socialism in Germany, by Castro and by Mao– the idea that society can and should produce good people, that is, people suited to life in whatever imagined optimum society, who then stabilize the society in its goodness so that it produces more good people, and so on. First the bad ideas must be weeded out and socially useful ones put in their place. Then the bad people must be identified... [*The Death of Adam,* essay *Puritans and Prigs*]

It is kinder to expect imperfection, which makes grace and forgiveness important, than to expect perfection, which makes them irrelevant.

Part II. Evidence for the Resurrection of Jesus

From his orthodox stance Pascal believed Jesus Christ must have risen from the dead in order for Christianity and its unique points to have any value. Accordingly Pascal offered reasons to believe the resurrection, most notably based on Man's wretched condition. Responding to the charge that the Apostles conspired to deceive people that Jesus rose from the dead, in *Pensée* 310 Pascal points to Man's wretchedness (weakness) as evidence for the historical veracity of the Easter event:

> The hypothesis that the Apostles were knaves is quite absurd. Follow it out to the end and imagine twelve men meeting after Jesus' death and conspiring to say that he had risen from the dead. This means attacking all the powers that be. The human heart is singularly susceptible to fickleness, to change, to promises, to bribery. One of them had only to deny his story under these inducements, or still more because possible imprisonment, tortures and death, and they would all have been lost. Follow that out.

Historical data document that the Apostles persistently claimed Jesus' resurrection, never flagging. This persistence flew into a strong headwind of many incentives to recant, such as bribery by Romans or Jews, and the fear of being tortured or killed. Pascal proposes that had the Apostles known that Jesus had not risen from the dead, then they would not have been able to keep up the charade. Rather, the fickleness and weakness of their human hearts would have caused them to abandon the conspiracy. Here Pascal draws upon the first part of the *Pensées*, where he laid extensive groundwork to demonstrate, from a study of human behavior, that humankind is weak. It is more likely that the Apostles really believed that Jesus rose from the dead than that they conspired to make it appear that he had. Moreover, the fact that almost all of the New Testament books were written within the lifetime of many eyewitnesses of Jesus' resurrection challenge any hypothesis that the authors concocted a legend about Jesus' resurrection.

In *Pensée* 322 Pascal suggests that it is also implausible that the Apostles were deceived themselves about Jesus' resurrection:

> The Apostles were either deceived or deceivers [if Jesus did not really rise]. Either supposition is difficult, for it is not possible to imagine that a man has risen from the dead.
>
> While Jesus was with them he could sustain them, but afterwards, if he did not appear to them, who did make them act?

In the days immediately following Jesus' death, the gospel writers record the disciples grieving Jesus' death, holing up in fear of the authorities, and going about their normal activities such as fishing. The disciples are described as having no inkling that Jesus would rise, consistent with Pascal's suggestion that it is not possible to imagine that a man has risen from the dead. Furthermore, while Jesus was alive the disciples are described as having no expectation that Jesus would rise and having no comprehension of Jesus' statements foretelling his death and resurrection (for example, John 2:19–22 reports the disciples not understanding Jesus' statement, "Destroy this temple, and I will raise it again in three days.") Moreover, the gospel writers and the Apostle Paul report Jesus appearing to hundreds of people after his resurrection, including to 500 at one time. [I Corinthians 15] This plus the fact that the Gospels were written in the genre of historical narrative challenge the hypothesis that the disciples were deceived.

Similar to Pascal's point in *Pensée* 322, C.S. Lewis proposes that the sanity of the disciples is one of the strongest pieces of evidence for the historical resurrection. As sane people they were neither deceived nor deceivers, making these approaches to explaining away the resurrection hard to reconcile with human nature and the data. It is therefore not unreasonable to believe the resurrection.

More generally, Pascal took the unique style of the gospels as evidence for their historical accuracy:

> The style of the Gospel is remarkable in so many ways; among others for never putting in any invective against the executioners and enemies of Christ. For there is none in any of the historians against Judas, Pilate, or any of the Jews. [*Pensée* 812]

What odd behavior from the Gospel writers! Experience suggests that it is human nature for a harassed group to reproach their tormenting enemies. Palestinians do so to the Jews, Jews do so to the Palestinians, Americans do so to Al Qaeda terrorists, right-wingers do so to left-wingers, left-wingers do so to right-wingers, etc. Why did the early Christians not rail against those who betrayed Jesus or were immediately responsible for putting him to death? Why did they not vehemently denunciate them? Pascal presents this as an impenetrable puzzle if looked at from a purely human perspective. In so doing Pascal hopes to stir a sense of wonder in his listeners, to provoke them to reflect on how special the Apostles were, and for this to warm their hearts to see that there could be a divine cause.

Part III. Classical Evidence for Christianity

Pascal intended his apology as a complete case for Christianity, and as such many *Pensées* address the traditional types of evidence. In Part III we will look at Pascal's presentation of this evidence. While many apologists have worked with this material, Pascal uses it in an original way. [*Pensée* 696]

Clues, Not Proofs. To frame the context for our exploration, note that Pascal did not present the traditional evidence as proofs per se, but as clues for the truth of the Christian religion. Pascal makes this clear in *Pensée* 835, which we previously considered in chapters 6 and 7:

> The prophecies, even the miracles and proofs of our religion, are not of such a kind that they can be said to be absolutely convincing, but they are at the same time such that it cannot be said to be unreasonable to believe in them... Thus, there is enough evidence to condemn and not enough to convince, so that it should be apparent that those who follow it are prompted to do so by grace and not by reason...

Pascal observes that people follow Christ primarily because of grace working in their hearts, and that God intended it this way. This *Pensée* teaches a lesson on how believers should wield the tool of the proofs of Christianity, not as a sledgehammer for banging truths into heads, but rather as a helpmate to relationships, service, art, hospitality, etc.– for most the primary means of instilling grace into hearts.

Outline of Pascal's Presentation of the Traditional Evidence. With that prelude, we will now explore Pascal's writings on several topics that he lists as supportive of Christianity. We will follow Pascal's topical ordering in *Pensée* 892:

> I prefer to follow Jesus Christ rather than anyone else because he has miracles, prophecy, doctrine, perpetuity, etc.

Evidence from Miracles. The fact that Pascal devoted a long section of the *Pensées* to miracles, fragments 830–912, suggests their importance for Pascal as evidence for Christianity. In *Pensée* 846, Pascal observes that Jesus offered miracles as the main proof of his Messiah-ship:

> Jesus proved he was the Messiah, but never by proving his doctrine from Scripture or the prophecies, but always by miracles.

Jesus did not point to his fulfillment of prophecies as evidence for his Messiah-ship until after the resurrection (for example on the road to Emmaus); during his lifetime Jesus' clear emphasis was on miracles. The gospels narrate dozens of them, which attracted crowds to follow Jesus and listen to his teaching. Miracles appeal to the emotions with high drama; witnessing Jesus healing a blind man arrests people to perceive something special about Jesus. In contrast, discussions of prophecy appeal to the intellect, and may have less impact because of the weaknesses of reasoning that Pascal describes. A miracle will amaze a child, while the fulfillment of prophecy may not.

In addition to their "wow" value, for the Jews miracles serve to ratify a person's special relationship with God, because they believed God is with people who perform powerful miracles. For example, in *Pensée* 846 Pascal notes,

> Nicodemus recognized by [Jesus'] miracles that his doctrine was from God. '*Rabbi, we know that thou art a teacher come from God, for no man can do these miracles that thou doest except God be with him.*' [John 3:2]

Therefore miracles have a double-layered appeal– to the uneducated they appeal directly to emotions and felt needs, and to the Jewish learned they have the additional appeal of fitting intellectual expectations of what a man from God should look like.

Toward the end of *Pensée* 846 Pascal goes so far as to say that if Jesus had not performed miracles, then no one could be expected to believe in him:

> The Jews had a doctrine of God, as we have one of Christ, and it was confirmed by miracles... They were, however, very much to be blamed for rejecting the prophets, because of their miracles, and Christ also, and would have incurred no blame if they had not seen the miracles. '*If I had not done the works... they had not sin.*' [John 15:24]. Therefore all faith rests on miracles.

Pascal states this more succinctly in *Pensée* 184:

> It would have been no sin not to have believed in Jesus Christ without miracles.

And in *Pensée* 903 Pascal describes miracles as a distinguishing mark of true religion:

> Miracles, mainstay of religion. They distinguished the Jews, they have distinguished Christians, saints, the innocent, the true believers.

Later in this *Pensée* Pascal calls miracles "the supreme effects of grace," observing that God in his grace uses miracles to stir up the Church and create true worshippers. Furthermore, in *Pensée* 859 Pascal suggests that

> Miracles are more important than you think. They were used to found the Church and will be used to continue it until Antichrist, until the end.

Miracles that founded the Church or continue it include creation, revelation, the giving of the law and prophets, the Incarnation, healings performed by Jesus and his disciples, the Resurrection, and the Ascension. Moreover, Jesus demonstrated by miracles that he could forgive sins. God chose to use miracles in all of the essential events of Christianity.

In comparison, miracles play no significant role in Buddhism, Confucianism, or in Mohammed's life, with Pascal enquiring, "What miracles does he [Mahomet] himself claimed to have performed?" [*Pensée* 243] Miracles make the Christian religion stand apart, giving the mind a reason to find it more credible than others.

On the other hand, Pascal acknowledged that miracles are often insufficient to convince, because they cannot necessarily change one's attitude. A person can witness a miracle and remain hard to God; for example Pharaoh hardened his heart despite witnessing 10 punishing plagues; and Jonah remained stubborn despite surviving the whales' belly. When Jesus encountered skeptics who said they would believe if only he performed a miracle, he declined, stating that they would still not believe, because of their closed hearts. But for those with open hearts and ears to hear, miracles are a mainstay for buttressing faith.

Do True Miracles Exist? To counter the heavy influence of Naturalism that asserts that miracles do not exist, C.S. Lewis wrote a book (*Miracles*) to show that it is not unreasonable to believe in miracles. Arguing on Lewis' side, Pascal addresses a common difficulty in believing them: many of us have never seen a true miracle, but have seen fake ones. Consider Pascal's reply to my skepticism:

> After considering what makes us trust imposters claiming to have cures, to the extent that we often put our lives into their hands, it seemed to me that the real reason is that some of them are genuine, for there could not possibly be so many false ones, enjoying so much credit, unless some of them were genuine. If there had never been a cure for any ill, and all ills had been incurable, men could not possibly have imagined that they could provide any, still less could so many others have given credence to those who boasted of having such cures. Similarly, if a man boasted that he could prevent death, no one would believe him, because there is no example of that happening...
>
> Thus instead of concluding that there are no true miracles because there are so many false ones, we must on the contrary say that there certainly are true miracles since there are so many false ones, and that false ones are only there because true ones exist. The same argument must be applied to religion, for men could not possibly have imagined so many false religions unless there was a true one. [*Pensée* 734]

At the end of this *Pensée* Pascal applies his line of reasoning for the existence of true miracles to the question, "How can Christianity be true given the global diversity of religions?" Surprisingly, Pascal proposes that the existence of so many false religions helps demonstrate that there is a true one! Thus Pascal turns the "problem" of religious pluralism into an argument for, not against, the truth of Christianity.

Evidence from Prophecy. To Pascal, as to many apologists, the fulfillment of prophecy constitutes the most compelling evidence for Jesus Christ:

> The most weighty proofs of Jesus are the prophecies. It is for them that God made most provision, for the event which fulfilled them is a miracle, continuing from the birth of the Church to the end. Thus God raised up prophets for 1,600 years and for 400 years afterwards dispersed all the prophecies with all the Jews, who carried them into every corner of the world. Such was the preparation for the birth of Christ, and since his Gospel had to be believed by the whole world, there not only had to be prophecies to make men believe it, but these prophecies had to be spread throughout the world so that the whole world should embrace it.

The prophets predicted that when the Messiah arrives the kingdom of God will spread over the earth. Pascal interpreted historical events such as the conversion of the Emperor Constantine to Christianity in the fourth century, and the spread of Christianity to predominance in the Western world, as fulfillments of this prediction. In *Pensée* 338 Pascal suggests that the history of mass conversions to Christianity is quite odd from a human perspective, but is sensible once viewed as a fulfillment of prophecy brought about by a "secret force:"

> What Plato had not been able to make a few chosen and highly educated men to believe, a secret force made hundreds of thousands of ignorant men believe the power of a few words.
>
> Rich men abandoned the luxury of their parents' home for the austerity of the desert. (See Philo the Jew.)
>
> What does all this mean? It was what was foretold so long beforehand: for 2,000 years no heathen had worshipped the God of the Jews and at the time predicted the mass of the heathen worshipped this one and only God. Temples are destroyed, even kings make their submission to the Cross. What does this all mean? It is the spirit of God spreading over the earth.

Pensée 326 further supports the importance of fulfillment of prophecy for Pascal.

> And what crowns it all is that it was foretold, so that no one could say it was the effect of chance.

With this *Pensée* Pascal addresses his gambling friends who dismissed the life of Jesus and Christianity as just one religious movement among many in history, a chance event like the rest of them. Some contemporary scientists such as Richard Dawkins offer this criticism, proposing that over a long enough period of time, chance genetic mutations and natural selection can lead to complex life forms and the emergence of culture and religion. I imagine Pascal asking Professor Dawkins whether chance mutations could bring about the Jewish people prophesying about Jesus for thousands of years, and the prophecies being fulfilled. Is Dawkins "blind watchmaker" model adequate for explaining the fulfillment of detailed prophecy? Pascal answers in *Pensée* 332:

> *Prophecies.* If a single man had written a book foretelling the time and manner of Jesus' coming and Jesus had done in conformity with these prophecies, this would carry infinite weight.
>
> But there is much more here. There is a succession of men over a period of 4,000 years, coming consistently and invariably one after the other, to foretell the same coming; there is an entire people proclaiming it, existing for 4,000 years to testify in a body to the certainty they feel about it, from which they cannot be deflected by whatever threats and persecutions they may suffer. This is of quite a different order of importance.

What do we have here? Pascal, the father of the science of chance, is saying that the nature of the prophecies is such that they could not have been made by chance. From Abraham to Moses to Isaiah to Jeremiah to Malachi, the same message for 4,000 years. Cultural evolution would never permit this kind of consistency, Pascal suggests, especially in the face of perennial threats and persecutions. The event of a whole body of people testifying about the coming Messiah for 4,000 years is a clue that a divine providence may be driving it all.

Uniqueness Point: Gentleness Not Terror. For the last word from Pascal on prophecy, consider his summary statement in *Pensée* 198 regarding it and the uniqueness of Christianity:

> I see a number of religions in conflict, and therefore all false, except one. Each of them wishes to be believed on its own authority and threatens unbelievers. I do not believe them on that account. Anyone can say that. Anyone can call himself a prophet, but I see Christianity, and find its prophecies, which are not something anyone can do.

Here Pascal suggests a useful test for screening out a false religion. Does it threaten you? Does it instill itself with terror? Does it say if you do not join their club then you will go to hell? Pascal says that anyone can make these threats, and any religion that threatens is false. In contrast, true Christianity instills itself into hearts with gentleness and grace, with no threats and no terror. [*Pensée* 172] Delivery of a religion through prophecies and grace, not through its own authority and threats, mark a true religion.

Evidence from Perpetuity of the Jewish People. Pascal marveled at the "perpetuity" of the Jewish people, in particular their continuous proclamation, for thousands of years, that a redeemer will come. Pascal suggests that the perpetuity of the Jews constitutes weighty evidence for the Christian religion. We begin with Pascal's summary of this evidence in *Pensée* 390:

> *Perpetuity*. Let us consider that from the beginning of the world the Messiah has been awaited or worshipped continuously; that there were men who said that God had revealed to them that a redeemer would be born and would save his people; that Abraham then came to say that it had been revealed to him that the [redeemer] would be born of his line through a son he would have; that Jacob declared that of his twelve children it would be of Judah that the redeemer would be born; that Moses and the prophets came next to declare the time and manner of his coming; that they said that the law which they had was only to last until the Messiah gave them his; that it would be perpetual until then but that the other would last for eternity; that in this way their law or that of the Messiah, of which it was the pledge, would always be upon the earth; that it has in fact always endured;

> finally, that Jesus Christ did come exactly in the circumstances foretold. This is all very remarkable.

A particular piece of evidence from perpetuity is that Christianity has roots in old books. Pascal suggests that the existence and age of the Old Testament Scriptures is foundationally important for the plausibility of Christian truth:

> *Foundation of our faith.* Heathen religion has no foundation today. It is said that it once had them in oracles that spoke. But what are the books that assert this? Are they so reliable by virtue of their authors? Have they been so carefully preserved that we can be certain they have not become corrupt?...
>
> [On the Jewish religion] Its foundation is admirable. It is the oldest book in the world, and the most authentic... Our religion is so divine that another divine religion merely provides its foundations. [*Pensée* 243]

The plausibility of Christianity is greatly enhanced by the fact that it emerged from an amazingly well founded and documented religion. In contrast, heathen and pagan religions that emerge, without reference to old and authentic books, have no basis for defining their principles and evaluating their application. They float as feathers on the wind. To Pascal a true religion must have a firm foundation.

Pensée 243 teaches us to value our historical roots. I believe Pascal would disagree with those within the Christian church who are quick to revise creeds and doctrines in response to cultural changes. In summer 2006, the General Assembly of the Presbyterian Church USA received a paper on the Trinity that proposed alternative metaphorical triads to the traditional "Father, Son, and Spirit," which is prominent in the Bible. The new proposals include "Compassionate Mother, Life-Giving Womb, and Beloved Child" as well as "Rainbow, Ark, and Dove." To abandon the Trinitarian naming used in Scripture is to create a new religion and a new God (Reverend Louise Holert, personal communication).

The uprooting of Christianity from the Scriptures and traditions erodes the distinctiveness of Christianity, making it look like a fad or trend, a grass-like religion that is here today, and the wind blows over it and tomorrow it is gone. *Pensée* 251 reveals Pascal's ethic to resist bending the interpretation of the Scriptures to fit cultural changes:

> Anyone who wishes to give the meaning of Scripture without taking it from Scripture is the enemy of Scripture. St. Augustine, *De Doctrina Christiana* [pages 111–127].

Pascal expressed awe and wonder at the prophet-bearers themselves– the Jewish people– and saw them as constituting weighty evidence for Christianity. In *Pensée* 451, entitled *Advantages of the Jewish people*, Pascal observed five "striking and singular features apparent in [the Jewish people]." First, the Jews are all brothers and sisters, descending from the single ancestors Adam, Noah, Abraham, etc. Second, the Jews have remarkable antiquity– at the time of Pascal's writing they were the oldest people group known to Man. Third, the Jews lasted for a singularly long time, indeed they still persist, which would impress Pascal. The longevity of the Jews is remarkable because it is "despite the efforts of so many powerful kings who have tried a hundred times to wipe them out." [*Pensée* 451] The Jews have faced enemies who hated them for thousands of years, yet they persist.

Fourth, the Jews have the oldest and most perfect law; the Mosaic law is the longest continuously observed law in history. The greatness of the Mosaic law can be seen from the fact that it has been widely adopted; Greek and Roman lawgivers borrowed from it in their chief laws, and today the laws of the United States and many other countries borrow heavily from it.

Fifth, the Mosaic law is the most severe and rigorous of laws. In Pascal's words:

> [The Mosaic] law is at the same time the most severe and rigorous of all as regards the practice of their religion, holding this people to its duty by imposing a host of peculiar and arduous observations on pain of death. Thus it is a really amazing thing that the law has been constantly preserved for so many centuries, by a people as rebellious and impatient as this one, while all other states have from time to time changed their laws, although they were very much more lenient. [*Pensée* 451]

Here we have a remarkable point. Because the Jewish law is the hardest and most difficult to obey, we would expect it to last only a little while. Normal human behavior would lead to the law being made easier over time, or to its abolition. So what was it that made the Jews preserve their stringent law in all perpetuity? Pascal beckons us to see the mark of divinity in this law, which is too perfect and too sustained to be invented and maintained solely by human beings. Pascal asserts this quite directly in *Pensée* 280:

> But the fact that this religion has always been preserved inflexibly shows that it is divine.

Pascal expands this point in *Pensée* 495, where he observes that God created the Jewish people for the express purpose of perpetuating the Mosaic law:

> They are clearly a people created expressly to serve as a witness to the Messiah. Is. 43:9, 44:8. They hand down the books and love them but do not understand them. And all this was foretold: that the judgments of God are entrusted to them, but as a sealed book.

Pascal observes that despite lovingly preserving every letter of the Old Testament for thousands of years, the (temporal) Jews could not comprehend that Jesus Christ is the center and thesis of the Old Testament.

Pascal goes on to write that this dual reality of the temporal Jews preserving the Scriptures yet missing their thesis is itself a piece of evidence for the veracity of Christianity:

> But it is the very fact of their refusal [to believe] that is the basis of our belief. We should be much less inclined to believe if they were on our side; we should then have a much better excuse [for not believing].
>
> It is a wonderful thing to have made the Jews so fond of prophecies and so hostile to their fulfillment. [*Pensée* 273]

By describing this strange paradox as wonderful, I think Pascal intends it as a hint that a divine cause might be behind it. For on purely human terms, it seems contradictory for a people to vigorously maintain prophecies unadulterated for 4,000 years, yet be against seeing them fulfilled. If this is accepted as a contradiction, then it logically follows that divine providence must be the cause. But as usual Pascal does not intend this as a logical proof, but rather as a winsome clue.

Pensée 454 most fully reveals Pascal's amazement at the unique history of the Jews, and his belief that this history constitutes a great and relatively clear piece of evidence for the Christian faith. A strength of this historical evidence is that it may be seen by anyone who looks, so that the basic points are resistant to dispute.

> I see Christianity founded on a previous religion, in which I find the following facts... It is certain that in certain parts of the world we can see a peculiar people, separated from the other peoples of the world, and this is called the Jewish people.
>
> I see then makers of religions in several parts of the world and throughout the ages, but their morality fails to satisfy me and their proofs fail to give me pause. Thus I should have refused alike the Moslem religion, that of China, of the ancient Romans, and of the Egyptians solely because, none of them bearing the stamp of truth more than another, nor anything which forces me to choose it, reason cannot incline towards one rather than another.
>
> But as I consider this shifting and odd variety of customs and beliefs in different ages, I find in one corner of the world a peculiar people, separated from all the other peoples of the earth, who are the most ancient of all and whose history is earlier by several centuries than the oldest histories we have.
>
> I find then this great and numerous people, descended from one man, worshipping one God, and living according to a law which they claim to have received from his hand. They maintain that they are the only people in the world to whom God has revealed his mysteries; that all men are corrupt and in disgrace with God, that they have all been abandoned to their senses and their own minds; and that this is the reason for the strange aberrations and continual changes of religions and customs among them, whereas these people remain unshakeable in their conduct; but that God will not leave the other peoples for ever in darkness, that a Redeemer will come, for all; that they are in the world to proclaim him to men; that they have been expressly created to be the forerunners and heralds of this great coming, and to call all peoples to unite with them in looking forward to the Redeemer.
>
> My encounter with this people amazes me and seems worthy of attention...

The Old Testament Points to Jesus Christ. Pascal believed that every word of the Old Testament points to God's redemptive plan that is accomplished by Jesus Christ. This is seen in *Pensées* 392 and 570:

> God wishing to create for himself a holy people, whom he would keep apart from all other nations, whom he would deliver from their enemies, whom he would bring to a place of rest, promised to do so and foretold by his prophets the time and manner of his coming...for in the creation of man Adam was witness to this and received the promise of a saviour who should be borne of woman.
>
> When men were still so close to Creation that they had not been able to forget their creation and their fall, when those who had seen Adam were no longer in this world, God sent Noah, saving him and drowning the whole earth by a miracle, which clearly showed his power to save the world, and his will to do so, and to cause to be born from the seed of a woman the one he had promised. [*Pensée* 392]

Pascal interprets the events described in Genesis as prophecies that God will send a savior into the world. For example Pascal suggests that the lives of Abraham and his descendants were intended as a witness for Jesus Christ. In *Pensée* 570 Pascal writes of Abraham's great grandson:

> *Christ prefigured by Joseph.* Innocent, beloved of his father, sent by his father to see his brothers, is sold for twenty pieces of silver by his brothers. Through this he becomes their lord, their saviour, saviour of strangers and saviour of the world. None of this would have happened but for their plot to destroy him, the sale, and their rejection of him.
>
> In prison Joseph, innocent between two criminals. Jesus on the cross between two thieves. He prophesies the salvation of one and the death of the other when to all appearances they are alike. Christ saves the elect and damns the reprobate for the same crime. Joseph only prophesies, Jesus acts. Joseph asks the man who will be saved to remember him when he comes in glory. And the man Jesus saves asks to be remembered when he comes into his kingdom.

Pascal's Apologetics is for Skeptics. To close Part III, I would like to emphasize that Pascal did *not* present the traditional evidence (i.e., based on the historicity of Jesus' resurrection, miracles, prophecies, and the Jews) dogmatically– he knew this approach would not be winsome for his skeptical interlocutor. Rather, Pascal emphasized the evidence that can be plainly seen by anybody without appeal to revelation:

> I see Christianity founded on a previous religion, in which I find the following facts. (I am not speaking here of the miracles of Moses, Christ and the apostles, because they do not at first appear convincing, and I want only to bring as evidence all those foundations of Christianity which are beyond doubt and cannot be called in doubt by anyone whatever.) [*Pensée* 454]

As a skilled observer of human nature, Pascal acknowledges that modern people are usually not persuaded by the traditional proofs, as they are too psychologically weak to convince. Elsewhere Pascal further addresses the limitations of traditional proofs, for example in writing,

> The proofs drawn from Scripture by Jesus and the Apostles are not conclusive, for they only say that Moses said that a prophet would come, but this does not prove that he was the one, and that was the whole question. These passages serve therefore only to show that there is nothing against Scripture in this, and that no inconsistency is apparent. [*Pensée* 840]

I find Pascal's precision about the limitations of his arguments refreshing. It is very different to say, "this proves Christianity is true," than to say, "this proves that Christianity cannot be proven to be untrue." If only more people on radio and TV would be so careful! Often arguments are delivered sloppily, like doing surgery with a chain saw, sometimes intentionally with intent of propaganda and manipulation. In contrast, Pascal delivers his arguments like a chief surgeon wielding a scalpel, with intent to probe and interpret reality with the utmost care.

Part IV. Christianity Compared to Other Religions

Pascal compared the Christian religion to deism and to Islam, and in Part IV we will consider these comparisons.

Christianity Compared to Deism. During the Enlightenment, deism emerged as a popular religion, to which many Christians converted yet still considered themselves Christians. The World Union of Deists defines their religion as "belief in God based on the application of our reason on the designs/laws found throughout Nature." As rationalists, deists reject revelation, the supernatural, and an interventionist God. Likely with Descartes in mind as an arch-example, in *Pensée* 449 Pascal points out the infinite distance between deism and Christianity, suggesting it is absurd for a deist to consider himself a Christian:

> They [deists] imagine that [the Christian religion] simply consists in worshiping a God considered to be great and mighty and eternal, which is properly speaking deism, almost as remote from the Christian religion as atheism, its complete opposite... All those who seek God apart from Christ, and who go no further than nature, either find no light to satisfy them or come to devise a means of knowing and serving God without a mediator, thus falling into either atheism or deism, two things almost equally abhorrent to Christianity.

Deism believes in the Creator but not the Incarnation nor the Redeemer. It believes in an aloof God without Christ, a God whom, after making humans, took leave from their affairs. In contrast Pascal's Christianity is Christ-centered, as beautifully expressed by Pierre de Bérulle, a major forerunner of the Jansenist movement. Bérulle agrees with Copernicus on the central position of the sun in the physical realm, and uses it as a metaphor for the Sun of Righteousness' central position in the spiritual world:

> An excellent mind of this century wishes to hold that the sun is at the center of the world and not the earth; that it is immovable, and that the earth, in proportion to its round shape moves in reference to the sun... This new opinion, scarcely followed in the science of the stars, is useful and ought to be followed in the science of salvation. Because Jesus is the sun, immovable in his grandeur and moving all things... Jesus is the true center of the world and the world ought to be in continual movement toward him.

Back in autumn of 1988, when I was a freshman comparing the religious ideas of Descartes and Pascal in a French literature course, this idea of the person of Christ in the center was ultimately what made Christianity more appealing to me than the deism I read about in

Descartes' *Meditations*. Christ is personally and inwardly transforming, not remote– a remote God cannot help me with my wretched condition.

Deism as Scientism. Deism, closely connected to modernism, purports that reason is the faculty we should use and trust for solving problems and creating a just and happy society. As we examined in chapter 3 Pascal critiques this path because it does not lead to faith:

> Faith is a gift of God. Do not imagine that we describe it as a gift of reason. Other religions do not say that about their faith. They offered nothing but reason as a way to faith, and yet it does not lead there. [*Pensée* 588]

Peter Kreeft (1993) observes that deism avoids the two basic truths of Christianity, sin and salvation– deism is a "proper" religion for respectable people, avoiding blood. Deists recoil from Christianity's dwelling on misery and death, as expressed, for example, in Pascal's summary of the Christian worldview:

> All Jesus did was to teach men that they loved themselves, that they were slaves, blind, sick, unhappy and sinful, that he had to deliver, enlighten, sanctify and heal them, and this would be achieved by men hating themselves and following him through his misery and death on the Cross. [*Pensée* 271]

The fact that deism avoids the uncomfortable topic of sin explains why it has been, and still is, quite popular. The remaking of the Christian religion with the blood removed can be seen in various organizations and sects that have spun off from Christianity. An example of a sect that avoids blood is Mormonism, which avoids any images of suffering in or on its buildings– no crosses are allowed and the art-work inside depicts only happy scenes. I visited a Mormon temple at its opening in Massachusetts in 2000, and there were many paintings on the walls, all of pleasant scenes with flowers and healthy people.

Another example is the Freemason fraternal organization, whose members believe in a "Supreme Being" but usually not in Immanuel. George Washington, Thomas Jefferson and many others in the upper crust of early American society were members, who as Enlightenment thinkers emphasized reason and dismissed the cross as the only way to know God. Most Freemasons are deists, as exemplified by the

Freemason's naming of God as "The Great Architect of the Universe" and the "Grand Geometer."

In contrast to respectable deism, Christianity comes across as quite odd, with its ghoulish emphasis on blood and suffering. How unique is the Christian religion for using the cross as its central symbol– a device used to put criminals to death in a humiliating manner! As Dick Keyes has mused, can you imagine churches adorned with hang-man nooses, or electric chairs, on top of their steeples? It seems strange– yet this is what Christianity is. Does any other religion have a central symbol anything close to an execution device?

Furthermore, Pascal points out that Jesus intentionally wished to die an ignominious death, that is, a death that makes him look like an accursed criminal that deserved to die:

> Jesus did not want to be killed without the forms of justice, for it is much more ignominious to die at the hands of justice than in some unjust insurrection. [*Pensée* 940]

How odd! From a human perspective, no one wants to die scandalized. Any deist, or almost any other human for that matter, would prefer an honorable or heroic death, or at least one without ignominy. This scandalized manner of dying that Jesus chose constitutes a clue that Jesus may have had a divine intent in mind that is unintelligible to a purely human analysis.

Continuing Pascal's comparison of Christianity and deism, consider another fragment of *Pensée* 449:

> [The Christian religion] teaches men these two truths alike: that there is a God, of whom men are capable, and that there is a corruption in nature which makes them unworthy. It is of equal importance to men to know each of these two points: and it is equally dangerous for man to know God without knowing his own wretchedness as to know his own wretchedness without knowing the Redeemer who can cure him. Knowing only one of these points leads either to the arrogance of the philosophers, who have known God but not their own wretchedness, or to the despair of the atheists, who know their own wretchedness without knowing their Redeemer.

Here Pascal classifies deists as arrogant philosophers who know God but not their own wretchedness, nor their need for a redeemer. Deism lauds human greatness while neglecting human weakness. Deist-type thinking has led to ambitious attempts to improve humanity, like Marxist communism, which historically has led to oppression and blood baths. Such failed systems went wrong in part because they excluded the wretched part of the human equation.

Christianity Compared to Islam. Pascal also saw stark contrasts between Christianity and Islam, which he suggests reveal greater credibility for Christianity. In *Pensée* 209 Pascal lists some of the major differences of their founders, Jesus Christ and Mahomet. First, while Jesus was foretold by prophets, Mahomet was not. Pascal queried, "What signs did Mahomet show that are not shown by anyone else who wants to call himself a prophet?" [*Pensée* 243] Second, Mahomet was a military leader that used violence and coercion to spread Islam, and taught his followers to disdain their enemies (Caner and Caner, 2002); while in contrast Jesus did not participate in military affairs, never used violence, and taught his followers to love their enemies and to spread the Gospel peacefully and non-coercively. In the area of violence these leaders are opposites, which Pascal summarized as, "Mahomet slew, Jesus caused his followers to be slain." [*Pensée* 209] The Caner brothers (Christian seminary professors who were converted from Islam) similarly contrast the two leaders:

> Jesus Christ shed his own blood on the cross so that people could come to God. Muhammad shed other people's blood so that his constituents could have political power throughout the Arabian Peninsula.

Third, Mahomet forbade reading, whereas Jesus' Apostles commanded it. Both religions claim to be the one true religion, but in their origins they took opposite approaches to making followers believe this. By forbidding reading, Mahomet asked Allah's followers to believe on sheer authority. In contrast, the early Christians were confident that the Scriptures express God's living truth in a manner akin to bread needed for daily nourishment, such that open reading of them makes them more compelling, not less.

In *Pensée* 243 Pascal observes additional differences between the religion's leaders. Fourth, Mahomet did not claim to perform any miracles, whereas Jesus performed a great many. Fifth, Mahomet did not teach mystery according to his own tradition, whereas Jesus taught a mysterious truth within the Jewish religion. Sixth, whereas Mahomet did not teach morality, Jesus is widely regarded as a great moral teacher.

Seventh, Mahomet did not proclaim a blissful eternal heaven, but only earthly pleasures continuing on after death. The Koran and traditional Islamic writings describe heaven in elaborate sensual detail; for example sura 56 verses 12–39 describes paradise entailing jeweled couches, purest wine, choice fruits and fowls, and dark-eyed virgins, chaste as hidden pearls and loving companions on one's right hand [Koran, translation by Dawood, 2000; also see Koran sura 55 verses 54–56 and sura 76 verses 12–22]. In contrast Jesus taught that paradise entails eternal bliss of a different kind (and of a higher order) than earthly pleasures, describing heaven as a consummation of spiritual marriage between himself and his people.

Pascal completes *Pensée* 209 with this summary of the differences between Mahomet and Jesus:

> In a word, the difference is so great that, if Mahomet followed the path of success, humanly speaking, Jesus followed that of death, humanly speaking, and, instead of concluding that where Mahomet succeeded Jesus could have done so too, we must say that, since Mahomet succeeded, Jesus had to die.

Pascal suggests that Mahomet's success was a success by human standards, achieved by conquering, winning, etc., and asks whether this is what we should expect from a true prophet heralding the true religion. He suggests it is more plausible that the unique true religion would be introduced by someone who is totally unique, and who does not fit the mold of human success. "Any man can do what Mahomet did. For he performed no miracles and was not foretold. No man can do what Christ did." [*Pensée* 321] Christ's uniqueness raises the hypothesis that he is unique in history as God's begotten who came for a divine and universal purpose.

What About the Crusades? Critics might object that if Christianity is radically different from Islam, being about peace and love, then how come the followers of Jesus Christ have also used violence to coerce conversions? Doesn't this suggest that both Christianity and Islam are fundamentalist dogmatisms that do more harm than good? While Christians are undeniably guilty of this charge and their only reasonable position is to acknowledge it and repent, this fact is not germane to the question of what the differences between the *leaders* implies about the differences between the religions. The facts that some followers of Christ botch their service of Christ horribly, and that some non-followers use the name of Christ to serve their own ends, do not invalidate Christianity practiced in a way that is true to the character of Jesus Christ. As the founder and model member of a religion has or has not integrity, so does the religion as correctly practiced.

The evil that is done in the name of religion is a popular modern argument for avoiding grappling with religious issues, and Christ's good character is an important counter-argument. Pascal would diagnose the modern's argument as an evasion technique, a form of indifference that he wrote blisteringly against. Pascal's *Pensées* on faith and reason, Man's pride, and God's hiddenness also contribute counter-arguments. It is a form of faith– not reason– that draws the inference that Christianity is false because some people do evil in Christ's name. It may be that God allows certain evils to be done by his followers, or by his feigned followers, for his own reasons that he keeps hidden. The point is this– human creatures *do not know* what the existence of evil deeds imply about the existence and nature of God. And Pascal insists that not knowing– acknowledging the limits of our knowing capacity– is critical for cultivating a humble disposition that is a pre-requisite for knowing God. (For example, God helped Job's faith by not telling Job why he allowed him to undergo great suffering.) To presume away mystery is irrational and cynical.

A True Religion May Contain Mysterious Paradoxes, But Not Contradictions. Although Pascal saw faith, not reason, as the most critical means for knowing God, he saw reason as an important tool for comparing different religions and drawing inferences that some are more rationally credible than others. This view can be seen in *Pensée* 257, where he proposes that if a religion has internal contradictions, then it must be rejected:

> *Contradictions.* A good portrait can only be made by reconciling all our contradictory features, and it is not enough to follow through a series of mutually compatible qualities without reconciling their opposites; to understand an author's meaning all contradictory passages must be reconciled.
>
> Thus to understand Scripture a meaning must be found which reconciles all contradictory passages; it is not enough to have one that fits a number of compatible passages, but one which reconciles even contradictory ones.

> Every author has a meaning which reconciles all contradictory passages, or else he has no meaning at all, and that cannot be said of Scripture and the prophets; they were certainly too sensible. We must therefore look for a meaning which reconciles all contradictions.
>
> Thus the true meaning is not that of the Jews, but in Christ all contradictions are reconciled.

Pascal insists that any religion, if it is to be accepted as true, must not have a single contradiction. He observes that when certain metaphorical Scriptures are interpreted literally, contradictions emerge. For example Pascal considers specific prophecies that were not fulfilled politically or militarily. But if the failed prophecies are interpreted figuratively, in terms of spiritual events wrought by Christ the Messiah, then they can be seen to be fulfilled. If we are to accept the Bible as a coherent document, then we must work to resolve the contradictions, and Pascal contends that Christ does indeed provide this resolution. Pascal's phrase "in Christ all contradictions are reconciled" may be equivalently expressed as "in Christ all apparent contradictions are found to be paradoxes." This wins for the Christian religion respect, for though it retains the grandeur of mystery, it does not contain flat contradictions.

In fact, Pascal suggests that a reasonable study of the Bible and the Koran will find that whereas mysteries but not contradictions persist in the former, *both* mysteries and contradictions abound in the latter. A reasonable analysis can detect this difference, Pascal purports:

> It is not what is obscure in Mahomet, and might be claimed to have a mystical sense, that I want him to be judged, but by what is clear, by his paradise and all the rest. That is what is ridiculous about him, and that is why it is not right to take his obscurities for mysteries, seeing that what is clear in him is ridiculous. It is not the same with Scripture. I admit that there are obscurities as odd as those of Mahomet, but some things are admirably clear, with prophecies manifestly fulfilled. So it is not an even contest. We must not confuse and treat as equal things which are only alike in their obscurities, and not in the clarity which earns respect for its obscurities. [*Pensée* 218]

Pascal suggests that a fair reading of the authoritative documents of the two religions reveals gaping differences. For example, a case can be made that the Koran contains clear statements that can be plainly contradicted by logic or known facts, whereas the Bible does not (appreciating the Bible's use of metaphor and figures, as discussed in chapter 6, is critical for making this case). As also discussed in earlier chapters, Pascal labored to show that Christianity better meshes with human experience– the Bible fully acknowledges the frailty and sinfulness of human beings, and also fully acknowledges their great dignity and capacities, whereas Islam and other religions provide oversimplified models that do not fit part of the human data. Islam does not hold the doctrine of original sin, for example, which Pascal found to be the key for making sense of human history and psychology. [*Pensée* 131]

Pascal's study of comparative religion convinced him that Christianity has the greatest rational plausibility. This inference under-girds his conclusion in the Wager that reasonable people do well to vigorously investigate the Christian faith.

Part V. Responding to Common Refutations of Christianity by Atheists

In this section I will raise four common refutations of the Christian religion made by atheists/scientific secularists, and summarize responses based on *Pensées* presented earlier. Pascal seizes what is often the atheist's advantage: he does not need to disprove the objections, but only to create serious doubt. In order to compel wagering, Pascal needs only to convince his interlocutor that Christianity is plausible.

Objection 1: Man Created God in his Own Image– Because of Science We No Longer Need God. Some atheists contend that humankind invented god as a necessary concept that modern scientific man no longer needs, and that in a matter of time superstition and ignorance will fade away. This objection states that before the age of science, humans had little control over nature, and thus had a psychological need for a god that benevolently controlled nature. But now that science has dawned, humans can sufficiently control nature to render the god concept unnecessary.

Pascal addresses such children of the Enlightenment in many ways; let us remind ourselves of four. First, recall Pascal's *Pensées* on the weakness of human reason: it is unreliable due to fanciful imagination, wrongly perceived sense data, a fly buzzing in the ear, passions, and self-interest. Reflection on contemporary culture and politics reveals that reasoning holds as weak a position today as when science dawned; for example, far from driving decision-making, scientific reasoning frequently takes a back seat to passions and self-interest. Second, humankind remains extremely vulnerable to nature (Man is a "reed, the weakest in nature" [*Pensée* 200]), as highlighted by several recent natural disasters. Descartes' hope that science would deliver control and safety has been dashed. Third, our ultimate vulnerability, to death, is the same today as for any other age. The fact that Pascal's description of our horror of death resonates so well with us shows that we have not materially progressed from his time.

Fourth, scientific secularism has not filled Man's vacuum of morality, justice, happiness, and meaning. This failure is explained by Pascal's observation that science delivers goods in the physical and intellectual orders, but not in the spiritual order. In the physical order, science may stave off disease and open up leisure-time, but disease eventually kills us and, apart from God, leisure-time is filled with diversionary activities devoid of true morality, justice, happiness, or meaning. In the intellectual order, even if science could provide a rationale argument delivering a modicum of these goods, its impact would flee away, "for it is too much trouble to have the proofs always present before us." [Pensée 821] In contrast we feel an aching hole in our heart automatically. If we feel this vacuum, we do well to acknowledge that science is unable to fill it, and to consider Pascal's suggestion that only God can fill it.

Objection 2: Man Invented God as a Psychological Crutch to Deal with his Fear of Death and Desire for Happiness. Some atheists contend that Man invented a god that will fix his problems because he wishes for such a god to be real; Freud called this a "wish-fulfillment dream." I dream for a god that dignifies me, loves me, and will bring me to paradise after I die, and my self-interest gives me an incentive to believe this dream to be true.

Pascal's *Pensées* on the Jewish people show a God not invented to provide themselves comfort. Their Old Testament is replete with prophets promising that God will severely judge the Jews, that they will be conquered and held in captivity by hated enemies. Why have the Jews– despite being fickle and proud like all other human beings– preserved their books and laws more inflexibly and more durably than any other people, even though these books and laws are severe and constantly shine a spotlight on their shameful ways? Why does the Bible describe God as totally rigid about the standard of behavior for the whole world? Why did God promise Abraham that he would bless his genetic pool, with purpose to bless other peoples outside of this pool? [see Genesis 12:3,

18:18, 22:18, 26:4, 28:14] The biblical God of Abraham, Isaac, and Jacob is not a god designed to satisfy one's self-interests, nor can he be manipulated. Why is the Jew's Messiah a suffering servant [Isaiah 53], a man who dies a scandalous and ignominious death? This is an odd contrast to other ancient narratives, which typically describe heroes. Wouldn't an invented god be a typical hero? In sum, a serious literary reading of the biblical texts is hard-pressed to conclude that this God was made in man's image.

Pascal's *Pensées* on God's hiddenness also respond to the objection. If Man made God in his own image, then why did Jesus Christ come in a way that is so unexpected? Pascal observes that the Old Testament reveals Jesus Christ as the Messiah in an intentionally obscure manner, veiled in figures, so that the spiritually minded will perceive him and the temporally minded will not. The inventor of a psychological crutch would be temporally minded– is it likely that such an inventor would be capable of constructing the Bible's obscure and double-edged narrative? Moreover, Pascal suggests that where other worldviews and philosophies fail to explain the riddle of Man (as paradoxically great and wretched), Christianity succeeds. This is an amazing achievement, casting doubt on a proposition that humankind could invent such an intricately accurate model from his base desire to assuage his fear of death. Lastly, Pascal's *Pensées* describing people as dispossessed kings cast doubt on the objection. We discover within ourselves both an idea of perfection and a feeling of wretchedness that we cannot attain. Pascal suggests that if we were merely animals, then we would not possess an idea of our lost perfection.

Objection 3: Religious Fundamentalism Does More Harm than Good. Some atheists including Sam Harris contend that Christianity, like other religions that believe in some absolute truth, do more harm than good. To address this objection, we begin by considering the meaning of the word "fundamentalist," which has become a smear word used against fringe groups. As Tim Keller (2008) points out, the word fundamentalist applies much more broadly than to fringe groups; in fact many of us are fundamentalists, defined as people who "strictly adhere to any set of ideas or principles." [Webster's dictionary] Secular scientists hold the fundamental that reasoning is the proper means for governing life; relativists hold the fundamental that no one religion possesses the absolute truth (i.e., tolerance); modern pagans hold the fundamental that people are free to engage in diversions and/or to be indifferent ("I refuse to care"); Christianity holds the fundamental that people ought to love everybody, even their enemies, even to the point of death. So the question is not whether fundamentalism is harmful or helpful, it is *which fundamentals* are harmful or helpful.

When stated thus, the Christian fundamental is obviously beneficent, and if every person in history calling themselves Christian had lived this fundamental, then there probably could be no objection. But, as mentioned above, the objection flows out of the historical fact that many people calling themselves Christian have exchanged the Christian fundamental for the fundamental of holding power, leading to all sorts of nefarious acts. Beyond the important response that Jesus Christ did truly live the Christian fundamental, how else do the *Pensées* provide a response to this objection?

First of all, Pascal himself said that the greatest evil is done in the name of religion. [*Pensée* 813] Pascal pointed this out not to suggest that Christianity as correctly practiced by its true adherents do evil, but rather to suggest that Man's wretchedness apart from God includes a willingness to use religion as a pretext to justify his self-interested behavior. Thus, the fact that people who invoke Christ's name do evil serves primarily as excellent support for Pascal's thesis in the first half of the *Pensées*.

But we must respond further, for if Christianity is true, then why has it not brought about a strikingly obvious revolution of goodness as the new kingdom is implemented? This question is fair, because Jesus Christ taught that his followers will be known by their love, and thus to be valid, Christianity must bring about actual goodness. Pascal's *Pensées* on God's hiddenness and the theory of orders support that it indeed has done this. For example, in *Pensée* 149 Pascal suggests that, "there is enough light for those who desire only to see, and enough darkness for those of a contrary disposition." There may be plenty of goodness brought about, but people who wish to debunk the faith cannot see it. This goodness, for example, may include the work of Christians to feed and clothe the poor, to struggle for civil rights and equality for women, to establish Universities and hospitals, and to free the Middle Ages from religious tyranny to an era that uses science where appropriate for delivering goods. In fact, many have argued that the Judeo-Christian worldview was indispensable for the emergence of science and its fruits (e.g., Schaefer, 1983).

A reason why the goodness of Christianity is not obvious to all is that the most advanced followers of Jesus Christ are the most humble and hence the least interested in making known their good deeds. (Pascal wrote that the finest thing about good deeds is the attempt to keep them secret, *Pensée* 643.) True believers in every age have quietly served the poor with no visibility, and people who treasure carnal or intellectual goods– but not spiritual goods– have very poor eyesight for detecting their good deeds. Moreover, Pascal's *Pensées* on Man's inability to reason stably and to detect justice raise the question of, "How can we reliably judge whether Christianity has done more harm than good?" Pascal would find it naïve to suggest that we can answer this through a straightforward scientific analysis. A reliable answer would have to be based on reliable sense data, and we have no assurance that history texts contain these. Furthermore, the fanciful imagination and self-interest of the evaluator prevents him from approaching certitude in answering this question. We are left with serious doubt about the claim that Christianity has done more harm than good.

Objection 4: Why is there Suffering in the World? Some atheists contend that if the Christian doctrine of a loving and all-powerful God were true, then there could not be so much suffering in the world. Hence the truth of Christianity is disproved. When I hear a newscast reporting the most recent natural disaster, my gut reaction is, "it seems unfair– how come God allowed the deaths and sufferings of certain individuals, while I am unaffected." However, this feeling that God is unfair only makes sense under an annihilationist worldview, which holds that this current life is all there is. From the annihilationist premise, equity is measured primarily by quality-adjusted length of life, and it is unfair for some to die in their sleep at 93 and for others to die violently at 3. In response, Pascal's *Pensées* contend that it is not reasonable to conclude that annihilationism is true– we do not possess the data or the faculties to infer absolutely that there is not an afterlife. But when the possibility of an everlasting afterlife is admitted– plus the possibility that events in this life may affect the quality of one's afterlife, then the whole calculus of what constitutes fairness changes. Based on Pascal's thoughts on the finite being 'swallowed up by the infinite' (e.g., in the Wager), once one admits the possibility of an everlasting afterlife, then death at 3 may not be less equitable than at 93, because 90 years is a blip of time that contributes only an imperceptible dot to the span of eternity, and because the 3-year old may have a happier afterlife, which far outweighs his misfortune of an early death. Moreover, Pascal's *Pensées* on death emphasize the universality of death– the fact that we all must die is infinitely more significant and terrible than the detail of the manner and time of our death. Pascal suggests that when we are honest about ourselves, we perceive our terror of death is so strong that only a complete reprieve would cure our terror and bring real peace. Thus the fact of death– and the possibility of an afterlife– challenge our gut instincts about what constitutes justice.

In addition, the thesis of Pascal's *Pensées* addresses the question of why is there suffering in the world, as summarized in *Pensée* 131: "There are in faith two equally constant truths. One is that man in the state of his creation, or in the state of grace, is exalted above the whole of nature, made like unto God and sharing in his divinity. The other is that in the state of corruption and sin he has fallen from that first state and has become like the beasts." Pascal's first truth– Man's greatness because he is like God in origin and redemption– includes the truth that Man has free will. A consequence is that God will not completely stop people from harming one another. The real possibility of suffering is a logical consequence of Man's possession of free will. Pascal's second truth– Man's wretchedness without God because of original sin– is terribly difficult for moderns to accept. Pascal understood our difficulty, remarking that the transmission of sin is the greatest mystery of all. [*Pensée* 131] But Pascal also insists that without this mysterious truth, "we can have no knowledge of ourselves." [*Pensée* 131] If the truth of original sin is accepted, then an explanation for suffering follows: through original sin Man made himself his own center, which logically must lead to strife and inequities; and because of original sin God subjected humankind to wretchedness, which includes disease, death, toil, and over-desires.

But is the doctrine of original sin plausible? It might be said that the whole point of the first half of the *Pensées* is to affirmatively answer this question. If Pascal's description of Man as a dispossessed king rings true, then you have accepted the reality of a set of effects that are perfectly consistent with the cause of original sin, making this doctrine a plausible hypothesis. Furthermore, Pascal's *Pensées* on the limitations of reason suggest that the assertions of modern atheists against original sin are presumption rather than reasoned arguments– Pascal claims that there are no grounds for laughing at those who do believe in the truth of original sin. [*Pensée* 482] Therefore the mind has reasons to accept the credibility of this truth.

The heart has its own reasons for believing this truth. Marilynne Robinson points out that John Calvin "considered the Fall of Man to be, on balance, a good thing. As a result of it, God's grace 'is more abundantly poured forth, through Christ, upon the world, than it was imparted to Adam in the beginning.'" Pascal also perceived this abundant grace, observing that, "God's mercy is so great that he gives us salutary instructions even when he hides himself." [*Pensée* 438] In a sense, then, humankind's sin provided opportunity for God's grand work of redemption, which demonstrates a greater love for people than would have been demonstrated had Man never fallen. This is the mysterious mercy in original sin.

In addition, there are mercies in suffering. One of Pascal's strongest themes is the necessity of knowing our wretchedness– this is the one thing we must know in order to find God. Therefore suffering is valuable in its function to help us perceive our wretchedness. Pascal wrote prayers to God asking him to use sickness in his life appropriately, for example praying, "If my heart has been in love with the world when I was in robust health, destroy my vigor to promote my salvation." (Houston, 1997) Thus when Pascal was enamored with diversionary gambling, he asked to be rendered unable to gamble, and enabled to be enamored with God. Without suffering, we would not feel our need for God; thus suffering is necessary for making relevant the seeking of God.

Furthermore, Pascal suggests that, in order to find God, we must accept the reality that some truths are mysterious and cannot be understood through reasoning. We must not dogmatically assume that revelation from a God outside of nature is impossible; given the frailty of our minds, on what grounds can this be presumed? Accepting mystery humbles our pride and fosters a disposition that enables us to seek God.

Lastly, Pascal suggests that suffering is an integral part of a person's journey from a wretched lover of self to a happy lover of God. For if over-desires have become our second nature, [*Pensée* 1616] then it will feel painful to give them up. Pascal's gambling friends and typical moderns cannot shed their hedonism without a whimper. Shedding them will entail changes such as less TV-watching, less gaming, and less cynical bantering. Shedding over-desires hurts because "anyone is unhappy who wills but cannot do." [*Pensée* 75] Moreover, becoming God-centered entails developing a character that is willing to love neighbors, which includes strangers. And loving people always incurs costs– it may mean canceling my planned entertainment to take care of a sick person, passing on an opportunity that would win me accolades to help a co-worker's career, or absorbing unfair criticisms without a word of retaliation. With each step away from self-absorption, a treasured over-desire, which I hitherto believed indispensable for my happiness, dies an excruciating death. Transformation into a lover of God hurts because it means, "putting myself out." [*Pensée* 32]

Conclusion. To conclude this chapter, consider G.K. Chesterton's suggestion, tracking Pascal's, that a survey of the history of Christianity provides a clue for its veracity:

> If I found a key on the road and discovered it fit and opened a particular lock at my house, I'd assume it most likely that the key was made by the lock-maker. And if I find a set of teachings set down in pre-oriental modern society that has proven itself with such universal validity that it has fascinated and satisfied millions of people in every country, including the best minds in history and the simplest hearts, that it has made itself at home in virtually every culture, inspired masterpieces of beauty in every field of art, and continues to grow rapidly and spread and assert itself in lands where a century ago the name of Jesus Christ was not even heard. If such teaching so obviously fits the locks of so many human souls in so many times and so many places are they likely the work of a deceiver or a fool? In fact it is more likely that they were designed by the heart-maker.

Pensée of the Day: Number 919

The PoD reflects on Jesus Christ as the living center of a Christian. It is a favorite of Earl Palmer, long-time pastor of Seattle's University Presbyterian Church, who carved it into driftwood.

> Do small things as if they were great, because of the majesty of Christ, who does them in us and lives our life, and great things as though they were small and easy, because of his almighty power.

Because of Christ's almighty power, great tasks can be taken on with confidence and with peace of mind and heart. In expressing this thought Pascal may have had in mind the struggles of Jacqueline, himself, and their Jansenist friends in the Jesuit-Jansenist controversy, wherein they courageously risked and expended their lives to uphold what they believed to be Christian truth. On the other hand, Pascal's suggestion to do small things as if they were great opposes the sacred-secular dualist who would propose that some activities are sacred and God cares about them, while other activities are secular and God does not care about them. Rather, because of the majesty of Christ and his living our life, all activities can be done as spiritual worship to God, and the tiniest act of charity has infinite value. Pascal expresses this in the bonus PoD number 927:

> The slightest movement affects the whole of nature; one stone can alter the whole sea. Likewise, in the realm of grace, the slightest action affects everything because of its consequences; therefore everything matters.

Synthesis Points of Chapter 8

1. To credibly be the one true religion, Christianity must be remarkably unique among religions. Pascal suggests it is unique because it is based on faith in Jesus Christ, with sub-points (1) it alone explains human behavior; (2) it is love- and grace-centered; (3) it is both wise and based on the "folly of the Cross;" (4) it perfects a person; (5) it is wonderful.
2. To Pascal the strongest traditional evidence for the Christian religion are its (1) fulfillment of prophecies; (2) miracles; (3) foundation on the amazing Jewish people, laws, and book.
3. Pascal presents the "proofs" not as mathematical certainties, but as clues and evidence for the rational plausibility of Christianity. Pascal proposes Christianity is more rationally plausible than other religions and that secular scientism. This greater evidence underlies Pascal's conclusion of the Wager that it is rationally compelling to begin an experiment to give the Christian faith a try.

9 CONCLUSION: FROM MONSTERS TO MEMBERS OF CHRIST'S BODY

> "Jesus came to this world and became a man in order to spread to other men the kind of life He has– by what I call 'good infection.' Every Christian is to become a little Christ. The whole purpose of becoming a Christian is simply nothing else."
>
> – C.S. Lewis, *Mere Christianity*

> "Jesus Christ is the object of all things, the centre towards which all things tend."
>
> – Blaise Pascal, *Pensée* 449

When setting out to write this guided tour, a number of alternative titles were tried. Notwithstanding *Pascal for Dummies* suggested by my wife, these included *Pascal's Pensées: Strong Coffee for Dispossessed Kings*; *Pascal's Pensées: Strong Coffee for the Great and Small*; and my favorite, *Pascal's Pensées: Strong Coffee for Monsters*. In the end these titles were rejected for concern that the Pascal-uninitiated would scratch their heads at their impenetrable meaning. But if you have now read the *Pensées*, perhaps you will agree with their suitability, as they acknowledge Pascal's approach to serve his interlocutor with the blackest kind of coffee– weak flavored coffee would be powerless to wake these indifferent, diverted, vain, presumptuous, and unduly selfish friends of his to take up an interest in seeking God. The chains attaching his friends to French parlor society were so secure that Pascal left no device unused in his efforts to loosen them.

In this closing chapter, I will summarize the themes of Pascal's *Pensées*, suggesting that the Wager is its coherent center, and that the *Pensées* as a whole provides compelling reasons for today's modern skeptic to give the Wager a try. I will conclude with Pascal's conception of the happy condition– humankind's true good– that awaits those rational enough to risk their lives for an infinite gain.

Man as Paradoxical Monster. The alternative book titles identify Pascal's interlocutor as a paradoxical creature with a strange, composite condition, in a word a "monster" (defined by Webster as "an animal or plant of abnormal form or structure"). As surveyed in chapters 2 through 4, Pascal attributes myriad oxymoronic dualities to this misshapen being. Man is terrified at death when safe yet unafraid when in danger; too bored to stay quietly in his room yet excitable merely by striking a billiards ball; and passionate about trivial things yet indifferent about great things (chapter 2). Man is colossal yet minute in the universe; skeptical yet dogmatic; and quick to exclude reason yet quick to exclude faith (chapter 3). Man is judge of the universe yet incapable of practicing justice; a prodigious thinker yet full of natural error; and possesses an idea of his duty to love God yet shuns it out of self-centeredness and over-desires (chapter 4). By showing his interlocutor his enigmatic condition Pascal aimed to "...go on contradicting him until he understands that he is a monster that passes all understanding." [*Pensée* 130] Man's monster-hood apart from God is the signature theme of the first part of the *Pensées*.

For Pascal, the essential mark of the human monster is his condition of being both very wretched and very great. We must know both to understand ourselves, presses Pascal, because without this key we are invincibly ignorant about our origin, our current state, and our destiny. Our dual condition reflects our status as dispossessed kings, who in our state of creation enjoyed happiness (entailing immortality, joy, justice, peace, purposefulness, virtue, wisdom, loving community), but in our fallen state suffer wretchedness (the loss of immortality and all the other qualities of perfection). The infinite dissonance we feel between our idea of perfect happiness and the wretchedness we experience helps us grasp the futility of seeking happiness on our own steam, and makes attractive a path of seeking happiness based on listening to God. The craving we feel as dispossessed kings helps us grasp that only our maker can help.

Jesus Christ: Resolver of Paradoxes. One of Pascal's most powerful techniques for winning seekers is to raise a paradoxical reality of the human condition, to pit different philosophical approaches against one another (especially those that hold sway with his friends), and to show that they uniformly fail to solve it. Pascal then brings in Jesus Christ as a surprising new element that uniquely resolves the paradox. A prototype case is the failure of optimist and pessimist philosophers to adequately explain the data on Man's morality. Jesus Christ shows us both our goodness and badness, bringing into focus a coherent picture of what constitutes a human being.

Pascal's Theory of Three Orders and Tyranny. Pascal's theory of orders, which addresses the physical, intellectual, and spiritual (or carnal, mind, and heart) realms of reality, contributes another signature of the *Pensées*. With this theory Pascal observes the disorder and tyranny that result when people use means appropriate to one order to obtain a good that can only be obtained by means appropriate to a different order. As we have seen, two chief tyrannical actors that Pascal criticized were the Jesuit Fathers and Descartes. Some Jesuit Fathers, while publicly acknowledging their chief duties to uphold Christian truth and shepherd souls, went about it by shrewdly devising systems that sustained their own power. This activity is tyrannical, states Pascal, because caring for the flock cannot be accomplished by building power– a carnal pursuit– but only by thinking well and loving well, which are intellectual and spiritual pursuits. Descartes and associated Enlightenment and deist thinkers, charged Pascal, attempted to achieve good in the spiritual order by applying means appropriate to the intellectual order. By replacing God's revelation with human reason, scientific secularism leaves people with only preferences to guide behavior, bereaving them of God's guidance principles for right living. Science is mute about spiritual matters involving ethics, duty, faith, hope, love, meaning; Pascal foresaw the tyranny, suffering and oppression that would result from Enlightenment presumptions that science could replace revelation. Speaking against a rushing current of rationalistic philosophy that urged staking future progress on human reasoning alone, Pascal reminded people that listening to God with a teachable heart is indispensable for living well.

Pascal considered it equally tyrannical to apply means appropriate for the spiritual order to attain intellectual knowledge. To Pascal science rightly proceeds by sensory observation of phenomena and reasoning, and is free from authoritative pronouncements that may contradict data and logic. Thus Descartes behaved tyrannically when he asserted that nature abhors a vacuum but did not support it with scientific experiments, and Church authorities behaved tyrannically when they burned scientists at the stake because they observed that the earth revolves around the sun. Furthermore, Pascal distinguishes two orders of religious people. The carnally minded misappropriate religion as a pretext to buoy their private or political agendas, whereas the spiritually minded practice religion honestly by *really* listening to God, abandoning their own agendas. By gradually being transformed to be like Jesus Christ, spiritually minded Christians in the long run become happy, reasonable, virtuous, and lovable. [*Pensée* 357]

Pascal's theory of orders reveals more than just Man's tyrannical inclinations. Pascal expresses amazement that many of his friends seemed to live without concern for matters of the spiritual order. Man's life span is an infinitesimal blip compared to the eternity that goes before and after it– if Man were not a monster, would he not care about his condition during eternity? (*Pensée* 427) It makes such a great difference to a person whether there is to be an everlasting state of torment, bliss, or annihilation, that a normal being will surely care about this question. Since carnal and intellectual means cannot prevent death, one should seek help through spiritual means, if only out of basic concern for one's being. Indifference to seeking help is doubly monstrous– first, Man is monstrous because he knows he will die soon, and second, Man is monstrous because he does not care to look for a preventative measure. The same double-monstrousness appears in the other great problems Man faces– his ignorance, unhappiness, emptiness, undue self-love. At least make some effort to return to completeness by seeking for good within the spiritual order, Pascal implores. Pascal would agree with Chesterton's observation that, "[men] scarcely reach sanity till they reach sanctity."

Living Well in all Three Orders. While Pascal stresses the necessity of seeking God with one's heart in the spiritual order, he suggests that effort in the other realms is also needed. To Pascal, the only path to completeness entails submitting one's whole being– including the physical, intellectual, and spiritual aspects– to God. Listening to God and growing in grace entails ongoing renewal in all three arenas; practically it means repenting of tyrannical behavior when it occurs and continually re-discovering truth and charity as goods that must be kept in view with every physical, mental, and spiritual movement. It means submitting all areas of life under the Lordship of Christ, and praying to God to make ones' whole self love God. This Judeo-Christian call on one's life is summed up by Moses' command to the Jews to "love the Lord your God with all your heart, and with all your mind and with all your strength." [Deuteronomy 6:4–5]

God's Hiddenness is Helpful for Seekers. Moreover, Pascal's theory of orders shows that God's hiddenness should come as no surprise. Because God cannot be found apart from seeking within the spiritual order, it follows immediately that those who care only for carnal or intellectual goods cannot see him. If a man's goal is to win fame by playing football or by proving theorems, then he will be blind to the (spiritual) greatness of a generous servant devoid of fame. Striving for physical or intellectual greatness cannot bring one nearer to God because such striving is fueled by pride, Man's vilest feature that cuts him off totally. Real progress toward God can be made only through humble seeking within the spiritual realm, through an open heart that submits itself to God's shaping. It is for this reason– that God is findable only through a humble disposition– that Pascal suggests God's hiddenness is useful for seekers. The sole point of a Christian's life is to become like Jesus Christ, and because Jesus Christ is supremely humble, it follows that for God to make any Christians, he must reveal himself in a manner that fosters humility. Had God continued to shine like the noonday sun to Adam and Eve after their rebellion, it would only have inflated their pride, severing any path of return. [*Pensée* 446] Yet God makes himself perfectly clear to the spiritually minded who desire only to see. [*Pensée* 149]

Grace-Centeredness. Pascal insists that a return to God is not brought about fundamentally through human effort, but through grace. Nowhere is this clearer than in Pascal's prayer asking God to use sickness in his life appropriately (Houston, 1997):

> But I confess, O my God, that my heart is so hardened, so full of worldly ideas, cares, anxieties, and attachments, that neither health nor sickness, neither talks, books, nor even your holy Scriptures, nor the gospel, nor your most holy mysteries, can do anything at all to bring about my conversion. Certainly it cannot be philanthropy, fastings, miracles, the sacraments, nor all my efforts, nor even those of all the world put together, that can do this. It is only the amazing greatness of your grace that can do this.

Pascal suggests that grace-centeredness makes Christianity unique among worldviews.

Restoring the Wager to the Heart of the Pensées. Despite the fact that many critics have pushed Pascal's Wager to the margins of Pascal's religious writings, I suggest that it coherently fits at the center of the *Pensées*. Preceding this center is the first part, which establishes Man's wretchedness apart from God, and the necessity for him to "hear from his master" [*Pensée* 131] to have any hope of restoration. This is Pascal's first key to open his friend to wagering on God– for if his interlocutor sustains his fine opinion of himself (as a respectable deist, for example), then he will either be disinterested in Christianity or dogmatically convinced that it cannot possibly be. Those who know they are monsters, however, are open to potential paths to restored happiness. Pascal's second key to open his friend to wagering on God is his rigorous case for the rationale plausibility of the Christian faith, demonstrating it is not contrary to reason to wager on God. These two keys are enough to motivate wagering, Pascal suggests.

Pascal's Apologetics are Winsome because they are Like Jesus Christ's Apologetics. There is a secret to the success of Pascal's approach to winning seekers by showing them they are monsters– this is the approach Jesus Christ took. Jesus began his sermon on the mount by observing that those who know their spiritual inadequacy are blessed– theirs is the kingdom of heaven. [Matthew 5:3] Jesus proclaimed he came for the sick, not for those who did not perceive their need for a doctor, and constantly acknowledged that God will remain hidden to the proud but will be found by humble seekers. When Jesus encountered people, he regularly suggested that some aspect of their perspective or worldview blocked their participation in the kingdom of heaven. For example, Jesus informed the rich young ruler that his attitude about his wealth and the poor were preventing him from having treasure in heaven. [Luke 18:18–23] At every turn Jesus would "go on contradicting" his interlocutors, pressing for them to recognize their need to undergo heart surgery by God. The ministry of Jesus, and of John the Baptist before him, may be summarized as calling people to recognize they are monsters that pass all understanding, and once they acknowledge it, to provide a cure. The secret of the whole *Pensées* is the acuity of Pascal's heart and mind to listen carefully to his Lord Jesus, the greatest apologist, and to imitate his approach.

Pascal's Pensées are for Today's Modern Skeptics. Many contemporary modern skeptics dismiss Christianity as irrelevant for the same reason as seventeenth-century modern skeptics. This fraternity spanning the ages believe that science provides a satisfactory explanation for history without the need to invoke a god; that accepting revelatory truth is anachronistic and leads to harm (leaving tolerance as the sole virtue that we can peg our hopes on for bringing justice and peace); and, above all, that diversionary pursuits constitute our happiness. As surveyed in this guided tour, Pascal's entire program exposes the vulnerabilities of these beliefs. Jesus Christ's deep understanding of the worldview and felt needs of his interlocutors under-girded the effectiveness of his apologetics; similarly Pascal's deep understanding of his interlocutors under-girded the effectiveness of his. Pascal's superb insight into his friend's monstrous condition stemmed from the confluence of his brilliance in science, rhetoric, and psychology, together with his life-experience in bourgeoise entertainments and in top scientific circles. Pascal was uniquely positioned to pen an awesome demonstration of the futility of his interlocutor's worldview.

Moreover, as A.J. Krailsheimer has observed, millions of moderns today exactly fit the mold of Pascal's targeted interlocutor, whereas only a small group of privileged bourgeoise folk fit it in Pascal's day. These two historical periods are divided by the industrial revolution, which, for the first time in history, led to a large middle class that had the time and education needed to pursue entertainment and science. And with recent inventions like TV and the internet, contemporaries may be even more steeped and stained in diversions and skepticism than Pascal's friends, making Pascal's 350-year old apology even more on target now than when it was conceived. The implication is that millions today, if they were to engage Pascal's *Pensées*, would be expected to discover within themselves doubt about the modern program for happiness, and a craving for something more. For those of us who feel this, Pascal encourages us to make a change in our lives according to the Wager.

Man's True Good: Membership in Christ's Body. Pascal's *Pensées* on the body of Christ, including *Pensée* 372, reveal the end to which Pascal hoped to bring his monstrous friend, the outcome of wagering one's life, the "point of it all:"

> To be a member is to have no life, no being and no movement except through the spirit of the body and for the body. The separated member, no longer seeing the body to which it belongs, has only a wasted and moribund being left... But in loving the body it loves itself, because it has no being except in the body, through the body, and for the body... *He that is joined to the Lord is one spirit [I Corinthians 6:17]*, we love ourselves because we are members of Christ. We love Christ because he is the body of which we are members. All are one. One is in the other like the three persons [of the Trinity].

From this *Pensée*, Pascal's "monster" can be rephrased as a "separated member" that has been cut off from the body– Pascal's image of the human condition is an amputated limb! The *Pensée* goes on to reveal wonderfully what to Pascal constitutes Man's normal state– a "member of Christ." Man was created for this, and only by living in and for the body does he attain the true happiness that makes Christianity attractive. Pascal's observation that a member "has no being except in the body" helps explain his description of vain Man as possessing an infinite God-shaped vacuum in his heart. The Wager's title, "infinity-nothing," further suggests Pascal's thesis that Man as separated member is null and void while Man as member of Christ's body is infinitely full. And the best news of all is that God himself transforms Man from empty to full, as in the story of the poor widow who brings to Elisha her empty oil-jars, who responds with love by miraculously filling them (2 Kings 4: 8-17). Indeed, the seeker's essential contributions to becoming full are to acknowledge his emptiness, to believe God can fill him, and to gratefully assent to God's work of grace.

While Pascal's purpose in the first part of the *Pensées* is to bring his listener to the doorstep of a spiritual experiment, through the discovery that he is dispossessed king, his purpose in the second part is to bring him to membership into Christ's body, through the discovery that Jesus Christ became dispossessed, becoming a vacuum ("he made himself nothing," Philippians 2:7), in order to restore him. Pascal quotes John 17 in his *Memorial*, which records Jesus' prayer on the eve of his death for believers to become perfect members of Christ's body:

> I do not pray for these [Christ's disciples] alone, but also for those who will believe in me through their word; that they all may be one, as you, Father, are in me, and I in you; that they also may be one in us, that the world may believe that you sent me. And the glory which you gave me I have given them, that they may be one just as we are one: I in them, and you in me; that they may be made perfect in one, and that the world may know that you have sent me, and have loved them as you have loved me.

Conclusion: Filling the God-Shaped Vacuum with a True State of Happiness. Pascal begins his case for seeking with, 'All men seek happiness,' yet, when they look, all they find is the empty print and trace of their original true state of happiness. Pascal ends with the 'joy, joy, joy' that is found when the infinite vacuum is filled with an infinite and immutable object, by God himself. While happiness sought through filling the God-shaped vacuum with mutable objects is inevitably thwarted by 'a thousand and one accidents,' a happiness sought in God is subject only to the immutable faithfulness and love of God. Pascal would approve of Augustine having the last word: "God alone is the place of peace that cannot be disturbed... only love of the immutable brings tranquility." [*The Confessions*, Book 4]

***Pensée* of the Day: Number 449**

The Christian's God does not consist merely of a God who is the author of mathematical truths and the order of the elements... He does not consist merely of a God who extends his providence over the life and property of men so as to grant a happy span of years to those who worship him... But the God of Abraham, the God of Isaac, the God of Jacob, the God of the Christians is a God of love and consolation: he is a God who fills the soul and heart of those whom he possesses: he is a God who makes them inwardly aware of their wretchedness and his infinite mercy: who unites himself with them in the depths of their soul: who fills it with humility, joy, confidence and love: who makes them incapable of having any other end but him.

Synthesis Points of Pascal's *Pensées*

1. Apart from God, Man is a monster that passes all understanding. "Monster" signifies abnormality– Man's normal state, for which he was designed, entails enjoyment of certain knowledge, everlasting life, happiness, meaning, the practice of true justice, and whole loving relationships with God and all created beings and things. But in his state of corruption Man finds himself unable to reliably find truth, dying, unhappy, vain, unjust, tyrannical, and self-centered.
2. Man tries to suppress his knowledge of monster-hood, through presumption, diversions, and indifference. Yet, this monster is great because it knows it is a monster (Man as paradoxical thinking reed). This monster is a "dispossessed king," who, in his current condition of wretchedness, retains a glimmering idea of his past felicity. To induce cure-seeking Pascal appeals to the craving in a person's heart (the God-shaped vacuum) to be restored to complete being.

3. Through Scriptures with figurative meaning and other means, God is revealed to all who seek him with humility, but remains concealed to all others. Hence there is enough light for all who desire to see Christ as he really is, and enough darkness for those who prefer their own private or political good. Sincere seeking entails effort in all three orders of reality, the body, mind and heart. As the principal organ for knowing God, the heart must not be supplanted by reason.
4. Pascal's Wager may be placed at the center of the *Pensées*, between the two parts. Once Pascal's friend appreciates that Christianity is not contrary to reason, and that he is a monster that desires restoration, he will be open to the Wager's call that for the sake of happiness (his "true good") he should give Christianity a try. The second part of Pascal's *Pensées* begins here, with objective to show Christianity is true. This experimental truth seeking entails diminishing one's selfish passions and acting as if one believes. The experiment entails replacing habits of concupiscence/over-desire with habits of the means of grace, including participating in Church fellowship, service, and prayer, as well as worshipping God in all areas of life.
5. Through this journey, Pascal hoped his monstrous friends would be transformed, through grace, into members of Christ's body, their normal state of complete being.

10 REFERENCES

1. Augustine [1960 (398)]. *The Confessions*. Translation by John K. Ryan. Doubleday: New York.
2. Augustine. *Sermo* 52, 16: PL 38, 360.
3. Augustine. *The Literal Meaning of Genesis*, Book 1, Chapter 19.
4. Becker E (1973). *The Denial of Death*. Free Press, New York, p. 15.
5. Borges JL (1956). *The Form of the Sword,* in *Ficciones.* Translated by Anthony Kerrigan. Grove Press, Inc. New York.
6. Brown WS, Murphy N, Malony HN (1998). *Whatever Happened to the Soul?* Augsburg Fortress, Minneapolis MN.
7. Caner E, Caner E. (2002). *Unveiling Islam: An Insider's Look at Muslim Life and Beliefs*. Kregal Publications, Grand Rapids, Michigan.
8. Cherbonnier E. La B (1955). *Hardness of Heart*: Doubleday: Garden City, New York.
9. Chesterton, GK [2001 (1908)] *Orthodoxy*. Shaw Books. Colorado Springs, Colorado.
10. Chesterton GK [1993 (1925)]. *The Everlasting Man*. Ignatius Press, San Francisco.
11. Collins FS (2006). *The Language of God: A Scientist Presents Evidence for Belief*. Free Press, New York.
12. Connor JA (2006). *Pascal's Wager: The Man Who Played Dice with God*. Harper, San Francisco, p. 96.
13. Custis, George Washington Parke (1860). *Recollections of Washington.*
14. Darwood NJ. Translation of *The Koran,* Seventh Revised Edition. Penguin Books, London.
15. Dawkins R (1996). *The Blind Watchmaker*. W.W. Norton, New York, Reissue Edition.
16. Dawkins R (2006). *The God Delusion*. Houghton Mifflin, Boston.
17. de Bérulle P [1984 (1856)]. "Discourse de l'état et des grandeurs de Jésus," Ceuvres complètes (Paris: Migne, 1856), 161. English translation in Anne M. Minton, "The Spirituality of Bérulle: A New Look," *Spirituality Today* 36, no. 3 (Fall 1984): 210–219.

18. Cunio T (1996). *Lectures on Pascal.* University Presbyterian Church, Seattle, WA.
19. Descartes R [1968 (1637)]. *Discourse on Method.* Translation by F.E. Sutcliffe, Penguin Books, London.
20. Dostoyevsky F [1990 (1879)]. *The Brothers Karamazov.* Translation by Pevear, Richard and Volokhonsky, Larissa. Farrar, Straus, and Giroux: New York.
21. Edwards J [1996 (1754)]. *Freedom of the Will.* Soli Deo Gloria Publications, Morgan, PA.
22. Edwards J [2003 (1765)]. *Dissertation Concerning the Nature of True Virtue.* Wipf & Stock Publishers, Eugene, Oregon.
23. Foster RJ (1998). *Celebration of Discipline: The Path to Spiritual Growth.* HarperCollins Publishers, New York.
24. Grayling AC (2005). *Descartes: The Life and Times of a Genius.* Walker Publishing Company, New York.
25. Groothuis D (2003). *On Pascal.* Wadsworth Philosophers Series.
26. Hacking I (1975). *The Emergence of Probability.* Cambridge University Press, Cambridge.
27. Hammond N (2003). *The Cambridge Companion to Pascal.* Cambridge University Press, Cambridge.
28. Harvard Women's Health Watch (2005). Five for 2005: Five reasons to forgive. Harvard Medical School, January 1, 2005.
29. Hoffman P (1999). *The Man Who Loved Only Numbers: Story of Paul Erdös and the Search for Mathematical Truth.* Harper Collins: New York.
30. Houston JM (1997). *The Mind on Fire.* Bethany House Publishers, Minneapolis, MN.
31. Huang C (2006). *When Invisible Children Sing.* Tyndale House Publishers: Carol Stream, IL.
32. James W (1956). *The Will to Believe.* New York: Dover Publications, p. 26.
33. Keyes D (1995). *True Heroism in a World of Celebrity Counterfeits.* Colorado Springs, CO.
34. Keyes D (1998). *Beyond Identity: Finding Your Self in the Image and Character of God.* Wipf and Stock Publishers, Eugene, OR.
35. Keyes D (1999). *Chameleon Christianity: Moving Beyond Safety and Conformity.* Baker Books, Grand Rapids, MI.
36. Keyes D (2007). *Seeing Through Cynicism: A Reconsideration of the Power of Suspicion.* InterVarsity Press, Downers Grove, IL.

37. Keller T (2008). *The Reason for God: Belief in an Age of Skepticism.* Penguin Group, Dutton Adult, New York.
38. Krailsheimer AJ (1980). *Pascal.* Hill and Wang, New York.
39. Kreeft P (1993). *Christianity for Modern Pagans: Pascal's Pensées Edited, Outline and Explained.* Ignatius Press, San Francisco.
40. Kristof ND, WuDunn S (2009). *Half the Sky: Turning Oppression into Opportunity for Women Worldwide.* Knopf, New York.
41. Le Mastre de Sacy (1699). *Les Psaumes de David.* Paris: G. Desprez, preface, pp. 5–6.
42. Lewis CS [2001 (1940)]. *The Problem of Pain.* Harper, San Francisco, New Edition.
43. Lewis CS [1982 (1942)]. *The Screwtape Letters. Revised Edition.* Collier Books. MacMillan Publishing Company, New York.
44. Lewis CS [2001 (1943)]. *The Abolition of Man.* HarperOne, San Francisco, New Edition.
45. Lewis CS [2001 (1945)]. *The Great Divorce.* Harper, San Francisco, New Edition.
46. Lewis CS [1978 (1947)]. *Miracles: A Preliminary Study.* Macmillan Publishing Company, New York.
47. Lewis CS (1952). *Mere Christianity.* Macmillan Publishing Company, New York.
48. Lewis CS [1994 (1963)]. *God in the Dock: Essays on Theology and Ethics.* William B. Eerdmans Publishing Company, Grand Rapids, Michigan.
49. Levitt SD, Dubner SJ (2005). *Freakonimics: A Rogue Economist Explores the Hidden Side of Everything.* William Morrow: New York.
50. Marsden G (2003). *Jonathan Edwards: A Life.* Yale University Press, New Haven.
51. McEntyre MC (2009). *Caring for Words in a Culture of Lies.* William B. Eerdmans Publishing Company, Grand Rapids, Michigan.
52. Medina JJ (2008). *Brain Rules.* Pear Press, Seattle.
53. Molière J-B [2000 (1673)]. *The Miser and Other Plays.* Translation by John Wood and David Coward, Penguin Group, New York.
54. Montaigne M [1958 (1580)]. *Essays.* Translation by J.M. Cohen, Penguin Books, Harmondsworth, Middlesex.
55. Morris T (1992). *Making Sense of it All: Pascal and the Meaning of Life.* William B. Eerdmans Publishing Company, Grand Rapids, Michigan.
56. Myers D (2000). *The American Paradox: Spiritual Hunger in an Age of Plenty.* Yale University Press, New Haven.

57. Newbigin L (1989). *The Gospel in a Pluralist Society*: William B. Eerdmans Publishing Company, Grand Rapids, Michigan.
58. Nietzsche F [1995 (1891)]. *Thus Spoke Zarathustra: A Book for All and None*. Translation by Walter Kaufmann. Modern Library, New York.
59. O'Connell M (1997). *Blaise Pascal: Reasons of the Heart*. William B. Eerdmans Publishing Company, Grand Rapids, Michigan.
60. Palmer E (2006). *Love Came Down*. November 26 sermon, University Presbyterian Church, Seattle, Washington.
61. Pascal B. [1967 (1656–1657)]. *The Provincial Letters.* Translation by A.J. Krailsheimer, Penguin Books, London.
62. Pascal B [1966 (1670)]. *Pensées.* Translation by A.J. Krailsheimer, Penguin Books, London.
63. Polanyi M (1967) *The Tacit Dimension.* Routledge and Kegan Paul, London.
64. Popper KR [1959 (1935)]. *The Logic of Scientific Discovery*. Harper and Row, New York.
65. Putnam R (2000). *Bowling Alone: The Collapse and Revival of American Community*. Simon and Schuster, New York.
66. Rauch J (2003). Let it be. *Atlantic Monthly*, May, 2003, p. 34.
67. Robinson M (2005). *The Death of Adam: Essays on Modern Thought*. Picador, New York.
68. Russell B (1957). *Why I Am Not a Christian*. Editor Paul Edwards, Simon and Schuster, Concord, MA.
69. Sagoff M (1990). *The Economy of the Earth: Philosophy, Law, and the Environment*. Cambridge University Press, Cambridge.
70. Schaeffer FA (1983). *How Should We Then Live? The Rise and Decline of Western Thought and Culture*. Crossway Books: Wheaton, IL.
71. Smith A (1989). A review of the effects of colds and influenza on human performance. *Occupational Medicine* 39, 65–68.
72. Solzhenitsyn A (1974). *The Gulag Archipelago1918-1956.* Translated by Thomas P. Whitney. Éditions du Seuil, Paris.
73. Stivers R (1994). *The Culture of Cynicism: American Morality in Decline*. Blackwell, Oxford, p. 73.
74. Strayer DL, Drews FA, Crouch DJ (2006). A comparison of the cell-phone driver and the drunken driver. *Human Factors* 48, 381–391.
75. *The Westminster Confession of Faith* [1990 (1647)]. Committee for Christian Education & Publications, Atlanta, GA.

76. Wright NT (1999). *The Challenge of Jesus: Rediscovering who Jesus Was and Is*. Inter Varsity Press, Illinois.

11 APPENDIX: BONUS PASCALIAN PROVERBS FOR LIVING WELL

On vanity

A trifle consoles us because a trifle upsets us. [*Pensée* 43]

On truth-seeking

It is absurd of us to rely on the company of our fellows, as wretched and helpless as we are; they will not help us; we shall die alone.

We must act then as if we were alone. If that were so, would we build superb houses, etc.? We should unhesitatingly look for the truth. And, if we refuse, it shows that we have a higher regard for men's esteem than for pursuing the truth. [*Pensée* 151]

On persuasion

Begin by pitying unbelievers; their condition makes them unhappy enough.

They ought not to be abused unless it does them good, but in fact it does them harm. [*Pensée* 162]

On truth

Those who do not love truth excuse themselves on the grounds that it is disputed, and that very many people deny it. Thus their error is solely due to the fact that they love neither truth nor charity, and so they have no excuse. [*Pensée* 176]

On education

As we cannot be universal by knowing everything there is to be known about everything, we must know a little about everything, because it is much better to know something about everything than everything about something. Such universality is the finest. [*Pensée* 195]

On manners

Some fancy makes me dislike people who croak or who puff while eating. Fancy carries a lot of weight. What good will that do us? That we indulge it because it is natural? No, rather that we resist it. [*Pensée* 196]

On humility

How little pride the Christian feels in believing himself united to God! How little he grovels when he likens himself to the earthworm! A fine way to meet life and death, good and evil! [*Pensée* 358]

On happiness

The Stoics say: 'Withdraw into yourself, that is where you will find peace.' And that is not true.

Others say: 'Go outside: look for happiness in some diversion.' And that is not true: we may fall sick.

Happiness is neither outside nor inside us: it is in God, both outside and inside us. [*Pensée* 407]

On seeking

Greatness. Religion is so great a thing that it is right that those who will not take the trouble to look for it, if it is obscure, should be deprived of it. What is there to complain about, if it can be found just by looking? [*Pensée* 472]

On persuasion

Authority. Hearsay is so far from being a criterion of belief that you should not believe anything until you have put yourself into the same state as if you had never heard it.

It is your own inner assent and the consistent voice of your reason rather than that of others which should make you believe. [*Pensée* 505]

On self-control

Abraham took nothing for himself but only for his servants. Thus the righteous man takes nothing from the world or its applause for himself, but only for his passions, which he uses like a master, saying to one 'Go' and [to another] 'Come'. [I Kings 12:31] *Thou shall rule over thy desire.* [Matthew 8:9] Thus mastered his passions become virtues; avarice, jealousy, anger, even God ascribes these to himself. And they are just as much virtues as mercy, pity, constancy, which are also passions. We must treat them like slaves, and give them food but prevent the soul feeding on it. For when passions are in control they become vices, and then they give their food to the soul, which feeds on it and is poisoned. [*Pensée* 603]

On good deeds

Fine deeds are most admirable when kept secret. When I see some of them in history… they please me greatly; but of course they were not completely secret, because they become known, and, although everything possible was done to keep them secret, the detail by which they came to light spoils everything, for the finest thing about them was the attempt to keep them secret. [*Pensée* 643]

On knowing our wretchedness

As I write down my thought it sometimes escapes me, but that reminds me of my weakness, which I am always forgetting, and teaches me as much as my forgotten thought, for I care only about knowing that I am nothing. [*Pensée* 656]

On humility

If you want people to think well of you, do not speak well of yourself. [*Pensée* 671]

On belief

We are usually convinced more easily by reasons we have found ourselves than by those which have occurred to others. [*Pensée* 737]

On truth

Truth is so obscured nowadays and lies so well established that unless we love the truth we shall never recognize it. [*Pensée* 739]

On trials

There is some pleasure in being on board a ship battered by storms when one is certain of not perishing. The persecutions buffeting the Church are like this. [*Pensée* 743]

On persuasion

There are two ways of persuading men of the truths of our religion; one by the power of reason, the other by the authority of the speaker.
We do not use the latter but the former. We do not say: 'You must believe that because Scripture, which says it, is divine,' but we say that it must be believed for such and such a reason. But these are feeble arguments, because reason can be bent in any direction. [*Pensée* 820]

On limitations of reason

Atheists. What grounds have they for saying that no one can rise from the dead? Which is harder, to be born or to rise again? That what has never been should be, or that what has been should be once more? Is it harder to come into existence that to come back? Habit makes us find the one easy, while lack of habit makes us find the other impossible.
Popular way to judge! [*Pensée* 882]

On humility

It is better not to fast and feel humiliated by it than to fast and be self-satisfied. [*Pensée* 928]

On comparisons

'Do not compare yourself to others, but to me. If you do not find me in those to whom you compare yourself, you are comparing yourself to someone loathsome. If you do find me, compare yourself to them. But whom will you be comparing? Yourself, or me in you? If it is yourself, it is someone loathsome; if it is I, you are comparing me to myself. Now I am God in all things.' [*Pensée* 929]

On submission

We must combine outward and inward to obtain anything from God; in other words we must go down on our knees, pray with our lips, etc... If we expect help from this outward part we are being superstitious, if we refuse to combine it with the inward we are being arrogant. [*Pensée* 944]

On the model person

Consider Jesus Christ in every person, and in ourselves. Jesus Christ as father in his father, Jesus Christ as brother in his brothers, Jesus Christ as poor in the poor, Jesus Christ as rich in the rich, Jesus Christ as priest and doctor in priests, Jesus Christ as sovereign in princes, etc. For by his glory he is everything that is great, being God, and by his mortal life he is everything that is wretched and abject. That is why he took on this unhappy condition, so that he could be in every person and a model for every condition of men. [*Pensée* 946]

On truth

Just as the only object of peace within states is to safeguard people's property, so the only object of peace within the Church is to safeguard the truth, which is its property and the treasure wherein lies its heart... And is it not obvious that, just as it is a crime to disturb the peace when truth reigns, it is also a crime to remain at peace when the truth is being destroyed? There is therefore a time when peace is just and a time when it is unjust. It is written: 'There is a time for war and a time for peace,' [Ecclesiastes 3:8] and it is the interests of the truth which distinguish between them... Truth is therefore the first rule and ultimate purpose of things. [*Pensée* 974]

ABOUT THE AUTHOR

Peter Gilbert is a research professor of biostatistics at the University of Washington, and focuses on HIV vaccine research within the Vaccine and Infectious Disease Division of the Fred Hutchinson Cancer Research Center. He provides leadership for the statistical design and analysis of HIV vaccine clinical trials, and frequently publishes and speaks on this topic. He lives with his wife and three children in Seattle, Washington, where he is a member of University Presbyterian Church.

14665727R00153

Made in the USA
Lexington, KY
12 April 2012